AF248575

Harwell Goodwin Davis

THE LEGEND
OF
LANDSEE

THE LEGEND OF LANDSEE

by

Harwell Goodwin Davis

THE STRODE PUBLISHERS, INC.
HUNTSVILLE, ALABAMA 35802

Copyright 1976
By Harwell Goodwin Davis
All Rights In This Book
Reserved Including The Right
To Reproduce This Book Or Parts
Thereof In Any Form—Printed In U.S.A.
Library Of Congress Catalog Number 76-40829
Standard Book Number 87397-106-X

To my wife

Lena Vail

I wish to express my gratitude to Mrs. Jean Buchanan Vess for her valuable aid in editing the original and for so beautifully typing the final manuscript.

Thanks also go to Mr. Hilary Milton, assistant professor and writer-in-residence, Samford University, for his helpful criticism of the first draft of the manuscript.

Contents

Prologue

This is memory's history of the village of Landsee and its countryside as it was once upon a time years ago. If you should wonder why an unskilled writer should dare to undertake such a task, the answer is a surmise.

We do not always comprehend the origin of some compulsions that force us to take certain actions. Especially is this often true when that which we do is not the result of a carefully considered and logical course of reasoning. But this lack of understanding is not always limited to the impelling act. It is sometimes true of a deliberate determination, such as my decision to attempt to tell the story of the land where I spent the early years of my life.

Perhaps this effort results from an urgent desire that others may know of Landsee, the people who lived there years ago, and their almost vanishing mode of life, with the hope that it will prevent their contribution to the present from being entirely forgotten. Or maybe it is the consequence of that sentiment with which old age adorns our youth as halcyon days intensely interesting to us and in our imagination important and worthy of the attention of others.

Does anyone ever completely lose interest in the experiences of his youth? The desire to see again your native heath may silently sleep for many years during your absence from it. Then one day you see or hear something that reminds you of that long ago, and suddenly without bidding your heart is flooded with a longing to go home. That is what happened to me.

After an absence of over half a century from Landsee, one summer evening while leisurely walking along a residential street I heard through the open window of one of the homes a young lady singing one of Stephen Foster's songs with its plaintive melody. It was a song that a group of us often sang those evenings we went serenading from home to home. All at once I was seized with an almost irresistible yearning to visit the place where I was born.

Although I lived many miles away, I decided to go in my automobile. With a growing anxiousness to be on my way I hastily arranged for a vacation, packed the clothing and articles I thought I would need on the trip, and on a clear summer morning I drove away homeward bound. At the least I thought of it as a trip going home.

In the state of nostalgia that obsessed me I failed to realize that, in all probability, most of my old friends and acquaintances had moved away from Landsee and that others had already made the "great adventure." Though reason, where it timidly asserted itself, warned me not to expect Landsee to be as it formerly was when last I was there, yet all through the returning way there persisted the hope that at my journey's end I would find familiar faces and long remembered places.

Within a few miles of my destination there was forced upon me the disappointing apprehension that my hopes were vain. The paved highway had abandoned the route of the old dirt road that ran with the contours of the land from one country home to another. Much of the shady forest, with its tall, long-leafed yellow pines, its white oak trees and dogwoods, had been destroyed, cleared away for an oily appearing gasoline station or an automobile repair shop. The large two-storied residences which served, when I was a young man, as a rendezvous for merry-making had been razed. While I did not expect to see Landsee Mansion as I had heard that it had burned, to my surprise it was difficult to locate even the site on which it had stood.

It was necessary to go to a motel for lodging which was in the charge of persons who had recently moved to Landsee and who were not familiar with its past and who did not know any of the oldtimers. Neither Mr. Henry May nor his "Drummers

Home," which he had owned and operated, were in existence.

After spending much time searching for an old acquaintance it dawned upon me that the place was a stranger to me and that I was a stranger to the place. Although a number of people moved along the sidewalk where I stood, I was almost overcome by a lonesome and "being forgotten" feeling. In the more than half century I had been absent from Landsee even the landscape had changed. There was hardly a familiar trace of the old community I knew as a boy and young man.

It was while alone in my motel room reminiscing, thinking of those who lived and labored here in the long ago when it was a land of beauty and of legend, that I clearly realized that I had to write about Landsee, its people of the yesteryears and the events of their times.

An incident occurred which made final my conviction that I must attempt to tell of the pioneers of this area. A light tap on the door of my motel room made me open the door with considerable curiosity to see who would be coming to see me. There stood a tall, neatly dressed, gray-haired Negro man. The first words he spoke brought recognition and made my heart leap with happiness. It was Ooden, a boyhood playmate of John Alston, Ben Davidson and mine. He lived several miles from the motel where I was staying. He had heard of a stranger being in Landsee who said he had lived in Landsee when he was young, and from what he had been told he thought it might be me. So he came to see.

We talked the afternoon through until twilight came, and until his grandson who had driven him was calling. After all, my visit was not an entire failure for those few hours with Ooden were worth the trip. As we walked together to his car he asked, "How do you like my tie? Miss Sarah sent it to me from Chicago last Christmas. She always remembers me every Christmas." Sarah was the only child of the one Jewish family that had lived in Landsee for a few years.

When a person attempts to relate an event of the long ago without the benefit of written records he is compelled to rely solely on his memory. So if you ask if this history is reliable, the answer is that it is meticulously true according to the record preserved on the pages of memory's book.

Memory is a mental echo of the yesterdays. A sound you

utter while in some quiet glen sometimes travels 'til it reaches a hidden cove or cliff and then turns and comes back to you a true repetition of the original sound but in a softer cadence. So memory, the mental echo, causes us again to visualize true in every detail some event of the long ago, except probably we see it in a softer tone than it appeared when happening. My facts are from memory's records.

It is recognized that the passing of years may cast a golden glow over the people and land we loved in our youth as at the closing of the day a beautiful twilight covers the land with a soft radiance. But also, the passing of many years may enable us to see with a clearer vision the true character of the people and the real significance of events than we were able to comprehend at the time of the occurrence.

As I am persuaded that memory, in recording facts and events for future recall, exercises wise discrimination, you are invited to come wander with me through memory's fields of yesteryears to meet the people and learn of the events of the village of Landsee*and its countryside, the place where I lived when I was young. May some gentle and patient muse guide the pen of this tyro to letters so that the kind reader may clearly envision the people as they were in their failures and in their victories, in their sadness and in their mirth.

The Village

"Truth Is Stranger Than Fiction"

Many a countryside is the stage on which is enacted, in actual human experience, a drama fraught with more tragedy and in which tenser human emotions are manifest than was ever dreamed by any playwright. Landsee Village was the center of such a stage, on which each of its citizens played an important or support part.

All of us are prone to consider our village "the loveliest village of the plain." Before the advent of the bulldozer and what is generally termed progress Landsee had many claims to this distinction.

There was the imposing house known as Landsee Mansion which Aunt Mymee claimed was haunted and which stood vacant for many years. Several hundred yards from the front gate in the fence surrounding the extensive yard of Landsee Mansion ran the public road lined with large shade trees. During the first development of the village the homes were erected along this road and generally as near Landsee Mansion as was practical.

The development of the Village changed with the coming of the railroad. The railroad ran parallel to the old public road for about two miles but its depot was about a mile from Landsee Mansion. After the coming of the railroad the buildings were constructed nearer the railroad depot.

One of the community landmarks was the Masonic

Building which was situated on the public road about where the old and the new development of the village joined. It was a two-storied building. The first floor served as a school room and the upper story was used by the Masons for their secret meetings.

The Masonic order was composed of select men from a wide area, and they yielded a strong influence throughout the county. Lon Williamson, Landsee's foremost merchant, was one of the prominent men who was not a Mason. Rumor was that he had applied for membership and had been rejected. As the Masons kept secret all their lodge proceedings, no one except the Masons knew whether or not this rumor was true. Mr. Williamson always spoke of the Masons sarcastically as a "bunch of old men playing at nothing."

Lon Williamson was perhaps the first to move his business to a site near the railroad depot. He built a large, rambling, one-story storehouse with sufficient room to accommodate all types of merchandise and supplies needed by the rural section he served.

Many years before the development of the village Williamson's father had operated a trading post far in advance of any white settlement. It is said that he often traded ten cents worth of beads to an Indian for ten dollars worth of animal furs. With the settling of the area by the pioneers the trading post became a general mercantile business. Lon Williamson, as an only child, inherited the business and considerable wealth. It was said that he not only inherited wealth from his father but that he also inherited his father's bead-fur trading qualities and improved on both.

South of Williamson's store on the public road was a cotton gin which not only ginned and baled cotton but also on Saturdays ground corn into meal for a toll of the grain. Several hundred yards down the road from the gin was a sawmill.

Miss Essie Gill, generally and respectfully called Miss Essie, a bachelor maid of an undisclosed number of summers, who taught the school held in the room of the Masonic building, dignified that part of the public road running through Landsee by naming it Broad Street. Many of those living in the community had gone to school to her and, to her, the community was her school room. Often she undertook to direct many of its affairs and as a rule her directions were followed. So when Miss Essie said that particular section of the public road, though narrow and unpaved, should be known as Broad Street, it became Broad Street.

A road was developed running by the depot perpendicular to the railroad and to Broad Street. It was named Commerce Avenue. Williamson's store was at the corner of Broad Street and Commerce Avenue.

On Commerce Avenue west of the railroad was the Baptist church, the residences of the Chaplain and Mr. Blossburg and other homes. On Commerce Avenue east of the railroad was the Methodist church. Across from the Methodist church was Mr. May's "Drummers Home." Further out Commerce Avenue was the ornate home of Lon Williamson, the Methodist parsonage, and other residences.

About twenty miles south of Landsee was the county seat with its courthouse and jail. About fifteen miles north was Snake Creek Beat, a section with a moonshine-making, lawless reputation. On the road a mile north of Landsee Mansion was what was called "the murder spot." No one was convicted for a killing which took place there but when the killing was first known people began calling it "the murder spot" and that designation became permanent.

Religion ranked high in the estimation of most of the citizens. There were two churches, each a small frame building with a steeple that housed a bell which was rung as a call to worship and tolled when there was a death. Each was a part-time church, with the Methodists holding preaching services on the first and third Sundays in each month and the Baptists on the second and fourth Sundays. The fifth Sunday was free for special services.

The pastors of the churches were regarded as leaders in both religious and civic affairs. As the Methodist preacher was not allowed to remain over four years at a church, he did not become as much a part of the community as did the Baptist preacher. The Rev. Paul Gordon, the Baptist preacher, owned his home in Landsee and had lived there many years. Because he was a former chaplain in the Confederate Army, he was always referred to as the Chaplain. He was an excellent carpenter and supported his family largely by following this trade. Each of the pastors had two churches situated several miles from Landsee at which they preached one Sunday each month.

Landsee was the home of the medical doctor that served the area for many miles around Landsee. Dr. Alfred Alston always looked tired. Sometimes astride his fine saddle horse with saddle bags full of drugs, sometimes in a buggy driven either by his son John or the Negro boy Ooden, he answered all calls, white or black, day or night. He knew that for many of the calls he would not receive any compensation and that for some calls his remuneration would be only a few bushels of ear corn or some sweet potatoes or some other kind of farm produce.

Dr. Alston was a widower. He lost his wife when his son John, their only child, was about ten years old. Dinah, her husband and their son Ooden lived in servants quarters on his place and kept house and tended his garden, stock and domestic chores. Dr. Alston and John were about as close to each other as father and son could become. Dr. Alston's home was perhaps the most beautiful inhabited residence in Landsee. It was next to the home of Benjamin Davidson, a friend whose son Ben, Jr., was the constant companion of John Alston. John, Ben and Ooden, all about the same age, were playmates. The Davidson home was also a fine place. Ben Davidson was a prosperous farmer.

The most ornate home was that of Lon Williamson. He was proud of what he considered as his reputation as being the richest man in that section of the state, and he was particular to give that appearance in every way he could, although his ideas of how to demonstrate his wealth did not often appeal to many people who considered his taste rather crude.

In the opinion of its inhabitants, Landsee was an important village. In the time about which this history is written it was the hub of activities of a large farming area. It was the market for cotton, which then was the money crop, grown within an area of twenty or more miles.

Landsee Mansion

In that far away day of long ago when America was young and the Southern region was being discovered, some men of wealth were among the vanguard of the pioneers searching out the undeveloped country. These men planned to acquire large acreage which they could develop and on which they could work quite a number of people. As landed aristocrats controlling all they surveyed, they would live in luxury.

It was such a person who purchased many acres of land and built what became known as Landsee Mansion. It was perhaps the first great residence in that territory. And in my youth the old-timers spoke of Landsee Mansion as having existed prior to their birth. It is difficult to estimate the importance to, and the influence it exerted on, the lives of the entire countryside.

To some it was a symbol reminding them of a legendary past around which previous generations had woven stories of mystery. Some professed to consider it only an abandoned relic. To many it was a haunted house on land under an old Indian curse that would not permit its use by a white man. But to all the people of the countryside, regardless of their expressed opinion, it was an inanimate object that silently, subtly, but surely in some mysterious way touched and tinged their lives.

An animist might contend that Landsee Mansion possessed a soul that made its overpowering influence felt by the people. But a person does not have to believe in the existence of spirits and demons to accept the truth that an inanimate object may greatly influence human life. We think of the man of the mountains as strong, large and rugged as the rock-ribbed peaks among which he lives. And we think of the man of the valley as gentle as the clear brook moving easily and without haste through the lowlands where he dwells. The inanimate which we constantly see leaves its imprint.

Landsee Mansion tall and towering was an object so impressive it could not be ignored. It was preeminently the most imposing residence in the state. It was a landmark known far and wide. The Mansion was built on a tableland from which all sides gradually sloped to a wide level plain that surrounded it. The terrain was such that the Mansion could be seen for miles from every direction. On a fair day there was a panoramic view from its cupola. In every direction the distance seemed to be unlimited. It is said this beautiful view so charmed the man who purchased the land that he refused to travel any farther to inspect other sites.

The house, according to legend, was designed by a distinguished French architect and its chandeliers and interior furnishing were imported. There are many stories extant with reference to the difficulty of transporting the imported materials to Landsee. The items came by boat up the river to a landing about thirty miles away. From this landing they were hauled by wagons to Landsee. As there were no roads through what was then a wilderness, the wagon train took several weeks to make the trip because at some places a roadway had to be cleared and at other times a creek had to be bridged. These stories of the difficulties encountered on these trips, such as the dangers of having to camp at night in the woods infested with wild animals, and of the use of foreign materials and artisans in the construction of the Mansion, caused it to be clothed in an atmosphere of mystery from the beginning. This mystery grew among the people through the passing of the years and still today the Mansion stands shrouded in mystery.

Its grounds were spacious including several acres enclosed by a pale fence which separated the yard from the slave quarters, the barnyard and the cultivated fields and pasture lands. There was little need of the fence except to keep the animals out, for the most courageous boy never dared to invade those premises.

The large high trees surrounding the building appeared to

be endeavoring to match in dignity the stately columns in front of the Mansion. But the boxwoods had grown scraggy and the entire premises were overgrown with bushes, tangled briars and weeds. The brick-paved driveways from the front entrances in the fence to the Mansion were covered with lichen and the whole premises evidenced neglect and abandonment.

A few years before the War between the States the owner of Landsee lost his wife. He sensed the coming of the war and did not wish to be involved in it, so decided to return to his native land overseas. He freed his slaves, distributed his personal property among them, and deeded Landsee to a nephew who lived in Boston. To Aunt Mymee, then a young girl being trained as a seamstress, he gave the sewing machine and all the utensils used by a seamstress, some money, and a plot of land near the Mansion. It was on this lot and with this money that Aunt Mymee built the cottage in which she lived the balance of her life.

The nephew to whom Landsee and its many acres were deeded placed it in the charge of an agent to rent or sell, but its reputation that misfortune had always come to its residents, and Aunt Mymee's insistence that it was haunted and under an Indian curse, prevented the agent from finding either a renter or a purchaser.

So, for many years Landsee Masnion was closed. The louvers of the window shutters had been left half open which would enable a person on the inside to see the outside, and a person on the outside to detect any light inside the house. Often some person would report that when he passed the Mansion at night he saw a light in one of the rooms. Some ridiculed these statements, contending that the party saw the reflection of the moonlight on the window panes.

The appearance of the place had become forbidding and hostile and tended to lend verity to Aunt Mymee's claim that it was haunted, and on ground bearing an Indian curse. The house, with its locked doors across which the spiders had spun their webs, and the partially closed louvers, stood like a silent sentinel guarding the past against any intrusion by the present

It was not always like this. Sometimes after a shower of rain had refreshed all the foliage and the sun was shining brightly, the Mansion momentarily put on a look of pride and evidenced the grandeur and beauty it once possessed. It was somewhat like that of a tired old soldier with shoulders sagging under the weight of old age, who suddenly forgot his weary worn body, straightened and stood at attention upon hearing the familiar bugle call of the army.

Aunt Mymee was diligent in keeping the public reminded of her contention that Landsee Mansion was the habitation of ghosts, and that the Indian curse would prevent any white person from living in peace on the property. While many derided Aunt Mymee's claim, still the Mansion and its quarters stood vacant many years. Even for good compensation, no one could be persuaded to live on the property and care for the house and yard. So the premises were unkept.

The lads were so afraid that Aunt Mymee was right about Landsee Mansion being haunted that when they passed it at night they quickened their pace and were careful to keep as quiet as possible. If alone, they generally ran. They sometimes thought they saw light shining through the window of a room upstairs, and always felt that, through the half-open louvers of the window shutters, malignant eyes of unseen beings stared at them, watching to see if anyone was guilty of any act that would offend them. I myself always drew a long breath of relief when I had finished passing Landsee Mansion at night and often, even in daylight, I felt somewhat uneasy when walking by it.

Landsee Mansion often caused discussion as to whether ghosts existed because, every now and then, some person would report observing a strange and unusual occurrence there.

Are there disembodied spirits of the dead which sometimes appear to the living? In my youth I knew some trustworthy white people and a large number of Negroes who believed in ghosts and claimed to have seen them. It is difficult to understand how an uneducated person could so vividly and convincingly describe the sight of ghosts unless he was relating an actual experience.

In concluding whether or not there are ghosts we must remember that the fact that we have not seen one does not prove they do not exist. Is it not possible that some may be attuned to seeing such visions and others not? And is it not reasonable to infer that ghosts might appear to those who believe in their existence and not to those who deride their being? We are compelled to acknowledge that there are many forces which affect our lives, that the eye does not see, and which we do not always understand. All of us at times have felt a presence that we could not touch with our hands. Where do we draw the line between what is a figment and what is some outside power?

Always we are standing on the brink of the revelation of new, greater and more astounding knowledge. We know that many universally accepted facts of today were yesterday considered fantasies. Our knowledge and experience are still limited. We may deduce logically from known facts certain legitimate conclusions but beyond that we cannot be sure. It may be true that whatever the mind conceives will some day materialize into a commonly accepted fact. So far as is practical, if Landsee Mansion were not a haunted house built on land bearing an Indian curse, it might just as well have been.

The Blossburgs

In the course of about two years two families came from distant and different places to live in Landsee. While their coming had no relation to each other, circumstances drew their families together and they, without any design on their part to do so, disturbed the usual quiet and serene social and economic status that had existed in Landsee for many years.

On an inspection tour to find a suitable place to locate a general mercantile business, Isaac Blossburg, a Jew, visited Landsee. He stopped at the "Drummers Home" of Henry May. Mr. Blossburg did not hesitate to let it be known that he was thinking of locating a mercantile business in the village.

He employed Mr. May to assist him in securing the facts he considered necessary to enable him to make a safe decision. Mr. May drove him through a good part of the farming area and introduced him to a number of the residents. After being in Landsee several days, Blossburg announced that he was interested in purchasing a lot on which to build a store and that he would like to purchase a residence suitable for his family.

The prospect of the unusual event of another large mercantile business being operated in Landsee stirred the interest of the entire village. People were coming to be more and more aware of the exorbitant charges made by Mr. Williamson and some had privately discussed organizing a business in competition with him. This coming of Mr. Blossburg seemed to them to be a blessing.

No one was more interested in, or concerned about, Blossburg's visit to Landsee than was Lon Williamson. Like his father before him, Williamson had always operated without any competition and had taken full advantage of this situation to arbitrarily impose such terms and prices as would enhance his wealth. Those who were in financial position to make effective objections to his high-handed methods were dependent on his business for so few items that they did not consider it worthwhile to question the morality of his business decisions.

He had also taken advantage of those in financial distress and made loans of money where he could not only be well secured and get a high rate of return but also where it would place him in a position to demand of the person to whom the loan was made services or favors he required. Years of such uncurbed activities not only placed a number of people under his power but developed in him the belief that he was superior to most men, and that he had a right to be granted his demands.

When Mr. Williamson first heard that Mr. Blossburg was making a survey to decide whether he would open a mercantile business in Landsee, he was of the opinion that a Jew would not care for the character of the rural trade he would find and would move on to some industrial center. However, he soon became aware that Mr. Blossburg was thinking seriously of coming to Landsee. He resented Blossburg's invasion of an area he had long considered his private preserve, to be exploited at his pleasure. Williamson was not of a character to relinquish without a fight a financial advantage he had long enjoyed. He determined to prevent Mr. Blossburg from coming to Landsee. Somehow he did not doubt his ability to do so.

Previously, he had always been in position to secure his wishes by coercion and had acted independently of others without any consideration of their opinion. After carefully evaluating his problem, he realized that in this case he would need the cooperation of a number of the local residents.

While Mr. Williamson did not relish going to the expense of serving a dinner at his home, he decided that the situation required him to do everything he could to assure a good attendance and a favorable reception of his proposal. So he sent a written, urgent request to those whose cooperation he felt he needed to come to dinner at his home to consider a matter of vital importance to the future of Landsee. Usually, the purpose for which a meeting of citizens was called was made known at the time the meeting was called but Mr. Williamson decided not to disclose the purpose until he had an opportunity to present it. Consequently there was considerable speculation as to the purpose of the meeting.

While he had kept his conjecture to himself, there was one man who thought he knew the purpose of the meeting. Afterwards, Henry May said that when he first received the request to attend the dinner meeting he decided not to go to Williamson's home. This decision resulted from an incident that took place at Sunday School that made him certain that Williamson was going to attempt to use the church against Mr. Blossburg.

He said that Mr. Williamson, who was presiding over the assembled classes as superintendent of the Sunday School, said to him in a voice he was sure would attract everyone's attention, "Henry, why did you not bring your hotel guest to Sunday School with you? Did you invite him?" May said he unwittingly played into his hands by replying, "Lon, you know that Mr. Blossburg is a Jew." Then Mr. Williamson said, "Yes, he is of the race that crucified Jesus and despises our Christian faith. It is fortunate that we do not have such a person in Landsee and I know all of you hope we never will."

When Henry May returned from Sunday School he told Mr. Blossburg about the incident and said, "I do not know how Lon expects to use the church to serve his selfish interest but this incident convinces me that he will and that it will be based on the fact that you are a Jew. I will not be a party to such an effort and I have decided not to attend his dinner meeting. He is holding the meeting in his own home to make it embarrassing for his guests to oppose him."

After thinking a little while Mr. Blossburg said, "Mr. May, I wish you could feel that it was all right for you to attend the meeting and let me know what happens. I am sure you can understand why it is important for me to know what action is taken. I had not expected Mr. Williamson to want me or any other competitor but I only anticipated that I would encounter keen commercial competition. If at this meeting the leading citizens express opposition to my operating a business here then I do not wish to come. Could you do me the favor of attending and letting me know if they organize against me?" Mr. May, considering this a fair request, agreed to attend the meeting and give him a full report of its proceedings.

Mr. Williamson arranged his meeting and the presentation of his plan with great care. When he decided the course he would pursue, he had a feeling of elation that fate was working with him by sending a Jew as the person to interfere with his beneficial situation.

Lon Williamson considered himself the most prominent churchman in Landsee and felt that it would appear natural for him to emphasize the religious in his plan and presentation. Mr. Williamson had suggested that he could serve as superintendent of the Sunday School and, as most church members are glad to have someone else assume responsible positions in the church, he became superintendent of the Sunday School. In the same manner, and by commenting that he was perhaps the largest contributor to the church, he became chairman of the Board of Stewards. At the expense of the church, he always attended the annual conference, which he said was to confer with the Bishop. He left the impression that the Methodist preacher assigned to the Methodist Church at Landsee served there at his pleasure. He felt that this background was perfect for keeping the religious theme dominant. He had invited both the Methodist and Baptist preachers with the belief that they would be compelled to support him. With their support, the others would fall in line with the plan he proposed.

After dinner they gathered in the parlor and Williamson took charge. He began by saying, "As this meeting concerns the preservation of our Christian heritage here in Landsee, I am asking the Chaplain to open our considerations with prayer, after which I have asked my daughter, Ina, to lead us in singing 'How Firm a Foundation'."

The Chaplain said, "May we bow our heads? Almighty God, we beseech Thy guidance in our actions this evening and may what we do be pleasing in Thy sight. Amen." Then Ina Williamson, a handsome young lady with an excellent voice, led the song announced by her father.

Mr. Williamson then said, "As stated, this meeting has been called to plan unified action to preserve our Christian faith. Heretofore our community has been entirely Christian in its belief and faith. There has been no one living in this community with a faith hostile to Christianity who would plant doubt in our children's minds and lead them astray. I know all of you, especially our preachers who are ordained to spread the gospel, desire with all your hearts to prevent any hostile influence against Christianity from entering our community.

"As all of you are aware, there is here a Mr. Blossburg who has announced his intentions to move to Landsee and open a business here. He is a Jew, one who denies the divinity of Jesus. We know nothing of his past. We do not know from whence he comes and why he is having to leave where he lives now. What we do know is that he will be endeavoring to convert our children to his belief. Could there be any greater threat to the spiritual welfare of our children? The danger to our Christian community is so dire that I have called this meeting that we Christians might unitedly take some effective action to prevent this invasion of Landsee by what might be correctly termed 'the devil's agent'."

Everyone present remained silent. Mr. Williamson's family were grouped around the door of an adjoining room. Mrs. Williamson listened without any indication of interest in what her husband was saying. Lon, Jr., was restless and quietly left the house before his father finished his talk. But Ina, his daughter, followed every word he spoke with evident approval and a face aglow as a holy crusader against the evil forces of Satan.

As no one spoke, Mr. Williamson decided he would commit the preachers and then use their stand to commit others. So he said, "I am sure our preachers agree that it is the better part of wisdom to keep our community with an undisturbed Christian atmosphere and that to do this it is necessary to prevent Mr. Blossburg from coming to Landsee. I am asking my pastor, Charles Jones, to express himself."

The Methodist preacher seemed to be studying a few seconds before he spoke. Then he said, "We have not been advised of the nature of the power you propose to use to prevent Mr. Blossburg from coming to Landsee. I am not willing to commit myself to any action until I know what that action is to be."

The failure of his preacher to support Mr. Williamson's contention promptly and without question, a support he felt he had a right to demand, angered him and, in a sharp reprimanding tone, he said, "Your answer is evasive. I only asked if you favored keeping evil influences from entering Landsee in the person of a Jew. It is deeply disappointing and a shock that you are not aware of this threat to our Christian environment." The preacher replied in a quiet manner, "Maybe, Mr. Williamson, instead of his coming posing a threat to our Christian environment, it can be an opportunity for you to win him to an acceptance of your faith." Mr. Williamson looked at the Chaplain with incredulity when he heard him say, "Amen." He returned to his attack on the Methodist preacher. He said, "You seem to forget he is of the race that crucified our Lord." The preacher replied, "I remember he is of the same race as Jesus, and Matthew, Mark, John and Paul. I also remember that it is to his race we are indebted for the Old Testament."

Mr. Williamson, desperate to rescue his leadership, replied, "You know very well that those you mentioned do not represent a Jew like Mr. Blossburg." And then returning to using threats to coerce, he said, "Your bishop, to whom I shall feel it my duty to report your attitude, will be mortified at your stand."

To the surprise of all present, the preacher stood and continued quietly, "It is evident that my presence is no longer desired by our host, so I will retire. I enjoyed the dinner and appreciate being included in such a select group. Before departing I suggest that each of you search his heart to be sure that you act from unselfish motives." There was no opportunity for a reply, for he was immediately out of the door and gone. If any one had been noticing Ina during this interchange they would have seen her look at the preacher with a searing hate in her eyes. To her he had committed an unpardonable sin, the opposing of her father.

Mr Williamson with bravado said, "Well, that cleared the atmosphere. We will now consider the plan to prevent this invasion of Landsee by Mr. Blossburg with his anti-Christian character."

Henry May said, "I have been with Mr. Blossburg several days. He has not done or said anything that was anti-Christian. He appears to be a refined gentleman. Anyway, I do not know any legal way to prevent him from coming to Landsee. If you are proposing a Ku Klux Klan, with our putting sheets over our heads and riding him out of town on a rail, you can count me out."

Regaining some of his self-assurance, Mr. Williamson said, "I am surprised and hurt that my friend Henry May would suggest that I favor or even endorse the illegal use of force. He should know I am too good a Christian to resort to violations of the law. I have invited to this meeting you Christian leaders who own property suitable for a store site. I propose that you pledge to each other that you will not sell Mr. Blossburg any property. When he finds he cannot secure a good location, he will abandon the idea of coming to Landsee. By this simple lawful plan this threat to our Christian environment will be averted. Also I am sure when he finds that the leading citizens oppose his coming to Landsee he will abandon his plan to locate here."

Henry May said, "Lon, your proposal requires us to surrender the right to sell our property when we see fit to do so. That is the same as your not being allowed to sell any goods unless all of us approve the sale. I know you would not agree to such an arrangement and I am not going to enter into such an unfair and impractical plan."

Mr. Williamson said, "I fear you do not appreciate the danger that confronts us, or perhaps you are not as interested in protecting our religion as you should be. Your analogy is inept, for you know I would not sell goods to be used in destroying our churches. What I have proposed is a small thing to do for a great cause."

It was evident that most of those present were becoming ill at ease but Williamson, interested in presenting a plan which he was sure could not fail, did not notice his guests' attitude. One of the party finally mustered sufficient courage to say, "I am sorry, Lon, it is getting late and you must excuse me. I have got to go, as I live some distance away." Then others said it was time they were leaving. But, intent upon securing favorable action on his plan, Mr. Williamson said, "Wait a minute, gentlemen, wait a minute. It will not take long to act on this proposal, and certainly we must take strong steps to protect our Christian faith. I have drawn up an agreement embodying the plan I have outlined to you and I have signed it. I will pass it around and each of you can sign it."

Mr. Williamson passed his document to Henry May, saying, "Henry, you can sign right under my name and then pass it to the one next to you." Mr. May said, "Listen, Lon, I am not going to sign any paper preventing me from selling my property when I please and to whom I please." Another man said, "I am afraid it would injure the title to our property and it might establish some kind of precedent that could embarrass us in the future. Would it not be necessary for our wives to sign to make it binding?"

Dr. Alston, seeing that they would never reach an agreement, and with the hope of saving Williamson from the humiliation of being refused by all of them to accede to his request, said, "Lon, your proposal is new to all of us. As you know, any written agreement affecting land title is something about which most of us need legal advice. Perhaps you should give us a little more time to consider it." In almost a chorus they agreed they needed more time and all arose to leave. Mr. Williamson finally recognized he could hold them no longer. He said, "I urge you for the protection of your children to think seriously about the danger that threatens them. I will call you together again soon for action."

Aftermath Of
Mr. Williamson's Dinner

The coming of the Blossburgs to Landsee was destined to disturb Lon Williamson's economic controls and, although he did not realize it, it would set in motion a challenge to his dominance of his church's affairs.

As the guests were leaving Williamson's home that night, the Chaplain quietly said to May, "Henry, I want to have a private talk with you." May replied, "You have to go by my house going home. We can walk together and talk." When they were out of the hearing of any other person, the Chaplain said, "I am concerned about what happened between your pastor and Lon tonight. I want you, as a member of the Board of Stewards of your church, to attend its every meeting and prevent Lon from having them take some detrimental action against him. You know that Lon resents the courageous stand that young man took tonight." Firmly May said, "I will take pleasure in complying with your request."

The Chaplain continued, "It will be necessary for you to do more than that to be sure he is protected. Lon has given the impression that your preacher serves at his will. Charles has been here four years and will not be eligible to return, but Lon could prevent him from securing a good assignment. You must be the one to represent your church at the Conference this year." Henry said, "Now listen, Chaplain, you are asking me to undertake a job I know nothing about. I am without any experience in such matters. In addition to that, I am not going to ask the members of my church to elect me."

The Chaplain said, "Henry, you have to go. We can't have Lon wreak his vengence on this young man. I am going to see some of my friends who belong to your church and I am sure they can elect you without your having to do one thing." Mr. May said, "Well, if I am elected, with your help, I will do the best I can."

Just as they were about to part, the Chaplain said, "Henry, there is one other matter I want to mention. Tell Mr. Blossburg not to permit Lon's attitude and actions to influence his decision about locating his mercantile business in Landsee." Henry nodded in agreement.

When Henry reached home he found Blossburg waiting for him and anxious to hear a report of the meeting. He gave Blossburg a full and detailed report and at the conclusion told him of the message the Chaplain had sent him. Blossburg asked, "What do you think of the situation and what do you think of the Chaplain's advice?"

Henry replied, "First, as to the advice of the Chaplain, I value his opinion as high as that of any man in Landsee. I fully agree with him. As I said, Lon's own pastor openly opposed him."

Blossburg said, "I had decided to locate in Landsee before I heard of Mr. Williamson's effort to organize some of the leading citizens against me. When I heard he had called a meeting to solidify the organization, I decided to await the outcome of this meeting before making a final decision. As he has failed to secure any cooperation on the part of the citizens in opposing my coming, I decide now to locate my business here. I would like to purchase your property just across the road from Mr. Williamson's store."

May and Blossburg soon reached an agreement and they arranged to go to the county seat the next day to have an attorney handle the transfer of the title of the property. Mr. May wished to complete the transaction before Lon Williamson could propose some other plan to prevent Isaac Blossburg from securing a suitable site for his store.

After purchasing the property, Mr. Blossburg carried the plans for the construction of his storehouse to the Chaplain and asked him to undertake the building of the store and have it ready for occupancy as soon as he was able to do so.

In a little over two months the building was available for occupancy. All during the construction period Lon Williamson endeavored to arouse prejudice, not only against the Blossburgs, but against those engaged in constructing the building. People would tell the Chaplain that Lon Williamson would say to them, "Over there is a preacher who on Sunday talks about the gospel and on week days engages for money in work that is contrary to everything he says in his pulpit. He and his helpers are bringing to Landsee persons who oppose our Christian religion."

Blossburg's store was quite different in appearance from the old rambling Williamson structure. In the front it had two show windows for the display of merchandise, one on each side of the main entrance. Inside, instead of wooden counters, he had glass show cases that served as counters.

As soon as the Chaplain notified him that the store was ready for occupancy, Mr. Blossburg ordered his stock of merchandise shipped and brought his family to Landsee. His family consisted of his wife and a daughter, Sarah. A house was readily selected by Mrs. Blossburg and within a few weeks the Blossburgs were residents of Landsee.

Blossburg arranged to have his store's opening on a Saturday. Ben Davidson, Jr., heard that Mr. Blossburg was inquiring for help and, with the consent of his parents, went to work for him.

The coming of the Blossburgs to Landsee not only interfered with Lon Williamson economically, but it also posed a threat to what his daughter, Ina, considered her popularity and dominance of her social set. A few days after Ben went to work for Mr. Blossburg, Sarah began coming to the store every day to help. Sarah was an intelligent and beautiful young lady. She had inherited her mother's wavy black hair and large, soft, and expressive deep brown eyes and her father's fair complexion. She had grace and a charming delicacy. As the Blossburgs residence lay in the same direction from the store as Ben's home, often after the store closed Ben would walk with her to her home. Sarah's beauty and Ben's attention to her did not go unnoticed by Ina Williamson.

To eliminate her as a competitor Ina began a subtle campaign. Whenever she had a chance, or could make a chance, she would remark in a confidential manner to one of the young people, "I feel sorry for that Jew girl (Ina always referred to Sarah as 'That Jew Girl') for there are no Jews here with whom she can associate, and you know a Christian will not care to go with her."

Ina saw to it that her remarks reached Ben. When she saw that Ben was still walking home with Sarah she carried her campaign directly to Ben. One day she made it a point to run into him and said, "Ben, everybody is surprised that you should be working for one opposed to our Christian religion. The other day some one told me you were showing that Jew girl a great deal of attention, and I told them I knew that was a mistake because you were too good a Christian to intimately associate with one who denied the divinity of Jesus. You should avoid the appearance of evil or you will lose your influence for good, as well as your Christian friends."

Ben listened in silence. He felt his anger rising in resentment at what she was saying. However, he had learned not to permit his anger to talk, so he walked in polite silence with her until he found an excuse to leave her.

While Ben's parents had consented for him to go to work for Mr. Blossburg, Ben had not discussed with them his going with Sarah. Ina's remarks worried him and he hesitated to mention them to his parents. Ben was one of several young people who believed that his school teacher, Miss Essie Gill, would know more about this particular problem than any one else. So he decided to go to her for advice. He told Miss Essie about Ina's remarks relative to his working for Mr. Blossburg and what she had said about his going with Sarah. Ben said, "My parents consented for me to work for Mr. Blossburg and I know that is all right. What I want to know, Miss Essie, is if it is proper for me to go with Sarah. As you probably know, I like Sarah."

Miss Essie said, "Of course it is all right for you to go with Sarah. Do not pay any attention to Ina's disparaging remarks. She has many fine qualities but one of them is not charity towards a prospective strong competitor in her social field."

Ina's Club

Mr. Williamson had failed in his effort to prevent Mr. Blossburg from locating in Landsee. That failure, though a severe shock, failed to prevent him from continuing his effort to eliminate Blossburg as a competitor. Each day as he realized that Blossburg was securing an increasingly larger portion of the business he had formerly received, he became more and more determined to find some means to drive him from Landsee.

Ina was in a somewhat similar situation. She had energetically spread her insistence that Sarah as a Jew was anti-Christian and that those interested in the Christian religion should not become socially intimate with her. Ina realized that in spite of her constant reference to Sarah as "that Jew girl," Sarah was making friends among the students, especially the young men.

Williamson realized that in order to restore the uncurbed operation of his mercantile business and his economic dominance to its former status, he must find stronger means than he had used. So also Ina realized that if she were to continue absolute control of the social activities of her age group which she had enjoyed prior to the coming of the Blossburgs, she must employ new and stronger tactics to accomplish her purposes.

Ina and her father acted independently of each other. Although they never consulted about the situations that confronted each of them, there was a sympathetic understanding of each other's problems, and each was confident that the other would be able to successfully solve his particular problem.

Ina was the first to act. She was like many others who considered religion a means to be used to promote their personal, private interests, regardless of how selfish those interests might be. She had listened with ardent admiration to her father when he urged religious reasons as a basis for preventing the Blossburgs from coming to Landsee, and now was convinced that these same reasons could be used to her advantage.

Ina announced to the students at school that she was inviting the members of the Sunday school classes of her age group of both the Methodist and Baptist Churches to a party she was giving at her home the next Friday evening, and that at this social gathering there would be organized a Christian Club for the purpose of providing entertainment suitable for young Christians.

Sarah knew this proposal of Ina's was a move to prevent her from participating in the social affairs of those of her age group. In fact, virtually everyone recognized this to be Ina's primary objective. Also, Sarah had been told by Ben of Ina's effort to prevent him from going with her and of his visit to Miss Essie to ask if Ina were right. Ben had told Sarah that Miss Essie advised him not to pay any attention to Ina.

One day after school, as Ben was leaving the school house, he looked back and saw Sarah walking alone in his direction. Sarah often walked alone. A sensitive soul, and conscious of Ina's remarks, she always deliberately timed her leaving school so that it would be clear that she was not forcing herself on anyone. Ben waited until Sarah had caught up with him and then said, "Sarah, let me have your books and walk home with you." Sarah had just passed a group to which she heard Ina, who had her back to her, say, "Some of those boys who are thoughtlessly associating with that Jew girl are going to be ashamed of themselves." Sarah said, "No, not this afternoon, Ben. I will tell you why some other time."

Ben was so surprised he just stood still and was standing there wondering when Ina came along. She stopped and said, "Well, Ben, did the hypnotizing siren leave you in a happy trance?" Ben replied, "If she did you have rudely disturbed it." Ina, who was seldom abashed by what others might consider a curt reply to her questioning criticism, said, "Many of your old Christian friends feel that some good influence should break your evil enchantment."

Fortunately for Ben, because his anger rather than his reason was about to reply to Ina, she continued hurriedly, "I know you and John will be glad to help make a success of the Christian Club we are going to organize next Friday evening at my home. Those with whom I have discussed the organization have suggested that you should be president, John vice president and treasurer, and that I serve as secretary and chairman of the program committee." Before Ben could reply Ina continued, "Oh! Yonder is someone I must see immediately. Excuse me. I will talk to you later. I will be depending on your support." And away she went to catch the other party.

Ben saw John Alston approaching and moved to meet him and they walked away together. Perhaps the legendary friendship of Damon and Pythias was no stronger than the friendsip that existed between Ben Davidson, Jr., and John Alston. They were such close friends that the problem of one was the problem of the other. They knew each other so well that every movement and expression of one carried a meaning to the other. When John looked at Ben he sensed that something had disturbed him. "Ben, has someone made you mad?" With considerable vehemence Ben replied, "Yes, that Ina and her persecution of Sarah."

Ben told John of Ina's conversation and her suggestion that they be chief officers of the Club when organized. Ben said, "You see what she intends to do. The Club will exclude Sarah from its membership and from participation in the social activities it promotes. By electing me as president, she will make me the spearhead of this effort to ostracize Sarah. You will also be prominent in her cursed movement. If we do not accept what she insists is the great honor of being officers of her club, then we will be in the embarrassing position of refusing to support a Christian effort." John said, "Yes, you will note she holds control of the activities of the Club by having charge of the programs, although she suggests others for what are considered the highest offices." Ben said, "Of course she holds control. She will dominate the Club and I do not want to be a member of any organization dominated by her. I do not know what to do."

They had reached John's home and were standing there talking when Miss Essie came along. Miss Essie always waited until everyone had left the school house and then she would check to see that all the windows were shut and all the doors closed. Miss Essie asked, "Why the sober and solemn looks? Are you thinking of attending a funeral?" While she was a strict disciplinarian at school and always appeared dignified and reserved, most of the students felt free to discuss with Miss Essie their personal affairs. She was a confidant of John and Ben and always listened with a sympathetic interest.

Ben said, "It appears that I am about to be forced into a position as hurtful as attending a funeral." Before Miss Essie could ask any questions John told her, "Ben and I are going to be seriously embarrassed unless we can find some way to avoid it. Miss Essie, maybe you can help us. Do you have time to talk to us about it?" "We can't discuss anything seriously standing here with our arms full of books and shifting our weight from one foot to the other," replied Miss Essie. "You two go home, put up your books, wash your hands and come to my house. I don't want you eating my cookies with dirty hands. I will expect you in fifteen minutes and we will see if there is any solution to your threatened troubles."

John and Ben were at Miss Essie's house within the time limit she had set. After they had generously sampled the delicious cookies Miss Essie had made, she said, "Now, tell me about your problem." They told her about Ina's scheme to exclude Sarah from all their social affairs, explaining that Ina was suggesting that they be made the principal officers of the club which would put them in the forefront of her effort. John said, "When Ina spreads, with shocking incredulity in her voice, our refusal to serve as officers of her Christian Club, we will look like hideous creatures."

When they had finished Miss Essie said, "It does seem that Ina is about to sail you two between Scylla and Charybdis. I have heard remarks now and then at school that gave me some idea of what Ina was doing. This caused me to think about an answer to her scheme. You are dealing with a foe worthy of your best steel, for Ina is resourceful, tenacious and shrewd. She has great confidence in her ability to compel others to serve her purposes and she will be relentless in her efforts. You will need time to create a plan that will give you a permanent reason for not joining her organization. Both of you must have some plansible excuse for not attending her party next Friday evening."

Ben said, "I would like to tell her that I have a previous engagement that evening with Sarah and watch her put on her act of horrification, but I know Sarah would not want me to do that. I don't suppose it would be plausible for both of us to claim we were sick." Miss Essie asked, "Is Jake Wilson invited to Ina's party?" Ben answered, "No, Ina invited only the members of the Sunday school classes in the Methodist and Baptist Churches and Jake and his family belong to the Primitive Baptist Church which is several miles from here."

Jake's father worked at the sawmill. Jake was about a year older than Ben and John and was large for his age. He was popular with the boys. When selections were being made to play baseball, Jake was always the first person chosen because he was the best catcher and batter in school. He was a special friend to John and Ben.

Miss Essie asked, "Hasn't Jake been trying to get you two to go 'possum hunting with him at Snake Creek Beat, where his aunt lives? His aunt is a fine person, although her husband has the reputation of belonging to that lawless gang living in that part of the county. She has a big house and I'm sure she would be glad to have you. Go to see Jake and ask him to arrange your hunt with his aunt. If the hunt can be arranged, then you can tell Ina that you had promised Jake sometime ago you would go with him on a hunt, that he had arranged it for this Friday evening and that you are compelled to go. I am told you will have some local boys on the hunt, so you can tell Ina there are others than you involved which makes it impossible to postpone it."

John and Ben readily adopted the suggestion and went that night to see Jake. They explained the situation to him for they knew they could trust him, and told him of Miss Essie's suggestion. Jake was delighted to have a part in helping them. He had no trouble in arranging the visit and hunt with his aunt. Jake's aunt told him that there were some men who lived in Snake Creek Beat who gave trouble to outsiders who hunted in the swamps unless they were accompanied by some of the local residents. However, Jake had two friends who lived in the Beat and who had some fine hunting dogs. His aunt suggested that she invite them to dinner with John, Ben and Jake and ask them to bring their dogs and act as hosts on a hunt. This, she said, would let everyone know that local people were in charge of the hunt.

Later, when Ina approached Ben and John to discuss the party, they expressed their regrets and explained why they could not attend. Ina was too smart to let them know how disappointed she was but it upset her plans. She was not accustomed to having her well-laid plans fail. Thinking that they would be flattered at being offered the highest offices in the club she was organizing, it never occurred to her that they would let any previous engagement interfere with doing as she suggested. Ina said, "Well, we will miss you. We might postpone the final organization of the club to a time when you two can be present. You have been so active in the Christian efforts of the young people of Landsee I know you will want to be active in this club. I will check with you before arranging our next social so you can be sure to be present."

Lon, Jr., had invited Amy White to accompany him to the party. Before they left Amy's home she said, "Lon, I have been wondering why Ina is organizing this club. From what she has been saying at school it appears that her purpose is to exclude Sarah from our social affairs. I do not like that. Suppose we just stay here." Lon said, "I would like to stay here, but if I did I would never hear the last of Ina's accusing me of not supporting her religious efforts."

It was fortunate that they attended the party for it was from Amy that John and Ben learned that Ina had announced how much they regretted not being able to attend and that because they so much wished to have an active part in the club, the election of officers would be postponed until the next meeting when they promised to be present. Amy's report was a warning that, while the 'possum hunt had bought them a little time, the sword of Damocles still hung over their heads. Every day Ben was becoming more deeply in love with Sarah. The prospects of being used to hurt or humiliate her severely agitated and disturbed him.

Legend Of Landsee

There was something so strangely fascinating about Aunt Mymee's recital of the Legend of Landsee that those who had heard it repeatedly returned to hear it again.

To many, Aunt Mymee was a person of mystery and they were always curious to hear what she might say. She was an elderly woman who stood tall and erect, and who quietly lived aloof and alone in her small cottage near Landsee Mansion. She seldom left her home and she had few visitors. Usually those who came to her house were on business. While a young slave she had been taught to be an expert seamstress. She was taught to read and write and used the dialect of her mistress. If she had any intimate friends they were Miss Essie, Dr. Alston, and after they came to Landsee, Mrs. Green and Ellen, her closest neighbors. Many were afraid of her. They claimed she would place you under an evil spell if you incurred her displeasure. The young people did not fear her but they did wonder if she did not possess occult powers.

Aunt Mymee was the oldest person in Landsee. She was the only one who had spent a part of her life in the Mansion itself. Also, she was the sole repository of the Legend of Landsee.

Once every two years she gave a recital of the legend. This was held at her cottage and the public was invited. This occasion developed into more than a recital of the legendary story. It became a tradition to which all looked forward with interest. It drew a larger attendance than any other occasion in

Landsee except the Brush Arbor Meeting.

There is planted in each of us a wondering and intriguing interest in the mysterious, and Aunt Mymee's story appealed to this instinct. A large number drove so many miles to attend the recital that they brought sandwiches as the recital was always after their supper time. This resulted in the residents of Landsee arranging long tables on which to place food and everyone would bring baskets of food for a picnic supper. In addition to furnishing their share of the food, the local residents furnished ice cold lemonade and ice cream. It became an occasion of visiting with acquaintances who lived far apart and seldom saw each other.

When the meal was finished, they arranged themselves around the porch of the cottage so as to be in a good position to see and hear Aunt Mymee. She sat in a large rocking chair on the porch while reciting the legend. Many spread blankets on the ground and sat upon them. Some of the older people brought chairs. While waiting for the time the recital was to begin there was group singing. They sang familiar melodies. It was beautiful singing for the people loved to sing.

Aunt Mymee had a shrewd sense of the power of the dramatic and she employed every means available to make her performance convincing and impressive. When she was ready to begin she would come to the door of her cabin, stand there until she had complete attention, and then take her seat.

There was no lighting outside of the cottage except that which came from the full moon. When Landsee Mansion was viewed from the cottage, the moonlight shining on the window panes sometimes made it appear as if there were a light in one of the upper rooms of the Mansion. And the moonlight, filtering through the shade trees around the cabin, cast shadows and patches of light over the yard. A light breeze cautiously moved the branches of the trees to and fro, causing these lights and shadows to silently and slowly shift positions and slightly change shapes, often to weird shapes.

From a strong lamp in the front room of the cottage a bright light came through the door, prominently illuminating Aunt Mymee sitting in her chair. The setting caused a strange and eerie atmosphere to pervade the crowd. Some magic influence constrained them to be silent and give Aunt Mymee complete attention.

Often the hearer of a legend has difficulty in deciding what part is fact and what part is fiction. Even where part of a story is fiction, the fiction is generally based on some admitted fact. The people went away from these performances with varying opinions. Some accepted the entire story as a true statement of actual happenings. To these, the more pragmatic said that distance not only lends enchantment to the physical view, but, in time, lends enchantment to mental decisions when considering events taking place in the misty long ago. Some will accept as possible the happening of an event in ancient days that they would consider impossible of taking place in the present. Some thought the legend originated with Aunt Mymee, but those who knew her and respected her were convinced that there was factual basis for the incidents she related. No one ever indicated that the phantoms which were such an important part of her story were invented by her, but some contended they were a figment resulting from her being indoctrinated when a young girl by the old Indian who told her the tale.

Although Aunt Mymee always had quiet and attention when she took her seat, she invariably rapped on the floor with a walking stick and then said, "When I was a girl between ten and twelve years of age, I do not know my exact age, there visited the slave quarters of Landsee Mansion an elderly Indian, a seller of baskets woven of stained strips of cane, who taught me the Legend of Landsee and charged me to keep the public aware of it. For reasons I will not now state, I do not dare ignore this charge, and it is in discharge of this responsibility that I hold this meeting once every two years.

"Once upon a time in the long ago all this land was the hunting ground of the Indians. How many years they had roamed these then forested acres and had sailed its rivers is not known. For a long period of time this high ground was near the border of the territories of the Choctaw and Creek tribes. Because of its location and the fact that from the site where now stands Landsee Mansion you could see in every direction as far as human vision reached, and also because down the slope on one side was a spring that furnished aboundant water, it became the meeting place for the pow-wows of the two Indian tribes. Because you could see such long stretches of land from its top, it was given the name 'Landsee.' And the great spring, with its full flow of cool and limpid water, was known as the 'Spring of Lifegiving Water.'

"To these pow-wows the chiefs would bring their families and spend several days discussing the affairs of their tribes and smoking the peace pipes. At one of these meetings a young chief of the Creek tribe and a maiden, the daughter of a chief of the Choctaw tribe, fell in love. He endeavored to persuade her to marry him and go with him to live with his tribe. As much as she loved him she hesitated to marry him. She was keenly aware of the difference in the attitudes of their tribes toward the white man. Her people believed they could live in peace with the white people, but his tribe, a proud and brave people, considered the pale face their enemy and thought that they should be driven from their hunting grounds. She knew his attitude meant constant strife and bloodshed and that they could never enjoy a happy home.

"Finally, she agreed to marry him if they could make their home at Landsee where they would be in close contact with both tribes, and if he would endeavor to influence his tribe to seek to live in peace with the white man. The chiefs of the two tribes agreed that they should have Landsee as a site for their home, and there in a beautiful Indian ceremony they were married, and there they made their home. They lived there happily for several years.

"Then came the great Indian orator from the North, preaching hatred for the pale face and calling the Indians to arms to drive them from their hunting grounds. This impassioned plea fell on fertile ground among the Creeks and they resolved to respond to the call. The young chief came home to tell his wife that his tribe was going to war against the pale face and his duty as a chief compelled him to go with them. They parted amid her protest and tears. He promised that at every opportunity he would ride home to see her and she promised to keep a light at night so that he could find his way home.

"One night when the young chief and two of his comrades were riding to Landsee under cover of darkness, he discovered, when they reached the place where he had always seen the light his wife kept burning, that there was no light. He was alarmed because he knew there was something wrong and he feared it was due to enemy action. They stealthily approached his home. Finally, when they entered the tent, they found his wife dead. While there was no evidence that her death was due to violence, he attributed it to the white man. With the help of his comrades, with night surrounding them, he buried her there on Landsee and they spread leaves over the grave so that no one except those who had buried her would know where her body was resting.

"When they had finished their solemn and sad task the young chief stood at the head of her grave and called upon his gods to see that for seventy-five years no white man could live happily at Landsee. He pledged his comrades that, at his death, to secretly bury him beside his wife, and he there consecrated his spirit to ride the grounds of Landsee and to haunt any house built there in order to make effective the curse he had placed upon it.

"He pledged that when the curse was cancelled his spirit would ride away as fast as any steed ever raced and the windows of any house built on Landsee would be bright with light, and that ill would come to anyone who looked upon him while he was making this last ride. He placed upon his comrades the responsibility of communicating this curse to one who, in turn, would choose his successor to keep it alive during its existence. And dire would be the disaster that would overtake the person given the responsibility to keep the public aware of this curse if such person failed to discharge this duty.

"The young Creek chief was killed in battle. His comrades, true to the promise made to him, placed the chief's lifeless body on his fine horse and brought it by night to Landsee where it was buried beside his wife. When they had finished spreading leaves over the fresh ground to conceal the new-made grave, the chief's riding horse whimpered, broke its tether and rushed away into the darkness. It was never seen again because, the Indians said, the spirit of its master had ridden it away to use when he rode the grounds of Landsee in enforcing his curse.

"The trail used by the white man in his westward trek ran by Landsee and, because of the spring of abundant good water and its shaded level ground near the spring, it became a wayside temporary camping ground where travelers would sometimes spend several days resting before continuing their journey.

"One day a wealthy man, traveling west in search of wide acres to secure and develop, stopped at this resting place. He walked to the high ground where Landsee Mansion is now situated and was enthralled with the beauty and breadth of the view in every direction. Then and there he determined this was the property he must own. After months of negotiations he acquired Landsee and several hundred acres surrounding it. He brought an architect to see the site before he drew the plans for its development. While he and the architect were looking at the property an old Indian appeared and told them the story of the young Indian chief and warned them not to build on that high ground. The owner did not believe in the Indian curse and paid no attention to what he had been told about it.

"A famous architect drew the plans for the Mansion and its slave quarters. Much of the material used in the construction was imported. It was brought up the river from the gulf and then hauled overland. Trained artisans were brought to Landsee to erect the buildings. Many accidents happened during the construction. The Indians attributed these accidents to the curse. When the Mansion was finally finished the owner brought his wife and slaves to live there. I was being raised by a Negro woman who was not my mother. She was owned by an Indian who was killed in the war at which time she was sold to the owner of Landsee. She brought me with her and thus I also became a slave of the master of Landsee. No one could have had a kinder and more considerate master than I had.

"Several years after I came to Landsee this elderly Indian basket maker told me the story of Landsee one evening when he spent the night at the slave quarters. We were in the same cabin. At midnight I heard a horse galloping around the yard. I crept to the door of the cabin in an effort to learn what was happening. The old Indian was also at the door. When we looked out we saw a light in one of the attic windows of the Mansion. We did not see the rider of the horse but we heard the receding sound of the racing horse and, when that sound ceased, the light in the attic window went out.

"I told the Indian that no one lived in that attic room and that it was seldom visited by anyone even during the day, and that I could not understand a light being on that night. He said it was the spirits of the Creek chief and his wife, his wife lighting the attic window as she had kept a light to guide her husband when coming home at night or when riding his horse away to battle. He said it was to impress me with the responsibility of warning the white man of the curse. While I did not doubt the Indian, I knew those who denied the existence of the curse would say I had heard a stray horse running around. I decided to find out what explanation they would give of the lighted attic room. The next morning I told the woman who was training me as a seamstress what the Indian and I had heard and seen during the night. I also told her what the Indian said about its being the spirits of the Creek Indian Chief and his wife. I hoped she would tell our mistress and that she, in turn, would tell our master.

"The woman in charge of the domestic servants overheard me telling about the night's experience. She had a harsh attitude toward those under her control and no one liked her. She was a white woman and said to be a distant cousin of our master. She accused me of manufacturing the story to frighten the Negroes. She said she was going to the attic room and if she could not find some evidence that someone had been there during the night she was going to have me whipped for lying. Frightened at the promised punishment which I knew she would make as severe as she could, I pleaded with her not to think I wanted to give trouble. I asked her to remember that never before had I been threatened with punishment or accused of telling a lie. She refused to listen and rushed away to the attic room. The seamstress said that she would follow her and try to influence her to change her attitude. In a few minutes I heard a scream and a noise of something falling. When I reached the foot of the stairs leading to the attic I saw the woman in charge of the domestic help lying there unconscious.

"The seamstress saw her rush out of the door to the attic room with a frightened look on her face, and when she reached the top of the stairs she lunged forward as if she had been given a severe push. She never regained consciousness. The master said that undoubtedly in her hurry she stumbled and fell, but all the servants knew she was the victim of the Indian curse.

"Several years passed with the affairs of Landsee seldom going smoothly. There were crop failures and hog cholera. The master owned a fine saddle horse which he prized highly and rode almost daily over some part of his estate. Often when reaching the Mansion, he would dismount and throw the bridle reins over the horse's head and the horse would walk to the barn where one of the servants would care for him. On one occasion when the master dismounted, the horse rose on its hind legs, plunged forward and then began running and staggering as if it did not know which way to go. The horse died that night. The man in charge of the stables said the horse had blind staggers but we knew it was the spirit of the dead Creek chief riding the master's horse to its death.

"And then again the Indian basket maker who was of the Creek tribe spent a night at our slave quarters, and again he and I heard the racing horse and saw the light in the attic window. The next morning I asked to talk to our mistress, and I told her what the Indian and I had heard and seen. She listened to me very carefully and when I finished she did not express any doubt as to my truthfulness but said, 'You, the seamstress and I will go to the attic room and see if we can find anything that indicates that someone has been in that room during the night. You know, if they were using a lighted candle, some of the tallow might have dropped on the floor.'

"When we reached the foot of the stairs leading to the attic, our mistress fainted. We carried her to her bed and sent for the doctor. In three days she was dead. The doctor said she had not been in good health for many months on account of a weak heart, and that undoubtedly the great excitement caused her to suffer a fatal heart attack. But somehow the opinion prevailed among the servants that our mistress' death was the result of the Indian curse. After the death of our mistress the master lost all interest in Landsee, and all the slaves lived an uneasy life.

"A few years after our mistress died the master called all his slaves together and told us that he had concluded that there was no prospect of his living with any pleasure at Landsee and that he had decided to close the Mansion and move back to his old home. He informed us we would be given our freedom and he would distribute his animals and farm utensils among us and give each of us money with which to start an independent life. Because I had no need for farm animals and equipment, he asked me what I would like to have. I told him that, as I expected to support myself as a seamstress, I would like to have the sewing machines and all the equipment used by a seamstress. He said the value of that which I had selected was not nearly equal to that which he was giving the others. Thinking of my responsibility to keep alive the Legend of Landsee, I said, if possible, I would like a plot of land near Landsee where I could build a cottage in which to live. He gave me the lot on which this cabin is built, the money with which to build the cottage, and such furniture as I wished from the Mansion to furnish it. I lived in the slave quarters until I moved into this cottage, and here I have lived ever since.

"The master appointed an agent to have charge of Landsee Mansion and the broad acres that go with it. This agent was to see that the property was rented or sold, and kept in good repair if not sold. The place has been vacant since the master's departure, for the agent has been unable to find a purchaser, and because of the fear of the curse he has been unable to persuade anyone to work on the place and keep it in repair.

"Several times at midnight while living in this cottage I have heard the racing horse and have seen a light in one of the windows of the Mansion. The light would always go out when I could no longer hear the running horse. Look at it as it appears under the curse, an abandoned great house with sagging shutters and peeling paint and crumbling parts. It is the home of unseen guests, the spirits of departed Indians. Remember, woe will come to the white man who attempts to live at Landsee Mansion before the curse is lifted. This ends my warning. Please depart quietly."

Aunt Mymee went into her cabin and closed the door, leaving the people to find their way by the light of the moon. Some lingered a few minutes gazing at lonesome-looking Landsee. Others moved quietly and quickly away as if they did not wish to be near the place where phantoms might appear and molest them. All were gone in a very short period of time.

The Educational
Aid Club

The o'possum hunt in Snake Creek Beat was quite a success. The young men of that precinct who had been invited by Jake's aunt joined John, Ben and Jake for supper at her home. They brought their hunting hounds and, as requested, conducted the hunt. Jake's aunt had let these arrangements be well known among the local residents who objected to outsiders hunting in the precinct without local guidance. It was thought that this required supervision was to prevent the accidental discovery by the outsider of moonshine stills.

To Ben the occurrence which gave him the most pleasure was not the supper they were served, as bountiful and delicious as it was, nor the hunt which was his favorite sport, but it was learning Jake Wilson's attitude with reference to Ina's effort to organize her Christian club. On their way to Snake Creek Beat Ben and John had told Jake that, in their opinion, Ina's proposal to form her Christian Club was for the sole purpose of excluding Sarah from all the social activities of the young people. Even though they were close friends, John and Ben did not know whether or not Jake had a prejudice against Jews. Jake, not only because of his friendship with John and Ben but also because of his innate sense of justice, became their strong ally in opposing Ina's scheme.

At school, the week following Ina's party and the o'possum hunt, Ina increased her activities in the promotion of the organization of her Christian Club. Ina, and several of those who always echoed everything she said, enthusiastically discussed how wonderful was the party given by Ina and how much they anticipated a summer of pleasant social affairs which would be planned by the Christian Club. Whenever possible Ina would promote these discussions in the hearing of Sarah. Ina was getting considerable secret pleasure in constantly reminding Sarah she would have no part in the social activities during the summer vacation.

Especially would Ina emphasize, when in Sarah's hearing, that Ben was going to be president of the club and that John was to be vice-president. On one occasion when she knew Sarah could hear what she was saying, but acting as if she did not know that Sarah was near, Ina said, "Ben is going to be happy to be president and actively promoting the club so as to show everyone that there is no truth in the report that he is being influenced by an anti-Christian person to the extent that it controls his thinking and his actions." It was this and similar remarks which Sarah overheard that prompted her to ask Ben and John to come by her home where she could talk to them privately and without being interrupted.

Sarah included John in this request because Ben had told her the reason for the o'possum hunt and she knew from this that neither John nor Ben wished to be officers of Ina's Christian Club. Sarah was convinced that if Ben and John refused to join the club, Ina would attribute their refusal to her anti-Christian influence, and would repeatedly and caustically criticize her for her evil influence, and John and Ben for their weakness in not supporting the Christian faith.

While John and Ben had avoided talking to Ina about the organization of her club, they knew about her comments, the purpose of which they realized was to compel them to accept the principal offices in her club.

Sarah was waiting for Ben and John when they arrived at her home, and immediately told them why she had requested them to come. She said that she had discussed with her mother the remarks made by Ina and others about making Ben and John the chief officers of Ina's Christian Club. Sarah had advised her mother that she knew that the boys had determined not to join Ina's club and she wanted to tell them her mother's adivce and suggestions in the matter. Her mother was of the opinion that if Ben and John did not cooperate with Ina in organizing and conducting her club, their failure to do so would be seriously misunderstood and would probably cause Ina to increase violently her charge that Sarah was an anti-Christian influence. As Jews, they had to be careful to avoid increasing any prejudice against their race. Her mother also told her to ask them to consider the fact that, as members of the club, they might shape the actions of the club.

Sarah concluded by saying, as she dropped her eyes and softened her voice, "Ben, Mother also said that you would be less apt to lose your old friends if you showed me less attention." John said, "Sarah, you know that neither of us is going to join Ina's club. We realize she will try to make us unpopular but we will make it hurt her as much as she makes it hurt us. Just thank your mother for us." As they left, gratitude glowed in Sarah's moist, large brown eyes and the slight tremble of her lips bespoke her emotions more eloquently than words could have conveyed.

John and Ben left Sarah to go and confer with their trusted mentor, Miss Essie. She was expecting them because they had asked her if they might come. After they had been invited in and were seated she said, "I have overheard enough at school to know that Ina is drawing her net tighter and tighter around you two. She thinks she is just about ready to pull you into the duties she has planned for you to perform. Have you arranged any way of escape without giving her good grounds to support her contention that you are no longer interested in the Christian religion? Ben, I can see Ina talking to her loyal followers, sadly expressing her regret at your desertion of the Christian faith and calling on all of them to pray earnestly for your return to the fold."

Ben, who had a feeling that he was trapped and was still so angry he could not think logically, said, "The only plan I have is to tell Ina and everyone at school that I am refusing to join the club because Ina is organizing it to ostracise Sarah because she is jealous of her, and that it is not being organized for any Christian purpose." John said, "Ben, you told Sarah you wanted to do that and she asked you not to because it could cause embarrassment to her and a lot of friction among the students. You promised Sarah you would not do it. Let us try to think of some other way."

Talking at high speed, Ben and John told Miss Essie what Ina and her followers were saying and doing at school. They also told her of Mrs. Blossburg's advice and of their telling Sarah they could not follow those suggestions. Finally Miss Essie said, "It would be a good reason for not joining Ina's club if you two were officers in another club which required a substantial part of your spare time." Ben remarked that they were not officers of any club, to which Miss Essie replied, "Ina does not have the exclusive right to organize a club. You can organize your own club and choose your own members and officers." After thinking a few seconds John said, "Ina would attack the formation of any such club as a deliberate move against Christianity. Don't you think that it would be apparent that our club was organized in opposition to Ina's club, expecially since no mention of such an organization has heretofore been made? Ina has enlisted and secured the promise of a number of the girls to join her club and I think it would be difficult to persuade them to join another club." Miss Essie, having thought of the questions which John raised, replied, "My idea was a boys club. This would make it unnecessary to approach any girl. You two have a sufficient number of close friends to secure the number needed for your club. You do not have to have a large number."

The two boys looked hopefully at each other as Miss Essie continued, "The club would have to have a public purpose that most everybody would recognize as worthy. This would require you to work at times that would interfere with engaging in sports. It is a question of whether you are willing to pay the price necessary to prevent being used by Ina, and if not used, being branded by her as a backslider or one who has fallen from grace, according to the church to which you belong." Ben said, "I would do most anything that would prevent Ina from making me front for her club."

John said, "Miss Essie, what kind of club could a few boys form that could do something for the public good, and how can we account for its sudden organization so that Ina cannot make monkeys of us for attempting to wreck her Christian efforts?" Miss Essie responded, "You could organize an Educational Aid Club." Ben asked, "What aid to education could I be? You say I do not even speak correct English."

Miss Essie replied, "Far be it from me to suggest making a

teacher of you. However, I can think of many ways a boys club could aid education. One of the first projects I would recommend would be to paint the Masonic building. The public has used the lower story of that building as a school house for many years without paying any rent. Certainly the public should help maintain the building. I have been endeavoring to get Mr. Lon Williamson, as Chairman of the Board of Trustees, to ask the Board to do the painting but he always replies, 'Let the Masons paint their own building.' I think the public is obligated to maintain this building. There are several of you' who can paint; there are others who could clean the old loose paint off; and others who could look after scaffolds, etc."

Ben said, "We would need money to purchase paint brushes and other materials." Miss Essie replied, "Yes, Ben, you would need some financing. I have heard some of the Masons say they had decided to paint the building, so it is likely the Masonic Lodge will finance the project. Ben, your father is Worshipful Master of the Masonic Lodge and John's father is a member. I think you two had better take your fathers into your confidence in this matter and see if you can get their cooperation. If the Masons do not offer to finance the project, we will find some other way to secure the money we will need. You can tell your fathers that, if they will cooperate and support you in this undertaking, I will aid you in organizing your club and supervise its operation. Also tell them that, to justify your organizing your club at this time, I will announce at school that its organization was at my request."

"Ben," said John, "you come go home with me and we will talk to Daddy and see if he is willing to support Miss Essie's plan. If he agrees to help us, then we will ask him to go with us to see your father." John knew his father would give them a sympathetic hearing and could persuade Mr. Davidson to join them in their scheme.

Dr. Alston listened attentively as they told him in considerable detail about Ina's proposal. They also told him of Ina's announced plan to make them chief officers of her club, and of how they had avoided Ina's first effort to organize her club. Then Ben, with considerable heat, told of Ina's statement that he was going to be happy to be president to show everyone that he was not under the anti-Christian influence of Sarah. Finally they told Dr. Alston of Miss Essie's plan and asked him if he and Mr. Davidson would aid them.

Dr. Alston got up slowly and, without saying a word, began to walk about the room as John and Ben anxiously waited for his reply. After a minute or two he told them, "I think we had better go over and talk to Ben. Miss Essie's idea of painting the Masonic Lodge is good even if the purpose were not to save you two from Ina."

They went to see Mr. Ben Davidson. Dr. Alston gave him all the information that Ben and John had given him and said, "You see, our sons are in a dilemma and this plan Miss Essie has suggested will prevent them from being placed in an embarrassing position by refusing to join Ina's club. I think the plan is good. It needs our help and cooperation and I think we should give it."

Mr. Davidson said, "I resent Lon Williamson and his daughter assuming they have a divine right to dominate and direct the life of every person in this community. It will give me great pleasure to help thwart their pretensions of superiority and their demand that we should bow down and grant their every wish. There will be no trouble in supporting Miss Essie's plan. The lodge has already given to me, as Worshipful Master, the authority to spend the necessary funds to paint the Masonic building. Miss Essie's plan will save the Lodge money. You can tell her that permission is granted her club to paint the building and that the Masons will finance the project."

John and Ben returned to Miss Essie in high glee. They reported to her that Dr. Alston and Mr. Davidson would cooperate with them and that the Masons would finance the project. Miss Essie then required them to make a list of those who they were sure would work with them. When the list was completed, Miss Essie considered it and marked out two of the names. She told them to go and see each one on the list and find out if he would join the club. She charged that they impress on each one that it was to be a secret organization like the Masons; that it would be a service organization which would require them to give time and work to accomplish its purposes; and that its meetings would be held at her house with her serving as adviser.

Ben and John knew Jake Wilson would help them. They

explained the purpose to him and then each took one-third of the names for solicitation. After one day's work, John, Ben, and Jake reported to Miss Essie they had not had a refusal by any one they invited to join. Then Miss Essie had them meet at her house and she again explained the purpose of the club and ascertained from each of them their willingness to serve for the public good. She then directed its organization.

Miss Essie explained to them the reason why they were asked not to join any other club. She said that it would often be necessary to have call meetings to discuss plans and projects and, as these meetings might be called at any time, they should keep free from any obligation that might conflict with their attendance. These meetings were to be held at her house and she would try to have some refreshments for them.

Ben Davidson, Jr., was elected president of the club, Jake Wilson, vice-president, and John Alston, secretary and treasurer. Then John told them that Miss Essie had suggested as their first project the painting of the school house, and that the Masons had agreed to finance it if the club would do the work. The club unanimously approved this project and committees were appointed to be responsible for certain tasks necessary for the efficient accomplishing of the project.

Miss Essie told them not to discuss the club with anyone except a member until after she had announced its organization and purposes at school. After agreeing on the date to begin the work, the meeting adjourned.

At the next general assembly Miss Essie spoke to the students saying, "I have an important announcement to make to you. All of you know that this building we are using as a school house belongs to the Masons. We have used it a number of years without paying one cent of rent. I think it is our duty to at least keep the property in good repair. Last night, I had a dozen of our older students meet at my house and I asked each of them if he was willing to make a sacrifice of some of his time usually devoted to sports and social activities and work to be of some service in accomplishing something beneficial to our community. As I had hoped and expected, each of them expressed pleasure at being so used. So the Educational Aid Club was organized. It is a secret organization so far as its club meetings are concerned. The officers of the club are Ben

Davidson, Jr., president, Jake Wilson, vice-president, and John Alston, secretary and treasurer." Miss Essie then read the names of the members.

Miss Essie continued, "In order to be sure that the club will be effective, it was agreed that each member should always be available for a called conference or the performance of some emergency duty and that it will not be practical for them to join any other organization.

"The first project adopted by the club is to paint this building. The club has already reached an agreement with the Masons and preparations are being made to begin the work. I have taken time to inform you about the Educational Aid Club and the fine service it will be rendering in the public interest in order that you might tell your parents. I am sure every one will commend these young men and encourage them in their work." When Miss Essie concluded, there was general applause.

As Miss Essie anticipated, the students carried the news to their parents and the Educational Aid Club was soon the general topic of conversation. Ina told her father of the organization, its project, and that it would wreck her plans to organize her Christian Club. Mr. Williamson said, "Miss Essie had no right to take such action without consulting me as the Chairman of the Board of Trustees. I shall order her to disband this club and I shall forbid the painting of the Masonic building." He immediately left the store and hurried to the home of Miss Essie to give her orders.

It so happened that John and Ben were at Miss Essie's and John, pulling a curtain slightly open, saw Mr. Williamson striding at a fast pace toward the house. Upon telling her of Mr. Williamson's approach, Miss Essie said, "I expect he is coming to make some protest about your club and its activities. Maybe it would be best for him not to see you two here. Suppose you go into the kitchen and remain there while he is here." They followed Miss Essie's suggestion and positioned themselves where they would be out of sight of Mr. Williamson but where they could hear the conversation between him and Miss Essie.

When Mr. Williamson walked up onto the porch Miss Essie opened her front door and said, "Come in, Lon. What brings you on a visit to me?" Standing in the doorway he said in an insulting tone, "What brings me here? I will tell you, and you had better understand what I say. It is your presumptuous and unauthorized act of forming this boys club and arranging for them to paint the Masonic building. You not only took this action without my approval as Chairman of the Board of Trustees, but I was not even advised of your high-handed action until Ina came home from school and told me about your speech. I am ordering you to dissolve this club immediately and to stop the painting. I warn you to comply with this order promptly or I will use the power I have to make you wish you had obeyed." Without giving Miss Essie an opportunity to reply, he turned and stomped away.

Ina's New Club

As soon as Mr. Williamson had left, Ben and John came charging into the room where Miss Essie stood. "Miss Essie, we are going to catch Mr. Williamson and make him come back and apologize for insulting you," fumed Ben. Miss Essie replied, "No, that would make matters worse. I am glad you two heard what he said and the manner in which he said it. Please tell your fathers what has happened and ask them to advise me what to do."

When they reached the home of Mr. Davidson they found him sitting in a big rocking chair on his front porch. As soon as he saw the boys approaching he sensed that something had happened to upset them. As they came up the steps he asked, "What has gone wrong with you two?" Ben replied, "John, you tell him." John told Mr. Davidson about Mr. Williamson's visit to Miss Essie and quoted verbatim his statement to her. They told him they were in the kitchen where Mr. Williamson could not see them but they could hear everything that was said. They also told him that they wanted to overtake Mr. Williamson and bring him back to the house and make him apologize to Miss Essie for his rudeness but Miss Essie told them only to report to their fathers what had happened and to ask them to advise her.

Mr. Davidson thought a few seconds and then asked, "Did you say that Lon told Miss Essie that if she did not do as he commanded immediately he would use the power he had to make her wish she had promptly obeyed?" John answered, "Yes sir, that is what he said. It was a threat and he sounded as if he really had the power to hurt her." Mr. Davidson again asked, "Did he or Miss Essie say what power he had over her?" John said, "No sir." Mr. Davidson did not know that Mr. Williamson had a mortgage on Miss Essie's home and that he was threatening to foreclose that mortgage if she did not do as he wanted. He had no idea that Miss Essie had fallen into the avaricious economic power of Mr. Williamson. Miss Essie had let her pride keep her from revealing this financial condition to her friends who would have rescued her.

After being silent for a few seconds Mr. Davidson said, "Well, I guess I had better have a little talk with Lon about this matter. He has already closed his store for today so I will have to wait and call on him in the morning." Ben, Jr., said, "Daddy, tomorrow is Saturday and John and I will not be in school. May we go with you when you call on Mr. Williamson?" Mr. Davidson replied, "I thought you were working for Mr. Blossburg on Saturdays." Ben, Jr., said, "Mr. Blossburg is always willing to let me off for any special occasion. John and I could tell you whether Mr. Williamson was stating the truth about what happened." Ben, Jr., was hoping Mr. Williamson would make his father mad and that his father would knock him down. He was anxious to see such a thing happen to Mr. Williamson. Mr. Davidson said, "No, this is a matter I must handle personally and alone. You two tell Miss Essie to ignore Lon's orders and proceed as if he had not talked to her. I will be present when the club begins its painting to see that no one interferes with them."

On Saturday morning Mr. Davidson went to the store to see Mr. Williamson. When Mr. Williamson looked up and saw him, he was surprised, for Mr. Davidson seldom came into his store except for mail and it was not mail time. When he noticed the determined expression on Ben Davidson's face and the briskness with which he was walking, he felt sure that Ben's visit was for purposes that might prove very unpleasant, and that it would be wise to avoid him. Without giving any indication he had seen Mr. Davidson, he began walking toward the back door of the store. Noticing his movements, Mr. Davidson called, "Lon, wait, I want to talk to you." Mr. Williamson replied, "I have a matter to which I must attend. I will see you later." Mr. Davidson said, "I want to talk to you now. I will walk along with you and we will talk as we walk."

Realizing that he was going to be unable to avoid the confrontation with him, Mr. Williamson decided he had rather talk to him in the store where others were present. Mr. Williamson turned and walked back to meet him saying, "Well, Ben, if it is urgent to you I guess I can wait. What is on your mind?" He indicated chairs. Mr. Davidson was a taller and larger man than Mr. Williamson and the latter felt more at ease if both were sitting. When they were seated Mr. Davidson said, "Lon, I hear you made a visit to Miss Essie yesterday afternoon." Endeavoring to sound as if he were amused, Mr. Williamson replied, "So Miss Essie has run to you with some exaggerated wild tale about my visit to her." "No," said Mr. Davidson, "I have not seen or talked to Miss Essie. It happened that John Alston and my son were in her kitchen and heard what you said to her. I am sure they gave me a truthful report. According to their report you were rude, insulting in your manner and threatening."

In an effort to prevent being placed on the defensive, Mr. Williamson mustered what he considered his most impressive pose and tone of voice and said, "Of course I was indignant that Miss Essie should embark on this scheme involving the student body without first securing my approval as Chairman of the Board of Trustees. Any one in my position would have been irritated at her for completely ignoring my authority. I did not intend to insult Miss Essie but it was necessary that she be made to understand just how out of line she had acted. I did order her to stop the whole matter until I submitted it to the Board of Trustees." Mr. Davidson still spoke in a calm manner but it was easy to detect that he was controlling his anger with difficulty. Mr. Williamson was aware of this but he forced himself to maintain his swaggering manner.

Mr. Davidson said, "The boys did not mention that you said anything to Miss Essie about submitting the matter to the Board of Trustees. If you had made such a statement, I am sure they would have told me. On the contrary, they said you told Miss Essie you would make her sorry by the use of your authority over her if she did not obey your orders without delay. Would you mind advising me what authority you were threatening to use?"

Mr. Williamson did not want Mr. Davidson to know that he was reminding Miss Essie that he could foreclose the mortgage which he held on her home. He answered, "The use of my authority as Chairman of the Board of Trustees, of course." He knew this was a weak reply and his voice lost some of its pomposity in making it, but it was the best he could do. Mr. Davidson said, "You forget that I am a member of the Board of Trustees and I know the Board has not given you any authority over Miss Essie and that, in assuming to reprimand her and give her orders, you have stepped out of bounds." Mr. Williamson hastily interrupted in an effort to maintain what he considered his superior position. "It was not necessary for the Board to pass a resolution giving me the authority I exercised because such authority is inherent in the office of Chairman." Mr. Davidson countered, "That statement is not true and if you are going to persist in acting as autocrat instead of representing the wishes of the Board, I will call a meeting of the Board of Trustees and it will elect a Chairman who will respect Miss Essie and act in accordance with its wishes."

Mr. Williamson, realizing he should find some compromise of the problem, said, "Ben, if you wish Miss Essie to have unbridled authority to use the student body and school in attempting to carry out her crazy idea, I will not object. I was only trying to protect us from trouble."

Mr. Davidson stood and said with vehemence, "So you brand the agreement I have made as Worshipful Master of the Masonic Lodge as a crazy idea which you are maliciously and wrongfully trying to stop! I remind you also that my son is president of that student group and I will hold you personally responsible if you dare to interfere with the carrying out of the group's agreement. I have sent Miss Essie word to ignore your threats and orders. I am going to have an attorney secure an injunction against your interference with the painting of the Masonic building by either act or word, and an injunction against your attempting to punish Miss Essie for ignoring your orders. If I can find any evidence of your violation of this injunction, I will see that you are tried for contempt of court."

The threat of the injunction, its exposure to the public of his indefensible and reprehensible action, and the financial expense to which it would subject him, caused him to wilt completely. He anxiously called after Mr. Davidson, "Wait Ben, you know a lawsuit is not necessary. We can settle our differences without that. I am willing to abide by your wishes in the matter."

When Ben Davidson left the store he went to the Masonic Lodge for a meeting which was being held that day. At the meeting he reported Lon Williamson's actions relative to the painting plan and his promise not to interfere with the painters. As they had little confidence in his promises, they decided to let Williamson know that the Lodge was taking action to prevent any interference on his part. That afternoon three men went to see Williamson at his store. One of them said, "Mr. Williamson, we represent the Masons. At the lodge meeting this morning we had a report on the plan to paint our building and your effort to prevent it. Of course, we resent your interfering in our affairs. We thought it proper to advise you we will have Masons present during the painting to prevent your interference." They left without waiting for a reply.

After they had gone only a few steps, one of the Masons turned and said, "Others will be calling on you to impress you that we are in earnest in protecting these young men while doing their work." When he thought of the prospect of other visits of this nature from other Masons, Williamson told Reuben Stone, his clerk who actually ran the store for him, that he was not feeling very well and that he was going home for the rest of the day.

Among those seeing and hearing what took place between Mr. Davidson and Mr. Williamson was Ina. She was sitting unobserved in the rear of the store. This was the second time she was shocked to find that her father did not dominate every person with whom he had any dealings. The first was when he failed to secure the cooperation of those he had invited to join him in preventing Mr. Blossburg from coming to Landsee, and now Mr. Davidson's compelling him to permit the Educational Aid Club to continue. But her confidence that her father was superior to all other men caused her to believe he would find a way to accomplish his purposes. However, she realized that in her campaign against Sarah time was of the essence and that she could not afford to wait for her father to take action against Miss Essie. She was even more convinced that she must immediately make plans to cope with the new situation when, the next Saturday morning, she saw the painting of the Masonic building proceeding apace with Mr. Davidson present and encouraging those taking part in the work.

Being pragmatic beyond her years, she set about finding a way to alter the organization of her Christian Club, and for the first time she resolved to be careful not to incite opposition. In her effort to analyze the situation she wondered about the sudden organization of the Educational Aid Club just at a time it would prevent her from completing her proposed Christian Club. She knew Ben was happy for an excuse that would prevent the social exclusion of Sarah. But Ina was sure that Ben neither conceived the idea of the Educational Aid Club nor undertook to organize it. She actually believed she was speaking the truth when she assured her girl allies that Ben was suffering a temporary and unthoughtful infatuation with that Jew girl which he would soon regret.

Finally, she decided that it must have been Miss Essie's idea. Then she considered whether or not the club was created to frustrate the organization of her Christian Club. Because Miss Essie had always encouraged her Christian activities, she reasoned that Miss Essie would not oppose the purpose of the Christian Club. While Ina did not know about the mortgage her father held on the home of Miss Essie, she was certain he had some control over her. It was significant to her that it was Ben who informed Mr. Davidson of her father's demands on Miss Essie. This indicated to Ina that Miss Essie personally did not dare defy her father. She thought that if Ben had not overheard what her father had said to Miss Essie and had not reported it to Mr. Davidson who then took charge, Miss Essie would have done what her father had ordered her to do.

Her conclusion was that Miss Essie was always starting something to promote education and that it just happened that she launched the Educational Aid Club when she did. So she decided to continue her Christian Club, which would exclude Sarah. Ina invited the girls who always accepted her leadership, and a few others she thought might be persuaded to follow her suggestions, to come to her home one afternoon.

After having refreshments, Ina asked for attention and presented her proposal. "All of you were present at the meeting

when we discussed the organization of a Christian Club to promote proper social entertainment for those interested in seeing
that our social life is always in harmony with the rules of our
churches. The plan considered at that time included the boys.
The organization of the Educational Aid Club will prevent some
of the boys from being a part of the club. I understand most of
them regret this situation but think they should go along with
Miss Essie's idea. There are a number of others willing to join
our club but, after giving the matter careful thought, I concluded that the club should be a girls club. As we know all the
social activities are planned and directed by the girls. Whatever
part the boys take in its planning is secondary. Such a girls club
could make a program of social activities for the entire summer.
There is need for such a club to prevent any anti-Christian ideas
or activities from creeping unnoticed into our pastimes.
Furthermore, our exclusive girls club could by agreement have
joint projects with the Educational Aid Club."

Ina mentioned civic projects that she thought could be
best handled jointly by boys and girls. She had prepared a con-
stitution and by-laws which she asked them to adopt by signing
as members. She passed several copies around to expedite the
signing.

One of the young ladies who did not belong to the group
that always agreed unquestioningly with Ina's suggestions said,
"I notice you have limited membership to those affiliated with
either the Methodist or the Baptist churches." Ina replied, "Yes,
because our activities will be in accordance with the rules of
conduct required by those two churches. That excludes anyone
who does not believe in the Christian religion." The one who
had made the observation continued, "There is a report that a
Mr. Green has bought Mr. Henry's business and that his family
will be moving here soon. I have heard that they have a
daughter about our age and that they belong to a Christian
church other than the Baptist or Methodist Church. Should you
not make the qualifications for membership broad enough for
their daughter to join?"

Ina had also heard of the coming of the Greens but she was
wary of bringing into her club some girl she could not control
or who might become her competitor. She replied, "We are not
sure the Greens are members of a Christian church. Even if they

are, it might be some sect entirely out of harmony with our local churches. If we find we would like to invite her to join our club, we can then amend the by-laws. I think it best to leave the qualifications as now stated."

All but two or three signed for membership. Amy White was one failing to sign. Although she failed to secure the signature of all she had invited, Ina was pleased with the results of her efforts. She was convinced that the membership she had enlisted would respond to any suggestion she made and that the club could control the social activities.

The next week she made it a point to advise Ben and John of the club and how enthusiastic each member was over the prospects of an enjoyable summer they were planning. She had asked that the first party be held at her home. She also told them they hoped to foster several worthwhile civic projects jointly with the Educational Aid Club.

The Greens' Ellen

One of the most important necessities of a farm area is a shop where woodwork and ironwork are done. Horses had to be shod; buggies, wagons and farm implements had to be mended; plow points and tools had to be sharpened; and various other jobs that required skill and know-how had to be done for farmers. Also, as there was not an undertaker in Landsee, such shops made coffins.

Mr. Elbert Henry had operated a shop of this character for many years, but he had lived over three score years, which was old in those days, and had become so seriously disabled with rheumatism that he was not able any longer to meet the demands made on him. He decided to sell his business. As he knew of no one living in his section of the country who could do the work required of such a shop, he advertised the business for sale in newspapers published in nearby cities.

Mr. Charles Green saw one of Mr. Henry's advertisements and thought that perhaps this business offered the opportunity he had been seeking. Mr. Green was a native of the state of Vermont, had been trained as a cabinet maker and had worked at that trade in that state for many years. He had moved south at the insistence of his wife who persisted in her desire to live in some southern rural village. As she had suffered a nervous breakdown, Mr. Green was anxious to comply with her request, hoping that by satisfying her wishes she would improve in health.

Mr. Green had moved to a southern city and secured work

in a cabinet shop. He assured his wife this was only temporary until an opportunity opened in a rural village where he could establish a business of his own.

Mr. Green decided to go to Landsee and investigate Mr. Henry's business. He was pleased with Landsee and was of the opinion that, with very little improvement, he could make the shop an excellent business place. He was surprised to find that Mr. Henry had operated the business without any help and that he had done both the woodwork and ironwork. He had anticipated that Mr. Henry would have an employee who shod horses and did other rough ironwork and that he would be able to retain such employee. He doubted the business would justify employing additional help. However, after conferring with Mr. Davidson and others, and considering the price at which the shop was offered, he took an option on the business for thirty days.

Within two weeks he returned and purchased the business. He brought with him a Negro man, Jim Jones, who was skilled in doing the work which Mr. Green did not do. With the help of Mr. May he purchased a home. The house needed repair but as Mr. Green did not wish to move his family until Ellen had finished the school term, he had time to do the needed work before moving to Landsee. So it was after the school at Landsee had closed when Mrs. Green and Ellen joined Mr. Green.

While Mr. Green was fast becoming acquainted with the men at Landsee because of his public business, Ellen and her mother lived almost in social isolation. In Mrs. Green's case this was easily attributed to the report that she was virtually an invalid.

Ina Williamson was like her father, each extremely aggressive and assertive in maintaining the leadership which they considered they held in their respective fields. Ina was not a beautiful young lady because she lacked that delicacy which is so essential to feminine charm. She was handsome and what is termed striking looking. She was rather large, but she had a good figure and was always well dressed and carried herself well. She was considered the best singer in Landsee. She conducted herself as if everyone understood she was the perpetual "Queen of May," and no one had ever questioned her leadership socially. She had never dreamed that what she considered her popularity with the young men would ever be threatened. Ina's first qualms that her dominance might be in some danger was when she recognized the influence the beauty of Sarah Blossburg was having on Ben Davidson, Jr. Ina considered Ben one of the choice young men of Landsee and one she felt she could claim whenever she so desired. Next to John Alston, whom she rated highest, stood Ben Davidson, Jr.

Now, just at the time she felt confident that she had made it difficult for the young men to show Sarah any attention by dubbing her as "that Jew girl" and excluding her from the parties given by her club, Ellen, with her beauty, appeared also as a threat. When Ina learned that the Greens belonged to the Lutheran Church, she was happy she had insisted that members of the girls Christian Club be members of either the Methodist or Baptist Church. This would make Ellen ineligible for membership. Ina determined, if possible, to crush any chance Ellen would have to gain popularity before she became generally acquainted and before the return of John and Ben and others from camp.

In that mysterious way that bad news has a way of becoming known, even though every conceivable effort is made to conceal it, the ingenious Ina learned that the illness of which Mrs. Green was suffering was mental and not physical. She also learned that she was ill only at times and for only a few hours. Ina did not delay using this information. Principally, by statements to her club members, she spread the statement that Mrs. Green was subject to spells and she would add, "You know this will probably be inherited by Ellen."

Mrs. Green, always extremely sensitive to what happened to Ellen, noticed that she was never invited to any of the young people's parties. She mentioned this to Mr. Green. At first he attributed the lack of Ellen's being included in the social affairs to a combination of circumstances. Their arrival after the close of school had prevented Ellen from making friends, and she was not able to attend church regularly because of her mother's illness. Also, Mr. Green mentioned that people hesitated to visit a home where there was illness.

However, one day Mr. Green heard of the remarks Ina Williamson was making about Ellen. He discussed the matter with Mrs. Green and they concluded that the exclusion socially of Ellen was due to Ina's efforts. They debated what they should do to protect Ellen.

What Mr. Green overheard Ina saying was, "That Yankee girl is real pretty and is real nice-mannered. It is a pity that her mother is suffering from a mental disease which Ellen will probably inherit. Mrs. Green has 'spells.' No young man can afford to take the risk of escorting Ellen anywhere because she might have one of these spells while alone with him."

Mr. and Mrs. Green finally decided to ask Ellen if she knew about Ina's statements and she told them that she did. They wanted to know what she had heard and why she had not told them about it. Ellen said, "One day I was at Mr. Blossburg's store and Sarah was there. She told me that she had heard that Ina has excluded me as well as her from her parties. I asked why she was excluded and she said it is because she is Jewish. Then she suggested that I ask Amy White why I had been excluded. I went to see Amy and she told me what Ina was saying." Ellen told them she did not say anything to them about it because she knew it would worry them and she did not think they could do anything about it.

Mr. and Mrs. Green spent several sleepless nights discussing the situation in an effort to find some way to insure the happiness of Ellen. As her happiness meant more to them than any other consideration, they decided to sacrifice their investment at Landsee and move to some place where Mrs. Green's condition was not known. They thought such a move would save Ellen from being subjected to the suspicion that she would someday become a mentally ill person. When they told Ellen of their decision, she strongly objected. She contended that wherever they went their situation would become known and they would be faced with the same problem they were now facing at Landsee. .

Ellen was so firm in her position that one day, when they were discussing the situation, Mr Green said he wished there was some person other than members of the family with whom they dared to discuss the matter. Ellen said, "You have discussed some of your matters with the Chaplain. I have great confidence in him. I do not see why we should not talk to him about this situation. I believe he will be willing to help if he can." The Greens agreed that they would seek the Chaplain's advice.

It happened that the very next day the Chaplain called at Mr. Green's shop. At that time Mr. Green said, "Chaplain, while I know we have no right to burden you with our family problems, yet we need to discuss with someone other than ourselves a very personal matter which is exceedingly important to us. Ellen has suggested that you would treat our discussion confidential, and would be willing to be of service to us if you can. I would appreciate it very much if you will let Ellen and me have a conference with you. We will come to your home at any time it is convenient for you."

The Chaplain suggested that, to prevent being disturbed, it would be better for him to come to the Green home some evening after supper. He said that often he had callers at his home who interrupted private conferences.

The Chaplain called one evening at Mr. Green's residence. Thus, Mrs. Green, who had not expected to be present at the conference, as she made it a rule not to leave her home except on a short visit to nearby Aunt Mymee, was present during the discussion and took part in it.

Mr. Green said, "Chaplain, as I stated to you before, we realize we are imposing on you by requesting you to aid us in solving our private family affairs, but my wife and I are unable to get Ellen to agree to what we propose and, as whatever course we pursue vitally affects her, we want her to be satisfied." He then related to the Chaplain the remarks they had heard that Ina was making, and the consequences of those remarks.

"We understand that Ina is a leader of the young people and, through her organization, virtually controls their social life in the community. If she and her club members persist in spreading this rumor, Ellen can never expect to make any friends or have any close associates. In view of this situation, Mrs. Green and I have decided that we should sell our holdings in Landsee, even though it will entail a great financial sacrifice, and move to some location where Ellen will have a chance of being happy. Ellen has vigorously opposed our moving."

Looking with affection at Ellen, Mr. Green continued, "Ellen insists that we would be confronted with the same problem wherever we went. She thinks that she should be the one to decide whether or not she can face the rumor, and she contends that she can live through it. She says the practical course to pursue is to remain in Landsee and face the problem here. Even if no one knew of her mother's condition, she feels she could not permit any young man to seriously consider marrying her without advising him of her mother's illness. I think this acquaints you with our dilemma. Can you suggest any course other than moving?"

After a pause the Chaplain said, "Please do not be offended by any questions I ask. They will not be asked out of idle curiosity but because the answers will be facts I will need to know if I am to be of any help. Mrs. Green, is there any basis for Ina's statement?"

It was Ellen who answered, "I told my father and mother you would have to have all the facts if you are to be of any help." Mrs. Green said, "Sometimes I have an hallucination that I am guilty of having committed some great wrong. These hallucinations are not violent and do not last very long, never over ten or twelve hours. I generally go to sleep and wake entirely normal. Because I have little warning of the approach of seizures I seldom leave home. I visit Aunt Mymee who understands my condition."

Then Ellen said, "My mother did not develop this condition until about seven years ago. She was then just past forty years of age. I think it was because she understood her condition and did not want her old friends to know about it that she insisted on leaving her old home and locating as far away from it as possible. The doctor who first treated her was able to ascertain that there had not been any antecedents afflicted with mental illness. Prior to her first attack she had been physically ill for about a year, and this attack closely followed the loss of her sister whom she loved very much. In her delirium she often mentions this sister. In fact, she is the only person she mentions except at times she calls me. The doctors said that probably her mental condition resulted from the shock of her sister's death while my mother was in such poor health. They expressed the opinion that if she could regain her physical strength, she would probably overcome these attacks. But she hardly eats enough to sustain life and remains weak. Mother has so strongly insisted that her mental illness will never affect me that I have sometimes wondered if I am an adopted child. I do not favor either my father or mother to any great degree."

Mrs. Green said, "Ellen was not adopted. If she had been, I would gladly produce the legal record of adoption and silence the rumors that are hurting her." Ellen interrupted, "No girl ever had lovelier parents than I have. Probably they love me too much. Let us get back to the facts the Chaplain needs to know." Mrs. Green continued, "Dr. Alston has seen me when I have been ill. He secured the names and addresses of all the doctors who previously have treated me. He said he needed the information they could give him. I do not know what he has heard and what opinion he has reached. You are at liberty to discuss my illness with him."

At this point Mr. Green said, "This gives you the facts." The Chaplain nodded as if satisfied. He had been intently studying Ellen during the conversation. He felt an increasing admiration for her logical conclusions and her evident courage to meet the situation without crying for sympathy. He said, "Ellen, my dear, you are wise beyond your years. Moving to another place will not solve your problem. Your beauty will activate the 'Ina's' wherever you go."

Turning to Mr. Green he continued, "My advice is to abandon any idea of leaving Landsee. It will, of course, be rough sailing for Ellen, but it would be as rough, if not rougher, at your next location. I feel sure that Ellen has the strength to master the situation. I appreciate your confiding in me and seeking my advice and I will attempt to find a way to help. Certainly something can be done to remedy so great a wrong. I will have to have some time to think over the matter before making any suggestions. You have given me permission to talk to Dr. Alston, but I would also like permission to discuss the matter with Miss Essie Gill. I can assure you she will treat the matter as confidential. She can prove a valuable ally and she has strong ties with some of the young people."

Ellen said, "Chaplain, thank you for your undertaking to help. You are free to use your own judgment as to whom you talk about the matter."

The Chaplain in leaving assured them that in a few days he would return to discuss plans of action.

Miss Essie's Plan

The more the Chaplain thought about what he had learned in his conference with the Greens, the more it disturbed him. He had known Ina all of her life and realized how much like her father she had grown. He knew the leadership which she, without resistance from any of her age group, had asserted in their social affairs, her ability to plan and execute her plans, and how greatly she valued her prestige. Ina, like her father, thought that money bestowed both prestige and power which demanded recognition and respect.

Considering Ina's actions against Ellen and Sarah, he was convinced that her effort to socially isolate them was not just the result of a frivolous or petty pique of youth that time would soon dissipate, but the beginning of a ruthless campaign which Ina would press determinedly until she had socially destroyed them. What to some might be deemed an insignificant rift among some of the young people, was to the Chaplain something sinister, and a harbinger of what could result in community discord. There was little in those days to distract the interest and attention of parents from promoting the happiness of their children, and the Chaplain knew that sometimes an incident that threatened their happiness could expand into a feud. So he had a compelling conviction that he should attempt to protect Sarah and Ellen.

The day after the Chaplain had his conference with the Greens, he went to see Dr. Alston with the hope that he could give him a statement that there was no danger of Ellen's inheriting her mother's illness. He told Dr. Alston that such a statement would rob Ina of any fact on which to base her contention that Ellen would probably become insane.

Dr. Alston said, "I agree with you that, if possible, we should stop Ina from continuing her effort, and that it could seriously affect the community. Just what help I can give is questionable. I am just a country doctor, a general practitioner, and I am not an expert in the field of mental diseases. Mrs. Green is the first case I have had in which I consider the illness to be a result of a mental condition. Her condition has confused me. The fact is that when she has these attacks, she not only seems to suffer physically but is confused mentally. I have seen her twice. She is not what we generally consider insane."

Shaking his head he continued, "On one occasion she told me, in a rather incoherent way, that she did not need any medicine, that she was not physically ill. However, she was mentally disturbed. She was deeply depressed and was suffering. She seemed to be in a semiconscious condition and even when you understood what she was saying you did not know whether to credit her statements. I have written each doctor who has treated her since her condition developed and have had replies from all of them. None of them is certain what causes her attacks. All of them are of the opinion that she is not insane but has depressions that exhaust her physically and confuse her mentally. I agree with this opinion. None of the doctors termed her attacks as hallucinations as has the family. Their guess is that her depressions might result from a conviction she is failing to correct some wrong that might cause great suffering. This is a mere surmise. So the best I can say is that I am not an expert on mental diseases, but in my opinion, Mrs. Green is not insane. This is also the opinion of three other doctors who have treated her. I do not think her condition will be inherited by Ellen. This leaves a lot to be desired, but I must be honest."

The Chaplain said, "That character of statement would help if we could somehow get it publicized. I am going to see Miss Essie. She has contact with many young people and can perhaps help us."

That same day the Chaplain called on Miss Essie. When she recognized who her visitor was, she said, "Good afternoon, Chaplain. Come in and tell me what you want me to do. You know you never come to see me unless you want me to pull some of your hot chestnuts out of the fire." The Chaplain replied, "And you always wave your magic wand and, lo and behold, it is done. Well, I am very much in need of your help and when you hear the facts I think you will agree that the problem is more in your field than it is in mine."

The Chaplain then told Miss Essie in full detail about his conferences with the Greens and Dr. Alston. He said, "I am concerned not only in preventing the hurt Ina's campaign will cause Ellen and Sarah but, in a community like ours, her campaign could result in a division among our people." The Chaplain told Miss Essie he had not been able to think of any effective plan to meet the situation. When he had finished both were silent for a while.

Miss Essie, almost as if talking to herself said, "If you did not know Ina and heard her sing a religious song, you would get the impression that she was the soul of purity and never thought or did an unkind act. I think she sincerely thinks of herself as being of that character."

She continued, "John Alston and young Ben Davidson have told me about Ina's drive against Sarah. They have had trouble in preventing Ina from jockeying them into a position of being the spearhead of her efforts to exclude Sarah from any part of the life of the young people. When I saw Ellen I wondered what would be her line of attack there. You have to admire her ability even though you despise her purposes and methods. I have given some thought to the problem but I need some time to consider the facts and suggest a plan of action. At present, I have an idea that it would not be good strategy to center our efforts on Ellen alone. I am of the opinion that it would be best to tie Ellen and Sarah together in any action we take. Perhaps you had better assure the Greens that we are working on the problem but will need some time before we can suggest anything." The Chaplain agreed with this suggestion.

Miss Essie added, "We don't want them to feel we have abandoned them. I will need the help of John and Ben. They will be home the last of this week. I need to get better acquainted with the Greens and gain their confidence. I know Sarah and the Blossburgs sufficiently well to know that they will cooperate. I do not know Ellen and Mrs. Green except to speak to them. It is Ellen who will have to carry the greatest burden in any effort we make. I think I can cultivate Mrs. Green through Aunt Mymee. You can help me with Ellen. Suppose you come to see me about two weeks from now." The Chaplain left with this understanding, confident that Miss Essie would find some way to help. He went to assure the Greens that he and Miss Essie were working to find some way to help.

Miss Essie did not tarry in starting to work. She knew Aunt Mymee had established close relations with Mrs. Green and that she had become extremely fond of Ellen. Miss Essie went to see Aunt Mymee and explained to her the problem and that they were attempting to find some way to protect Ellen. Aunt Mymee not only readily agreed to cooperate with them, but assured Miss Essie she wanted to do everything in her power for Ellen. Aunt Mymee soon had made Miss Essie a welcomed visitor to Mrs. Green.

As soon as John and Ben returned from camp, Miss Essie took them and Sarah and Ellen into her confidence and explained to them the plan she was going to propose to the Chaplain. She knew she could not carry out this plan without Sarah's and Ellen's unequivocal approval. She secured their wholehearted assurance of cooperation. Then she had a conference with the Blossburgs and the Greens to get the parents' consent to use Ellen and Sarah in her proposed program.

When the Chaplain and Miss Essie met again for another conference the Chaplain said, "I hope you have been able to think of some effective action. For a time I considered denouncing Ina's actions from the pulpit but, upon consideration I realized that would not accomplish anything except stir up hostilities among our people. Then, I considered appealing personally to Ina and her father, but I have never had any influence with them. Lon has hardly spoken to me since I refused to support his effort to prevent Mr. Blossburg from coming to Landsee. So it all depends on you."

Miss Essie replied, "I have been working on a plan which I hope will meet with your approval. I don't think we can hope to stop Ina but I think we can lessen her effectiveness and the hurt of her efforts. Ina's campaign has been somewhat sub rosa, quietly planting her detrimental suggestions in a confidential tone here and there, whenever and wherever she could do so. To answer her accusations it will be necessary to force her attacks into the open. The public must be told that it is known what Ina is doing, that she is responsible for these rumors and that we are branding her efforts as evil. Assassins of character seek the shadows for secrecy and darkness is their ally. Light and publicity are their enemies."

The Chaplain nodded assent as Miss Essie continued, "Now as to the plan. You will recall that for a number of years I have had a picnic for my students each summer at the Spring of Living Waters. In this manner I kept in touch with the students during the holidays. The last two years I have not given the picnic. Most people thought that my failure to do so was because of my age but that was not the reason. I was not able financially to cover the expenses it entailed. I regret having to reveal my private affairs but I am compelled to do so in order that you may understand why I need financial assistance to carry out my proposal."

Pausing a moment for breath, Miss Essie resumed, "My plan is to renew holding the picnic this summer and invite all the young people to attend. I will ask some of the mothers to aid in serving lunch in order that they will hear the afternoon program. If I secure sufficient financial support, we will advertise that fine food will be served free and that valuable attendance prizes will be awarded. I want this to be the best attended picnic ever held in Landsee."

The Chaplain shifted his chair a bit as Miss Essie went on, "As you know, Chaplain, I have always had a program at these picnics. I propose to use the afternoon program in a manner that will bring Ina's efforts against Sarah and Ellen into the open. This part of the program will be advertised as 'the Surprise Feature' without stating its character or purpose. This will not stop Ina but it will reduce her following and give anyone who wishes a good excuse to refuse to be aligned with her. It will, at the least, dull the cutting edge of her disparaging remarks. We will invite everyone who wishes to attend the surprise feature and the awarding of the prizes in the afternoon. I hope a number of grown people will attend that afternoon."

The Chaplain interjected, "What about the Blossburgs and the Greens?" Miss Essie, a bit annoyed at his anticipation of what she would say next, replied, "I have discussed with them what I expect to do and all of them have agreed to cooperate with me. In fact, Sarah and Ellen are strongly in favor of it. As I thought, Mr. and Mrs. Blossburg readily consented for Sarah to take the part I suggested for her. The fact is, Sarah's part presents no difficulties. The only thing she has to combat is prejudice and she is fully competent of presenting a good argument against that."

Leaning toward the Chaplain, Miss Essie continued, "It is different with Ellen. To answer Ina's suggestions against her, she will be compelled to talk about intimate personal family conditions. Mr. and Mrs. Green were opposed to Ellen's taking the part and making the talk I suggested. They contended that it would be humiliating and embarrassing and that she should not be subjected to such an ordeal. If it had not been for Aunt Mymee's and Ellen's insistence that it was the only way to publicly answer Ina and check her, they never would have consented. It will take a lot of stamina and courage on Ellen's part but I am convinced she has both." Miss Essie then told the Chaplain that only Aunt Mymee, John, Ben, and the families involved had been told of the entire program.

When Miss Essie finished the Chaplain said, "Well, no one but you could have conceived of such an audacious attempt to meet such a delicate situation. I am sure you can make it succeed. I did not know what plan you would evolve but I anticipated there would be some expense. Mr. Blossburg, Mr. Green, Dr. Alston, Mr. Ben Davidson and I will see that you have the funds needed. We are meeting tomorrow in order for me to report to them concerning my conference with you and, after our meeting, I will get in touch with you."

Miss Essie confessed, "I have been using the preparation for the picnic to get John and Ellen acquainted. John had left for his summer camp just before the Greens moved to Landsee. I think he will like Ellen. If we do no more than keep Ben and John interested in Sarah and Ellen we will have accomplished much."

The Chaplain thought a minute and said, "I have been thinking that your program would be more effective if Ina were present to hear what is said and see how it is received by the audience. I am afraid she will resent your using Sarah, Ellen, Ben, and John in your preparations for a program that she will not attend."

Miss Essie responded quickly, "I have discussed the picnic with Ina and have told her that I was using Sarah, Ellen, Ben, and John to help me and that I was doing it to give Ellen an opportunity to get acquainted with some of the young people. She voiced her disapproval of what I was doing. She first ventured the opinion she would not attend and would advise the members of her Christian Club not to attend. She told me that she was surprised and that I did not seem to appreciate that, in promoting Jews in any respect, I was hazarding the Christian religion. She even intimated that she thought I was under moral obligation to cooperate with her father in his effort to prevent this 'invasion' of Landsee by the Jews."

Remembering the conversation, Miss Essie smiled and said, "I just let her talk herself down. I had one purpose to accomplish and that was to get Ina to attend the picnic. When she had finished her lecture to me, I simply reminded her that this was going to be the largest picnic we had ever held and I was planning a large amount of group singing and had expected her to lead the singing, even hoping that she would sing a solo. I did not think she could forego the pleasure that this prominence would give her. She is helping me to arrange the music now. I had John to bring her over to my house one evening to work on the program and that pleased her." As the Chaplain prepared to leave, Miss Essie suggested that it might be well for them to inspect the old brush arbor and ascertain if it were in good enough condition for the picnic.

When the Chaplain next came to see Miss Essie, he told her that Mr. Blossburg was donating two bicycles, one for a young man and one for a young lady, to be given as attendance prizes. To be eligible to win one of the bicycles, the party would have to show that he or she had attended the entire picnic. He told Miss Essie that Mr. Blossburg would place the two bicycles on display in the show windows of his store with a placard stating that these were the attendance prizes to be awarded at Miss Essie's picnic.

Miss Essie then began to put on an intensive advertising campaign in an effort to secure a good attendance. The preachers at both churches announced the resumption of the annual picnic. Miss Essie had distributed a number of leaflets giving information concerning this event. These flyers, left at every home, featured four things: (1) that Ina would lead the group singing and sing a solo (this was to assure Ina's presence); (2) the abundance of delicious food, including ice cream and ice cold lemonade (ice desserts were considered very special because ice had to be shipped from the nearest city, generally in a large crocus sack insulated with sawdust); (3) that in the afternoon there would be a surprise feature on the program and everyone was invited to the afternoon program; and (4) the attendance prizes would be awarded at the conclusion of the program.

In compliance with Miss Essie's suggestion, John and Ben had aroused as much curiosity as they could about the surprise feature. Miss Essie authorized them to offer two dollars to the one who guessed what the surprise feature would be. It was the principal topic of conversation among the young people for the entire week before the picnic.

The Picnic

As the day for the picnic approached, Miss Essie felt satisfied that everything had been done which she thought would contribute to its success. On the morning of the picnic, the sun was shining and the skies were clear. One could not have asked for nicer weather for the occasion. By ten o'clock Miss Essie knew that, from the standpoint of attendance, the picnic was a success. The attendance exceeded her most sanquine expectations. The merry greetings and happy laughter evidenced the good will that existed among those who were gathering, and every omen promised a good and pleaant day.

At eleven o'clock the Chaplain rang a bell for attention and when there was quiet he requested everyone to assemble under the arbor so Miss Essie could advise them of the order of the program. Their interest was so high and their curiosity so great that it took only a few minutes for all of them to gather and be seated. Each took a seat as near the stage as he could, so as to be sure to be in a good position to see what took place.

Miss Essie, erect and with her characteristic dignity, stood at the center of the stage and said, "For a number of years I gave a picnic here every summer for my students. They always enjoyed coming together on such an occasion and it gave me an opportunity to see them during the holiday season. It was with regret that, during the past two years, I was not in a position to hold it. This year, the financial assistance of several friends made it possible for me to give the picnic again and invite all the young people. It makes me glad that so many have come today.

The attendance is the largest of any previous picnic I have given. It is my earnest hope that each one of you will always remember today as one of the most pleasant days of your life."

Glancing around and pleased that she had everyone's rapt attention, Miss Essie continued, "Now here is the order of today's program. Because all of you like to sing, we will have a lot of singing. Ina Williamson has aided in arranging that part of the program and she will have charge of the music. Evan Agee with his fiddle and the Banjo Boys will play several numbers. At the end of the musical program the Chaplain will say grace and you will then come to the tables for the feast. As others prepared the food, I can without embarrassment truthfully describe it as a feast. After we have eaten, we will assemble in here again at one o'clock and finish our program. Ina will now take charge."

Ina was in glory when she was chief director of affairs. She was capable and acquitted herself well. She had arranged a program of familiar songs many of them had sung together on serenades. Most of the songs were those taught them by their parents. They were songs of tender melodies and songs of love. First, she led them in singing "America." They sang it like patriots with hearts taught to love their country. Among the songs they sang was "Swanee River." They sang it as if their homes were near that river and the Okefenokee Swamp from which it flows. Evan Agee played "Turkey in the Straw" on his fiddle. The Banjo Boys drummed away two pieces on their banjos. Ina led them in other group singing and then announced, "We will sing 'Down By The River Side' and then the Chaplain will say grace."

When they reached the tables they found an abundance of delicious food and drinks so arranged that everyone could serve themselves. The mothers, requested by Miss Essie to assist her, had brought plates, saucers, cups, knives, forks, spoons, etc. All agreed that Miss Essie was justified in calling it a feast.

At one o'clock, after the Chaplain had assembled them once more under the arbor, Ina again took charge. A large number of adults came after lunch to see what the surprise feature would be.

Ina said, "As announced, we will have one chorus and my solo and then Miss Essie will take charge and present the surprise feature. After that, there will be the drawing for the attendance prizes. Miss Essie has suggested that, to show that we are now one nation, we sing the first and last verses of the 'Battle Hymn of the Republic.' Ned Hinds has brought his trumpet and will take part in this chorus. Also Evan Agee with his fiddle and the Banjo Boys will participate. After this, I will sing, as the solo requested by Miss Essie, 'The Sweetest Story Ever Told.' Then Miss Essie will conduct the remainder of the program."

The singing of "The Battle Hymn of the Republic" was a stirring performance by the entire audience, singing ardently while Ned Hinds sounded battle calls on his trumpet. The Banjo Boys kept a beat like the tramping of soldiers, and Evan Agee's fiddle beautifully emphasized the melody. Ina was at her best singing her solo.

When the music was finished, Miss Essie walked to the center of the platform and, as she did, there was a burst of applause. After there was quiet and she had the attention of the audience, she said, "It is now time for the surprise feature of our program. As most of my life has been spent as a teacher, I hope it will be more instructive than surprising. In order that you may better understand the reasons for this feature of the program, you must listen carefully while I give you a short lecture."

After a meaningful pause, Miss Essie began, "Education seeks to destroy ignorance because ignorance often destroys that which is good and true. The children of ignorance are many and of various characteristics. Most of its offspring are evil and hurtful. Ignorance is the fertile soil in which the charlatan thrives and false and malicious rumor flourishes. Perhaps the most dangerous child of ignorance is suspicion. Many are prone to think evil of those they do not know. They suspect them of having been guilty of serious wrong. Suspicion publishes a false and slanderous rumor in a soft and confidential voice and with a smile. Thereby it can destroy the reputation of an entirely innocent person. Thus, sometimes a lovely person is injured for life."

Miss Essie's expression grew stern as she continued, "The way false and harmful rumor begins and grows is somewhat like this: some person states in a manner that intimates suspicion, 'we do not know anything about that party. I wonder why he came here.' Another who hears that statement repeats it and adds, 'Of course we know nothing about his past.' Then another, ready to accept any derogatory statement which he has heard, will add, 'He might be a convict escaped from prison.' Soon it is an accepted fact that the person is an escaped convict and thus a reputation is assassinated. One is almost defenseless against such a surmise. This is what the surprise of this program is about."

As some feet shifted nervously in the audience, Miss Essie went on, "Within the last fifteen months, two families have moved to Landsee. Few if any of us know anything about them, from whence they came, or why they came. Our ignorance of them and their past could soon cause the suspicious imaginations of some to start a rumor that could create an image of them that would be entirely false. I am informed that, already, there are some whispered expressions about the two newcomers to Landsee. From these expressions a damaging rumor could develop and the person responsible would unwittingly, yet unjustly, cause them injury and pain. We, the people of Landsee, consider ourselves good and just people who would not knowingly hurt anyone."

Reassured by nods of assent, Miss Essie proceeded, "So, to protect them from false and hurtful speculation and to prevent unfair insinuations being made about them, I have asked Sarah Blossburg and Ellen Green to tell you about their families and themselves, their past, and why they came to Landsee." Then she addressed herself to Sarah and Ellen, who were still sitting in the audience, saying, "Sarah, you and Ellen come and have seats on the platform." The two girls went to the platform and took the seats indicated by Miss Essie. She then said, "I am now calling on Sarah to tell you about her family and herself."

Sarah went to the center of the platform and began: "Miss Essie told me that I was going to be given this opportunity to inform the public about my family and myself in order that each of you may judge whether or not a pernicious suggestion about us is true. I appreciate her concern and I will make a brief statement in accordance with the purposes she has outlined. However, I must advise you first that Miss Essie has not had any part in preparing what I will say."

Sarah's poise and her steady voice assured Miss Essie that she would acquit herself creditably. However, she had never been apprehensive about Sarah's being able to carry out the role assigned to her. Her anxiety was for Ellen because Ellen was going to be forced to talk about private family affairs, which could be twisted to support the charges Ina was making against her, and she was not sure that one so delicate looking as Ellen would not break under the severe stress she would have to undergo.

When the little rustle that ran through the audience had died away, Sarah continued, "Before I talk about my family I wish to express my appreciation for being permitted to work with Miss Essie in preparing for this picnic. It gave me the happy feeling of being an accepted part of the community. I have enjoyed the picnic, especially the music. Ina's solo was beautiful."

Then, turning slightly toward Miss Essie, and with a smile wreathing her face and merriment in her voice, she said, "Miss Essie, there are some present who would have recognized immediately who you were requesting to give an account of herself if you had said you were calling on 'That Jew Girl'." Then turning and looking at Ina who had remained seated on the platform, Sarah, still smiling, continued, "I understand the appellation Ina has given me is 'That Jew Girl' and that is the only name by which she and her friends know me. Of course it is entirely proper to speak of me as a Jew Girl. Just what the word 'that' which they use preceding 'Jew Girl' is intended to signify I do not know. I am of the same race as was Moses, King David, Solomon, Deborah, Isaiah, and many others you read about in what you term as the Old Testament. There was also one known as Jesus of Nazareth who was a Jew."

Sarah paused just long enough for the audience to wonder what she would say next. When she was assured she had complete attention, there was evident a note of pride tinting her Charleston accent when she said, "I am not ashamed that I am a Jew. Pride in one's own race is necessary if he is to acquire dignity and demand respect." Again there was a slight pause as if to give time for her last statement to be understood. Then she continued, "Of course I know a person should be judged by his own individual worth and not by the race to which he belongs.

We are not responsible for our race but we are responsible for our character. I try to be a good person. So, if you can truthfully say that Jew Girl is a good girl, I will be happy."

Solemnly now, Sarah spoke, "I have been told that some are saying we are enemies of the Christian faith and we are seeking to destroy it. I challenge anyone to produce one fact to support this malicious and false charge. We have always believed a person's religious faith is a purely personal matter and that he has a right to choose the way he exercises that faith, and that no one should interfere with this right. We ask for this right for ourselves and we grant it to others."

Stepping back a pace, Sarah said, "Now about my family. Soon after the close of the War Between the States, my father and mother and my father's twin brother and his wife came to the United States from Germany. It was virtually their wedding trip for both of them had been married not quite two years when they migrated. My father and his brother had heard from a distant relative then living in America that this land offered Jews the greatest freedom and the greatest opportunity of all the nations of the world. So they decided to immigrate to the United States. A Christian minister, who had known my father and his brother all their lives, volunteered to write for them a letter of recommendation certifying to their good characters. We highly value that letter and both families preserve a copy of it as part of our family history. The original letter is written in German. If any of you can read German, and are interested, we will be glad for you to see it. My father furnished a copy of this letter, translated into English, to the Chaplain when he made his first visit to Landsee. Our families came to Charleston, South Carolina, where they lived until we moved to Landsee."

Sarah waited a moment as some in the audience cleared their throats and then resumed her story, "While they brought some money with them from Germany, my father, his brother, and their wives worked, economized, and saved in order to accumulate sufficient funds to establish a mercantile business. They had been brought up in this type of business. Both they and their wives became naturalized citizens in Charleston. I was born in that city." Sarah brushed her hair back and went on, "A few years ago, my father and his brother decided that their accumulated capital was sufficient to justify their making the venture of establishing a store for the sale of merchandise. They were undecided whether it would be best in some growing rural community or in some city. They agreed that one would open a business in a city and the other in a rural village. It was also agreed between them that, after several years, they would be able to ascertain which location was the most advantageous. At that time, one would sell his business and they would become partners in the place where they considered they could prosper most. So, my father came to Landsee and his brother went to Chicago."

Nodding in the direction of Mr. Henry May, Sarah said, "When my father made his first visit to Landsee he brought letters from some of the officials of the city of Charleston, some outstanding citizens of that city, and bank letters of credit. He showed these to Mr. Henry May, Dr. Alston, Mr. Davidson, and the Chaplain. I have a written statement from these parties which they have given me permission to refer to on this occasion. This statement says that these letters established my father's good character and financial integrity and, they added, that they encouraged my father to establish a mercantile business in Landsee."

Smiling again, Sarah continued, "This brings us to Landsee where we hope to prosper financially and make some worthwhile contributions as good citizens. Many of you have accepted us and have been kind to us. To those I wish to take this opportunity to thank you publicly. Especially am I grateful to Miss Essie and the Chaplain for giving me this opportunity to let all of you know who we are and where we have lived before moving to Landsee. Please remember that this 'Jew Girl' (and turning to look at Ina with a victorious smile) or should I say 'That Jew Girl' would like to be your friend. Thank you."

As Sarah took her seat, there was loud applause. Ina realized that a number of people were looking at her. So she made herself smile and, with studied dignity, joined slightly in the applause.

The issue faced by Ellen now was entirely different. When Miss Essie thought of the timidity with which Ellen seemed to speak of her mother's illness, she could not completely calm her fears that Ellen might be abashed when she endeavored to speak publicly about the health of one she dearly loved, and of the probable effect by inheritance her mother's illness might have on her. Miss Essie's fears were not allayed when she looked at Ellen again. She was charmed by her delicate appearance, her sensitive features with her large violet eyes shaded by long eyelashes when looking down. Ellen did not appear to be one who could endure stating facts which could be cruelly misconstrued by those desiring to ostracize her, to make her a social leper. It was an undertaking that was apt to cause an older and more seasoned person to falter and fail.

Miss Essie had attempted to impress upon Ellen the trying nature of the experience she would have to undergo, and Ellen had assured her that she was able and ready for whatever ordeal might lie ahead of her.

Afterward, Miss Essie commented that she was amazed at how in a moment of stress so many thoughts raced unbidden through her mind. She said that while Sarah was making her speech, she tried to concentrate on what she was saying but somehow could not control her thoughts. Among the thoughts that crowded into her mind concerned how many people, when they think of courage, think only of some physical display in the face of threatened danger to the body. Yet often such a display is a braggart's showmanship which covers moral bankruptcy. And she thought how few would realize how superior was the spiritual or moral courage Ellen must have in making her speech. She said she was astonished when it occurred to her that there is no standard or method of measuring this type of courage before the time it is necessary to use it.

The applause given Sarah was subsiding and soon Miss Essie would have to present Ellen. Miss Essie later said that, at that time, she regretted ever proposing the plan. In spite of her determination and strong effort to control her emotions, a keen observer who knew Miss Essie well could have detected anxiety in her generally unrevealing features. If any one had been observing the Chaplain, who was sitting in the rear, they would have noticed that his usually relaxed body was tensed.

Miss Essie had offered and almost insisted on helping Ellen in preparing her statement but Ellen held that the statement was her sole responsibility and no one else should have to bear any blame that might result from it. Now, Miss Essie did not know what Ellen was going to say nor how she was going to say it. Her anxiety was increased when she noted that Ellen did not have a manuscript nor did she even have any memorandum to use to refresh her recollection during her speech. But when Miss Essie made herself present Ellen, the titian-tressed, violet-eyed young lady never faltered nor hesitated. She walked steadily and gracefully to the center of the platform, faced the gathering and smiled as if only happiness was in her heart. She stood there, five feet and five inches of unafraid loveliness. Ellen's smile, showing what complete self-control she had, erased the anxiety from Miss Essie's face and brought relief and admiration to her eyes. And that smile banished the uncertainty that had toughened the Chaplain's body and it softened his stance. And that smile convinced John Alston that he would always love Ellen better than anyone else and it caused him to release the tight grip he unconsciously had with both hands on the seat of the bench on which he sat.

Ellen began, "This opportunity to speak to you today is a special privilege which I appreciate very much and I wish to thank those who made it possible." Then, in a jesting manner she said, "If it was necessary for Miss Essie to introduce Sara as 'That Jew Girl' for some of those present to understand to whom she was referring, then, when she presented me she should have told you that she was presenting 'That Yankee Girl.' I am reliably informed that Ina and those she influences always refer to me as 'That Yankee Girl' with the emphasis on the word 'that.' I am a Yankee if that means being born north of what is called the Mason and Dixon line. If that is correct definition of the word, then a majority of those who fought as soldiers in the Revolutionary War and won our independence were Yankees. I understand that in all foreign countries every person from any section of the United States is called a Yankee. So being called a Yankee should not carry any stigma except perhaps to the ignorant steeped in sectional prejudice."

Now it was clear that Ellen had determined to leave no doubt that her attack was on Ina and her sycophants and that attack would be as fierce and as strong as she could make it. Hardly anyone would have dreamed that Ellen's winsome personality housed a moral strength of steel. Who was it that said, "The bravest are the tenderest and the loving are the daring?"

"But I am charged to tell you who we are, from whence

we came and why we came to Landsee," continued Ellen. "My parents and I are natives of the state of Vermont. One of my forefathers was a revolutionary soldier. My father was too young to serve in the War Between the States. My parents were married in 1880 when my father was twenty-one and my mother was eighteen years of age. My father was trained as a cabinet maker and was prospering at that trade when my mother insisted that we should move to the South. My father owned his home and had acquired some additional valuable property. Are you wondering why we left such a favorable situation? Later I will answer the question at some length. At present, a sufficient answer is that my parents sought to better their situation and the public interest should be limited to a desire to be assured that we are good citizens. When my father came to Landsee to investigate the desirability of purchasing Mr. Henry's business, he brought a number of letters of introduction that covered his entire life. These letters were furnished to a number of citizens here. Ina's father, Mr. Lon Williamson, Sr., the Chaplain and others urged my father to purchase Mr. Henry's business and pledged him their support in building his business. If you wish to verify this fact, the Chaplain is sitting in the rear of the arbor and you can ask him if this statement is correct." The Chaplain smiled and nodded in agreement.

Ellen continued, "This should be sufficient to brand as malicious slander any suggestion that we left Vermont to avoid the result of some shameful action on the part of some member of the family. Don't you know that with all the energy exercised to discover something with which to discredit me, if I had been guilty of some wrongful act, they would have found it and it would have been shouted from the housetops? Those seeking to malign me would not have been driven to making discrediting suggestions in an assumed confidence and in a hypocritical tone of voice.

"This brings me to the most difficult part of my talk. We were taught that it was not good manners to discuss family affairs in public. But there is always an exception to every good rule. I am assured by some in this audience that a current rumor, which seriously affects my social life, and which is fostered by Ina, creates such an exception. As much as I desire to avoid discussing delicate private affairs publicly, I am compelled to do so to destroy what I consider to be a vicious and injurious rumor.

"I am told that Ina has told several of the young men that she understood my mother had 'spells' and has warned them that I might have such a 'spell' when alone in their company if they escorted me anywhere, and that I might fall into their unwilling arms. I wish to assure all the young men that it is not my desire to have your chivalry and courage tested by any such acts of mine.

"It .is said that there is always a small thread of truth woven into every damaging, though untrue, statement, else it would not be believed by anyone. It is true my mother is in bad health. Of course, I realize that if my mother is insane there is a chance I might inherit her affliction. This makes it necessary for me to discuss her condition.

"About six years ago my mother's health began to decline. She lost her appetite and failed to eat sufficiently and, consequently, she gradually grew physically weak. The doctors were unable to find the reason for her condition and attributed it to grief over the loss of her sister who died about the time my mother's illness began. They expressed the opinion that if she would rest and eat better, she would soon be well again. She did not improve and, one day, she witnessed a terrible accident in which one of her closest friends was killed. She fainted. When she began to recover from her fainting, and while she was in a semi-conscious state, she kept mumbling something about righting a great wrong. Since that time she sometimes grows so weak physically she has to go to bed and occasionally during one of these attacks, she talks about righting some great wrong. She is never violent. She never states what wrong she should right and always, after a little rest, is entirely normal mentally.

"Dr. Alston has seen my mother during two of her illnesses. He has secured a report from all the doctors who have treated her. Among these doctors is one of the finest mental specialists in the East. He searched her family history and found that none of her forebearers ever suffered from insanity. Because my mother talked about righting some wrong, the specialist sought to find if she had ever committed some wrong. They found she had not I knew that no one as good, as kind and as considerate of others as my mother, could have ever been guilty of wronging anyone. All the doctors, including the specialist, agreed that my mother was not insane. They agreed that her condition is physical and that her slight delusion about righting some wrong is the same kind of hallucination a normal person would sometimes have when suffering from fever. All of the doctors assured me that there is no reason to conclude that I will suffer a like illness.

"My mother is very sensitive about her condition. To prevent her old acquaintances from learning about it, she begged my father to move far away to some rural village where she could live a quiet and secluded life, and where perhaps her condition would not become known. Fate has not been so kind to her. But we like Landsee and here we expect to remain.

"This finishes my statement of facts. We have been advised there are legal remedies to which to resort. But this would cause extra hurt and I do not want to hurt any person, not even those who, for selfish reasons, are willing to hurt me. I know that old adage is true that says that 'hate hurts the hater more than it hurts the hated.' No one can fatally crush justice. A great majority of the people are good people, and when they know the facts, will be kind and just.

"The Good Book says the truth will make you free. I have told you the truth which makes you free to form your own opinions of the truth rather than of the spurious speculations of one who lacks good will towards me. And I expect it to make me free to live a normal and useful life. I see no reason why we all should not be friends. My earnest prayer is that, if tomorrow's winds are adverse winds, I will recognize them as temporary winds, and I will have the courage and moral strength to live as if all of us were friends and with the assurance that in days to come this will be true. Thank you for your kind attention."

As Ellen turned to leave the center of the platform, Miss Essie realized she had spent herself in making the supreme effort necessary to control her emotions while speaking and that she seemed a little unsteady on her feet. Miss Essie took her by the arm and quickly guided her to a chair on the platform.

There was no applause when Ellen closed her remarks as there had been when Sarah had finished. There was a stillness and a quiet that seemed to hold everyone motionless. Perhaps it was this condition that attracted the attention of the entire audience to Amy White, who had been sitting on the front row, when she arose and walked up onto the platform. Miss Essie, who was approaching the center of the stage to make an announcement, stopped to see what Amy was going to do. Amy moved a chair close to Ellen who was sitting with her hands folded in her lap and her eyes downcast. Amy sat down and, without saying a word or being aware that she was attracting so much attention, reached over and placed her hand on Ellen's hands. The audience recognized this gesture of friendship and approval and, as Ellen raised her moist eyes to Amy in appreciation, the audience burst into deafening applause. Afterwards, one of the boys was asked why he had not applauded Ellen when she finished, as he had for Sarah. He replied, "I was for Ellen but when she finished I felt like I was in church and you don't applaud in church."

All left the platform when Miss Essie announced they were going to award the attendance prizes. Ellen and Amy simply went down and sat on the front bench. Ina, with her face flaming with anger, marched to the rear seat and sat alone. This was Ina's first experience of having her conduct challenged or criticized. She considered it the height of insolence for Ellen, a newcomer, to dare to brand her actions as improper. But her vanity received an even greater shock when she saw John Alston, during the preparation to award the prizes, leave his seat, walk past her without speaking, and go to the front and sit by Ellen.

The Murder Spot

So long had Landsee been a peaceful and law abiding village that it was difficult for a great many of its citizens to believe the report that someone had shot and killed Mr. Sydney Steele. Mr. Steele was a prominent citizen and a prosperous farmer who lived a few miles from the village. For several days it was not known who fired the fatal shot and suspicion and rumor ran riot.

The first that was known of this tragedy was when Mr. Steele's oldest son, a lad about twelve years of age, arrived in a run at Mr. Williamson's store, frightened and out of breath. He attempted to make those present understand from his incoherent statements that his mother had sent him to ask Dr. Alston and the deputy sheriff to come to their home because someone had shot and killed his father.

It happened that Mr. Lawrence Dunn, a close friend of the Steele family, was present when the lad arrived at the store and was the one who first understood the boy's message. Mr. Dunn told the lad to go with him and he would help him find Dr. Alston and the deputy sheriff and then go back home with him. In a short time Dr. Alston, the deputy sheriff, Mr. Dunn and the lad were on their way to Mr. Steele's home. When they reached the home they saw a farm wagon, to which two mules were hitched, standing near the front gate of the fence which surrounded the yard of the home. Mrs. Steele stood bareheaded in front of the mules holding the driving reins near the bridle bits, evidently to prevent the mules from moving the wagon.

Mr. Steele's lifeless body was lying on his right side on the wagon seat.

Mr. Dunn addressed Mrs. Steele, saying, "Clara, you and your son go into the house. We will look after what is to be done out here. I know where the mules and wagon go and will take care of them. You should arrange a bed for Sydney's body. Later, if you feel like it, the deputy sheriff will want to get such information as you can give him." Mrs. Steele, an attractive and generally well liked woman, obviously struggling to control herself, without replying called her son and they went into the house.

The deputy sheriff waited until Mrs. Steele and her son were out of hearing of what was said and out of sight of what they did. He then suggested to Mr. Dunn and Dr. Alston that they closely observe the position of Mr. Steele's body and the entire situation so they would be able to accurately describe it in court if it became necessary.

The deputy then asked Dr. Alston if he could examine the body to ascertain the cause of death before moving it into the house. Dr. Alston said it was not only practical but better to examine the body there in the wagon, and proceeded to do so.

Mr. Steele's body was lying on his right side with his right arm under him. When they moved his body, they found his pistol on the seat under him but not in his right hand. The pistol was fully loaded and had not been fired. The safety catch was still on. While Dr. Alston was making his examination, Mr. Dunn unhitched the mules from the wagon, carried them to the lot, unharnessed them and put them in their stables.

Upon examination of Mr. Steele's body, Dr. Alston reported that death resulted from a gunshot wound and that the weapon used was evidently a shotgun loaded with buckshot. The wound where the buckshot entered the body on the left side was a few inches above the waistline and ranged upward, indicating that at the time he was shot, Mr. Steele was standing in his wagon and the person who shot him was standing on the ground. Dr. Alston also expressed the opinion that, from the bunched manner in which the buckshot entered the body, the shot had been fired at close range, probably from about fifteen feet away.

In those days there were no undertakers in small rural villages like Landsee. So, when Dr. Alston had finished his examination, they carried Mr. Steele's body into the house and laid it on the bed Mrs. Steele had prepared for it and drew a sheet over him. Mr. Dunn then asked Mrs. Steele if she felt able to talk to the deputy sheriff and give him such information as she could about her husband's death. One could see that she had bathed her face to wipe away the stain of tears and had attempted to arrange her hair which had been blown askew by the wind while she was standing in front of the mules without her bonnet. She was making every effort to brace herself and control her emotions. She said she was willing to talk to the deputy sheriff.

In answer to the deputy sheriff's questions Mrs. Steele told him the following facts: "Sydney drove to the village to get some commercial fertilizer. He seldom used commercial fertilizer but he decided he would purchase one sack each of several different types and test them in order to find out their worth. I was sitting on the front porch when I saw the mules in a trot pulling the wagon without a driver. As they approached nearer the house I could see Sydney lying across the wagon seat. I, of course, realized there was something seriously wrong. I ran out the gate and met the mules as they pulled the wagon where it was when you arrived. I stopped the mules and called Sydney. When he did not answer I went to the side of the wagon where I could see him better and could reach him. When I touched him and saw the blood I knew he was dead and that someone had murdered him. I was so stunned I must have stood still for a minute or two before I realized I must have help. I regretted having to send Sydney, Jr., on his mission for help but he was the only one I had. When Sydney, Jr., left, I took my stand in front of the mules to prevent them from moving the wagon. I simply stood guard until you came. That was all I knew to do."

The deputy asked Mrs. Steele if she had any idea who had shot her husband. Mrs. Steele answered, "Of course, you know I did not see the shooting. There is only one person who hated Sydney enough to kill him. He had a falling out with Ed Stanley over a matter in which he caught Ed Stanley in a lie. Ed Stanley was afraid of him. I think you will find that he shot my husband. He is too big a coward to have given Sydney an even chance." The deputy sheriff thanked her and told her that the sheriff and his deputies would find out who killed her husband.

Mr. Dunn said to Mrs. Steele, "Clara, I will remain here until others come. Dr. Alston and the deputy sheriff are going back to Landsee. They will notify the Chaplain and he will arrange with you for the funeral. The deputy sheriff has agreed to bring my wife to be with you. So you and Sydney, Jr., try to get a little rest because you have a long trying time ahead of you."

Mr. Dunn walked out of the house with Dr. Alston and the deputy sheriff. When they got to the gate Mr. Dunn asked them to help him roll the wagon to the barnyard. This they did. He said it would be some time before he could wash the wagon and he did not want it with its blood-stained seat and floor to be where everyone that came to the Steele's home would see it.

Attendance at the funeral of Mr. Steele was large. The Masons had charge of the graveside services. Mr. Steele was a forceful man, outspoken and forthright. His friendship was valued highly because he was known to be extremely loyal. However, some considered him a high tempered and dangerous man to those with whom he had serious differences.

After the funeral and the meager facts learned by the deputy sheriff became generally known and no arrest had been made, several of Mr. Steele's friends formed themselves into a committee to aid in apprehending the party committing the homicide. They urged the sheriff to employ an expert criminal investigator. They branded the killing as an assassination and pledged themselves to seek evidence that would expose the guilty party. Some of the most partisan left no doubt that they suspected Mr. Stanley.

Along one side of the public road, where it was afterwards ascertained the killing took place, there ran a zigzag rail fence ten rails high. If a man should slightly lower himself, he would be concealed from sight by a passerby until the passerby was directly opposite him.

One day a friend of Mr. Steele brought to the sheriff a Negro man who stated that he was walking along the public road going to Landsee on the day Mr. Steele was killed. He saw Mr. Ed Stanley standing in a corner of the rail fence. Mr. Stanley had his shotgun with him. A short time after he passed Mr. Stanley, he met Mr. Steele driving two mules hitched to a wagon. Mr. Steele was seated and traveling toward his home in the direction which would carry him past where Mr. Stanley was standing. Shortly after Mr. Steele drove past him he heard a gun fire. He did not see the shot fired but it sounded as if it came from the direction where he saw Mr. Stanley standing in the fence corner. He said that the laces of one of his shoes had become untied and he had stepped in a corner of the fence to tie them and was tying the shoe laces when he heard the shot. When he went to where he could see up the road, he did not see any person but he saw the mules running with no driver visible. When asked why he had not let the sheriff know what he had seen, he said that when he heard that Mr. Steele was killed he was afraid to let anyone know he was near the killing, and that he did not tell anyone whom he thought would report it until he was questioned by Mr. Steele's friend who promised to protect him if he would tell the truth.

After securing the facts from this Negro witness, the sheriff, his deputy and a friend of Mr. Steele went to that section of the public road where the Negro said he had seen Mr. Stanley standing. In one corner of the fence they found the grass and weeds trampled, as if a person had repeatedly walked over them. They also found an empty shotgun shell which was of the gauge that Mr. Stanley's shotgun was known to be. Mr. Steele's friend stated he could testify that the shell had been fired by Mr. Stanley's shotgun because he was familiar with his gun and that its plunger made a peculiar indenture on the cap of the shell. He called attention to the fact that there was the same indenture on the empty shell they had found. With this evidence Mr. Dunn said he would swear out a warrant charging Ed Stanley with murder.

While Mr. Stanley did not have the staunch friends Mr. Steele had, he did have a large number of family connections. His family connections constituted a clannish crowd and they had their friends. These became active in Mr. Stanley's behalf as soon as they heard he was under suspicion of killing Mr. Steele. The sheriff's discovery of the evidence that definitely implicated Mr. Stanley was immediately and publicly known.

Before Mr. Dunn could go to the county seat and have the prosecuting solicitor draw up the papers charging Mr. Stanley with murder, Mr. Stanley went to the sheriff and gave himself up. It was learned that when one of the relatives of Mr. Stanley heard of the evidence secured by the sheriff, he went to see a lawyer in behalf of Mr. Stanley. The lawyer had advised him to surrender to the sheriff before he was arrested.

Mr. Stanley's relatives influenced some of their friends with large ownership of property to accompany Mr. Stanley to the county seat when he went to surrender to the sheriff. They had agreed to go on his bond. Soon after Mr. Stanley surrendered, his attorney secured a court order fixing the amount of his bond and the bond was readily made. He was in jail only a few hours.

Mr. Thomas Hallmark was a cousin and lifelong friend of Mr. Steele and also a friend of Mr. Stanley who was often his hunting partner. He was so completely convinced that Mr. Stanley had lain in wait and killed Mr. Steele that he secured the cooperation of some of Mr. Steele's friends and raised a purse to employ a special attorney to assist in the prosecution of Mr. Stanley.

Mr. Stanley was considered a rather harmless character and, in addition to the support by his relatives, there were others who sympathized with him in view of what they considered the dangerous reputation of Mr. Steele. When it was learned that a special prosecutor had been employed, Mr. Stanley's relatives and sympathetic friends raised funds for his defense.

Thus this act of violence not only affected the family of the killer and the Steele family but also virtually divided the village into two separate hostile camps. People spoke to each other in passing but with an evident lack of cordiality. The grand jury indicted Mr. Stanley and charged him with murder in the first degree, a crime for which the death penalty could be inflicted.

The Trial
Of Mr. Stanley

The trial of Mr. Stanley is said to have been the most sensational criminal case ever tried in the county. It was a long and bitter one. The weekly newspaper published at the county seat had carried news items about the case for several weeks prior to the trial. The paper had published a list of the names and addresses of the men on the regular jury panel for the week of the trial as well as a list of the names and addresses of those drawn on the special venire for the trial of Mr. Stanley.

It took most of the first day to select the jury. Every prospective juror was asked at least three questions. "Have you contributed to funds for either the prosecution or the defense?" "Have you expressed an opinion or do you have a fixed opinion as to the guilt or innocence of the defendant?" "Are you related by blood or marriage to either the defendant or the deceased?" So many of those living in the Landsee community answered at least one of these questions in the affirmative that there were only three or four from that community who qualified to serve on the jury. Those who qualified were struck either by the state or the defendant for fear they might have a deep sympathy for one or the other side. As a result, there was not a single person from Landsee community on the jury that tried Mr. Stanley.

The courtroom was crowded with partisans of each side. Not only were the benches full, but a number of people were standing around the walls. The first day of the trial had not reached noon before the partisans of Mr. Stanley were sitting on one side of the courtroom and those of Mr. Steele on the other side of the room.

Anyone observing the people inside the bar of the courtroom saw a vivid and distressing picture of how violent acts can engulf innocent persons and force them to follow a course of conduct that causes them to endure anguish and agony. Those who were compelled to be inside the bar for the trial of the case were the officers of the court, the defendant, the attorneys for the prosecution and defense, and the witnesses while they were testifying. But it was not these persons who caused the picture to be in cruel colors. Beside Mr. Stanley sat his wife, appearing uncomfortable, and beside the prosecuting attorneys sat Mrs. Steele, motionless and donned in widow's weeds. Mrs. Stanley and Mrs. Steele had been girlhood friends and that close intimate relationship continued through their married life. Sitting there they seldom raised their eyes and when they did they were careful not to look at each other. When they moved they made sure there would not be a confrontation that would require them to speak to each other.

The poignant part of the scene that was heartrending to a sensitive soul was the involvement of the two children of the families. Beside Mrs. Stanley sat their ten year old daughter. She was just a little trusting and affectionate lass who had neither reached the maturity nor had gained sufficient experience to enable her to separate the ugly charges levied against her father by the attorneys for the prosecution from the proven facts. No one knows what corroding stain the deluge of brutal and criminal charges made against her father would be indelibly printed on her tender mind and cause her to have disturbing memories that ever afterwards would affect her faith in the goodness of her father.

It was said that Mrs. Stanley had arranged for her daughter to stay with friends during the trial and had objected when it was suggested she should sit with her father during the trial. The defense attorneys, however, had impressed on her that the life and liberty of Mr. Stanley were at stake and that they considered it necessary to use every available means to secure the sympathy of the jurors, and that the presence of his young daughter by his side during the trial would be of great value to the defense. Finally, she reluctantly agreed to do as they requested. She could not stand to think that if she refused to have her daughter sit with them in court and her husband was convicted, that he might have been saved if she had followed the advice of the defense attorneys. She almost regretted bringing her when the child moved as close to her as possible and looked back and forth at her father and mother with wide open distressed eyes while the prosecuting attorneys were speaking of her father as an assassin.

Beside Mrs. Steele was sitting her twelve year old son, Sydney, Jr. He was sitting erect and with a dignity that indicated that he already realized that soon he was to become the responsible man of the house. Mrs. Steele had also objected to the fact that her son should be seated by the prosecuting attorneys during the trial. The prosecuting attorneys told her that Mrs. Stanley and her daughter would be sitting with the defendant to remind the jury that they were supporting him, and that the jury might infer from her son's absence that he was not in sympathy with the prosecution of the man she had said she believed assassinated her husband. She stated she was not going to permit her son to hear what the defense attorneys might say against his father.

She finally agreed that she and her son would sit with the prosecuting attorneys during the selection of the jury, they would be allowed to retire to the jury room while the attorneys were stating their case to the jury, and that she would be the first witness called by the State. When she was called to the witness stand her son would come out of the jury room with her and again sit with the prosecuting attorneys. But after she had testified, she could ask the Court to excuse her and then she and her son could go home.

In accordance with this agreement Mrs. Steele was called as the first witness by the prosecution and testified to the same facts she had related to the deputy sheriff at her home the day Mr. Steele was killed, except she was not permitted to tell whom she thought killed her husband. The defense, aware that she was making an extremely favorable impression on the jury and wishing to avoid increasing their sympathy for her, asked her no questions on cross-examination. When she was told she would not be questioned further and that she could come down from the witness stand, she turned to the judge and said, "Judge, may my son and I be excused from attending the rest of the trial? We need to go home as there is no one there to look after the stock and other matters needing attention." With the consent of the attorneys, the Court excused her.

This simple request of Mrs. Steele probably reminded the jury more forceably than any other action she could have taken that they were trying the man who had deprived this woman and her son of their mainstay, support and protection. It was a hushed courtroom as she took her son by the hand and walked with him out of the court. Even the proceedings of the court were halted until they had cleared the room.

The prosecuting attorney in presenting the State's case to the jury made the following terse statement: "Gentlemen of the jury, we expect the evidence to convince you beyond a reasonable doubt that Mr. Stanley hated and feared Mr. Steele, and that he lay in wait for him in a fence corner on the road he knew Mr. Steele would be traveling on his return to his home from Landsee, and that when Mr. Steele arrived opposite his hiding place he assassinated him."

The opening statement of the attorney for the defense was as concise as that made by the attorney for the prosecution. He said: "Gentlemen of the jury, we expect the evidence to show you that Mr. Steele was generally known to be a dangerous man who always went armed by carrying a pistol in his right hip pocket. He had threatened to kill Mr. Stanley and, when they met the day he was killed, Mr. Steele attempted to carry this threat into effect, and that as Mr. Steele reached for his pistol, Mr. Stanley shot him in self defense."

Over two days were used in taking testimony. The defense was constantly imposing technical objections that caused the proceedings to move slowly. There were only two persons who were present when the killing took place and who could testify as to what happened, Mr. Steele and Mr. Stanley. Death had sealed the lips of Mr. Steele. The prosecution was certain that Mr. Stanley would testify to facts constituting a case of self defense and depend on no person being able to contradict him. Consequently, the State would have to depend on circumstantial evidence to a great extent to show that Mr. Stanley was not telling the truth. The strategy of the prosecution was to introduce only a sufficient amount of evidence to make a prima facie case, thereby compelling Mr. Stanley to disclose his defense. The prosecution hoped by cross-examination not only to discredit Mr. Stanley's testimony, but to lay the predicate for the introduction of circumstances that would destroy the contentions of the defense. This would give the State the opportunity to close the case by its rebuttal with its most persuasive facts and circumstances.

After Mrs. Steele had testified, the State called the Negro man who swore that he saw Mr. Stanley in a fence corner on the side of the public road at the place where it was said Mr. Steele was killed. He testified that Mr. Stanley had a shotgun and that after he had passed Mr. Stanley he met Mr. Steele driving two mules hitched to a farm wagon. He said that Mr. Steele was sitting on the wagon seat and spoke to him as they passed each other and that about the time Mr. Steele should have reached the place where he had seen Mr. Stanley, he heard a gun fire. At the time the gun fired he was in a fence corner where he had stepped to tie a loose shoe lace and so did not see who fired the gun. When he returned to the road he saw Mr. Steele's mules pulling the wagon on a run but Mr. Steele was not sitting on the wagon seat. At that time he saw no one on the road near where he had seen Mr. Stanley when he had passed him. As the facts to which he testified were not disputed by the defendant, the witness was asked only a few questions which failed to develop any new information.

The State introduced evidence to show that Mr. Stanley and Mr. Steele were not on speaking terms and that extremely bad feelings existed between them.

Dr. Alston testified that he had examined the lifeless body of Mr. Steele while it was in the wagon. That wagon was standing in front of Mr. Steele's home. He said that the body was lying on its right side on the wagon seat with the legs hanging down to where the feet were on the floor of the wagon bed. Mr. Steele's right arm was under him and there was a pistol on the wagon seat under him. There was a safety catch on the pistol which had to be released before it could be fired and the safety catch had not been released. The pistol was fully loaded with no empty shells in it.

Dr. Alson further testified that from his examination he determined that death resulted from gunshot which entered his left side a few inches above the waistline and ranged upward.

The gun had been loaded with buckshot and death was almost instantaneous. Mr. Steele was shot at close range. On cross-examination Dr. Alston was asked where were the reins and he said that, according to his recollection, they were lying loose on the floor of the wagon bed. He was then asked if he saw the pistol before the body was moved and he said that he did not see the pistol until they had lifted the body to carry it into the house. He was then asked how much the pistol was moved from its original position in moving the body. Dr. Alston said he could only venture an opinion. When he saw the pistol it was about ten or twelve inches from Mr. Steele's right hand.

The deputy sheriff testified that on the day Mr. Steele was killed he stopped along the road from time to time on his return from the residence of Mr. Steele and upon noticing that one of the fence corners appeared different from the others, he examined it. This was the corner the black witness later identified as the place in which he saw Mr. Stanley. The grass and weeds in that area were trampled down as if someone had repeatedly walked around in the corner. He found a large number of cigarette stubs that were of the brand of cigarettes Mr. Stanley smoked. He also found an empty gunshot shell of the same gauge as Mr. Stanley's gun. He was familiar with Mr. Stanley's gun and it made a peculiar indenture on a shell fired by it where the plunger struck the shell. He then produced the shell and called attention to the mark made on it by the gun's plunger.

The deputy sheriff said that after finding this evidence he went to the home of Mr. Stanley to question him and was told he was not at home. He visited the residence of Mr. Stanley the next two days in an effort to interview him but was told that he had gone to see some parties on business. On the third day, he saw Mr. Stanley and three other persons leave Landsee and go toward the county seat. As he had been ordered to attempt to get Mr. Stanley to go to the county seat for questioning by the prosecuting attorney, he followed them. He was present when Mr. Stanley surrendered to the sheriff and heard him say he was surrendering on the charge of killing Mr. Steele. With this the State rested its case. It was then almost noon and the judge recessed court until one o'clock p.m.

When court reconvened that afternoon the defense first

put two witnesses on the stand who testified to the good character of Mr. Stanley. A third witness said Mr. Steele had the reputation of being a dangerous man who always went armed by carrying a pistol in his right hip pocket. This last witness admitted on cross-examination that he had contributed to a defense fund for Mr. Stanley.

Then the defendant was placed on the stand in his own behalf. He stated that on the day Mr. Steele was killed he had gone to hunt birds in a small clump of woods situated on the road leading from Landsee in the direction of Mr. Steele's home. On his return from the hunt he had had an urgent call of nature that forced him to stop in the fence corner where the witness stated he saw him. When he started to step out onto the road he saw Mr. Steele driving toward him with his mules in a trot. He and Mr. Steele had had some trouble and Mr. Steele had told him that if he ever crossed his path again that he would kill him.

He did not think Mr. Steele had seen him and, in hopes that he would pass without noticing him, he drew back as far as possible into the fence corner. Evidently Mr. Steele had seen him for he slackened the pace at which he was driving and just as he reached opposite to where he was, he stopped his mules, stood up in his wagon and shouted, "There you are, you skulking coward, hiding in a fence corner. We will settle our differences now for good!" At the same time he reached for his pistol. When he saw Mr. Steele reach for his hip pocket and saw the pistol, Stanley said he fired without taking aim and had no idea whether or not he hit Mr. Steele until he fell. At the firing of the gun the mules were frightened and started running.

Mr. Stanley further testified that he was not very well at that time and it all happened so unexpectedly and so suddenly that he was completely unnerved. He realized he was trembling and was nauseated and he stepped back into the fence corner to lean against the fence and try to compose himself. It was at that time in his anxiety he smoked so many cigarettes and constantly moved about in the fence corner and trampled the grass and weeds. He said he went home and told his wife what had happened and that he was going to see one of his cousins who would help him secure a lawyer and bondsman. He had suggested to his wife he would need several days to make necessary arrangements before he went to jail and that she had better not know where he was. As soon as he had secured bondsmen he had surrendered to the sheriff.

Mr. Stanley also stated that he did not know his gun was loaded with buckshot. After he heard that Mr. Steele had been shot with buckshot he recalled that he had bought some shells loaded with buckshot several months before for a deer hunt in the swamps of Snake Creek Beat and that he had one of those shells left. He had pitched this shell on the shelf where he kept his shells. He had forgotten he had such a shell and evidently picked it up by mistake.

Mr. Stanley was subjected to a long and vigorous cross-examination. The first question the prosecution asked was, "How many times before the day you killed Mr. Steele had you gone bird hunting without your bird dogs and with your gun loaded with buckshot?" Showing confusion he answered, "Never." He was asked if he did not know that a shell loaded with buckshot was heavier than one loaded with birdshot. He answered the weight was so slight that it was easy not to notice the difference. He was asked if he had not seen Mr. Steele that morning in Landsee before the shooting and had hurried home, loaded his gun with buckshot and gone and waited in the fence corner and shot him. Stanley denied seeing Mr. Steele that morning prior to the killing.

The prosecution on rebuttal introduced a witness who testified that he saw Mr. Stanley and Mr. Steele pass each other in the village the morning of the killing. He placed the time of this meeting at a time which would give Mr. Stanley time to go home after the meeting and get his gun and then go and hide in the fence corner, but would not give him sufficient time to hunt birds in the woods as he claimed. The prosecution also introduced the owner of the woods in which Mr. Stanley said he went bird hunting. The owner lived on the edge of the clump and he testified that he was in the woods all that morning selecting trees to use for firewood and that he never saw Mr. Stanley. There was much more testimony but this touches the emphasized issues. It was the general opinion that Mr. Stanley did not make too favorable an impression as a witness.

That the alienation between the group of citizens who sympathized with Mr. Stanley and those supporting the prosecution had widened during the trial was evidenced by the fact that when court would adjourn, one side would wait until the other side had left the courtroom before attempting to leave in order to avoid contacting each other.

The arguments of the attorneys took about three hours. The defense emphasized that the burden was on the State to prove beyond a reasonable doubt that the defendant was guilty and that it had failed to do this. Mr. Stanley was shown without contradiction to be a peaceable man of good character. His statement of facts established that he acted in self defense and no person had disputed his testimony. Mr. Stanley's statement was corroborated by the fact that Mr. Steele was an aggressive and dangerous man who always went armed and that he had pulled his pistol from his hip pocket to shoot Mr. Stanley was evidenced by the pistol being out of his pocket and within a few inches of his hand as testified by Dr. Alston.

In closing its argument the prosecution contended that Mr. Stanley saw Mr. Steele in the village of Landsee the morning of the killing and hurried home, got his shotgun, loaded it with buckshot and then hid himself in the fence corner until Mr. Steele came along and then assassinated him. Briefly they contended that Mr. Stanley saw Mr. Steele in Landsee that morning prior to the killing as established by the testimony of a disinterested witness whose credibility was not attacked. Mr. Stanley had not gone bird hunting because he did not have the time to do so, because he did not carry his bird dogs that might have given away his hiding place. Furthermore, the woods was not a hunting ground for birds, and the owner of the woods in which Mr. Stanley said he hunted had testified he was in the woods that morning and had not seen Mr. Stanley. It was not reasonable to believe an experienced hunter like Mr. Stanley did not know he was loading his gun with buckshot. The prosecution also stressed the fact that, if Mr. Steele were stopping his mules to shoot Mr. Stanley, seeing Mr. Stanley armed he would have his pistol out of his pocket with the safety catch off before he was opposite Mr. Stanley. The State said the facts proved that Mr. Steele realized Mr. Stanley was about to shoot him and he quickly stood to get in a position to defend himself and was killed before he could turn and face the defendant.

The prosecutor closed by saying, ".The defense contends

no person saw the killing and, therefore, the defendant's statement must be accepted. While no person saw the shooting,
many facts contradict his story. And there is such a multitude
of circumstances crying out that he is not telling the truth that
you must be convinced his entire story is a fabrication."

The judge gave a rather lengthy charge and the jury retired
about the middle of the afternoon to consider their verdict. The
jury did not reach a verdict that day. The next morning at
eleven o'clock the jury asked to report. The judge asked,
"Gentlemen, have you reached a verdict?" The foreman of the
jury replied, "Judge, we are unable to agree. We considered the
evidence several hours yesterday and since eight o'clock this
morning and we are convinced that there is no reasonable
chance of our agreeing. We are asking to be discharged."

The judge said, "Gentlemen, this case has taken several
days to try. It has cost the county a large sum of money and has
caused considerable inconvenience and expense to a number of
people. It is your duty, if possible, to render a verdict and make
a final disposal of the case. I am asking you to return to the jury
room and make another sincere effort to reach a verdict."

About three o'clock that afternoon the jury asked to
report. When the judge asked if the jury had reached a verdict
the foreman answered, "Yes, sir." The judge ordered the clerk
to read the verdict. The clerk read, "We, the jury, find the
defendant not guilty." The momentary stillness that followed
the reading of the verdict was broken by the crying of Mrs.
Stanley. She could not control her pent-up feelings. Then the
attorney who had been employed to aid the prosecution said,
"If the court please, I request that the jury be polled." The
defense attorney said, "The State has no right to have the jury
polled." The judge said, "This is the first time I have ever been
requested by the State to poll a jury but I know of no reason
why the State is not entitled to exercise that right." The judge
then began asking each individual juror, "Did you agree to this
verdict?" The first five jurors questioned replied, "Yes." The
sixth said, "Yes sir, in a way."

The judge asked, "What do you mean by 'in a way'?"" The
juror answered, "Well, Judge, six of us doubted if the evidence
proved the defendant guilty beyond a reasonable doubt and six
of us were convinced that it did. That was the way it stood

when we reported that we were unable to agree and asked to be discharged. When we returned to the jury room, after you instructed us to endeavor again to reach a verdict, we agreed that we would review all the evidence and then vote, and that if on that vote there was a majority either way, we would make the majority vote the verdict. After we went over the evidence again, one of the jurors who had previously voted for conviction said, 'Maybe there is a reasonable doubt about the defendant's guilt' and then voted 'not guilty.' This gave those voting 'not guilty' a majority. Then, in accordance with our agreement, we made the verdict 'not guilty.'"

The prosecuting attorney said, "If the Court please, that statement shows that the verdict is not properly a unanimous verdict. I ask for a mistrial." The judge then asked the juror, "Did you agree to this verdict voluntarily?" The juror answered, "Yes, sir." The Court then denied the motion for a mistrial, ruled the verdict valid, and discharged Mr. Stanley.

Legally, the verdict acquitting Mr. Stanley settled the case, but Landsee community was probably more divided than ever. The friends of Mr. Stanley contended that the verdict was a complete vindication. The friends of Mr. Steele contended the verdict was based on a technicality and not on the merits as shown by the facts. Citing the statement the juror made when the judge polled the jury, they held that the real verdict was that six of the jury was convinced beyond a reasonable doubt that Mr. Stanley had assassinated Mr. Steele, and that the other six jurors believed him guilty but feared it had not been proved beyond a reasonable doubt.

Institute Promotion

In a small rural village, such as Landsee, where communication with the outside world is limited, little stirs and retains the interest of its people except that which happens locally. Social wounds heal slowly. When an incident has affected the entire community and has served to almost sever long existing friendships and damage the cordial relationship that existed between many, the community suffers from a social sickness that depresses every individual and blights the whole countryside.

Several months had elapsed since the trial, yet the animosities engendered by the killing did not appear to have abated. It deeply concerned the Rev. Paul Gordon, the Baptist minister, always called the Chaplain, and the Rev. Peter Matthews, the Methodist minister. There was lacking the camaraderie which existed among the citizens of Landsee prior to Mr. Steele's death. The estrangements not only existed among the adults but were influencing the conduct of the children. It was seriously affecting the fellowship of their members. The pastors realized that in such a social atmosphere a slight incident might be so magnified as to cause serious hostilities. They were anxious to find some means to counteract this condition. They freely confessed to each other that their preaching had not been successful in improving the situation. After they discussed ways and means at length, they decided they needed the opinions of some others. In a community like Landsee, there are always three or four people in whom virtually everyone has confidence and on whom the citizens rely in the event of an emergency. In Landsee these were Dr. Alston, Mr. Ben Davidson, the Chaplain and Miss Essie. The Methodist minister was new in Landsee but was soon to be recognized.

The two preachers secured a conference with Dr. Alston, Mr. Davidson and Miss Essie. After reminding the group of the social situation they were advised that they had been requested to meet to help find some way to remedy the condition. There was much discussion and several suggestions as to what might be done, but no suggestion met with unanimous approval. During this discussion Miss Essie had been silent. Finally the Chaplain said, "Miss Essie, you have not said one word and you are usually full of plans. Do you not have a plan?" Miss Essie replied, "Oh yes, whether it is good or bad, I always have a plan." The Chaplain said, "Let us hear it."

Miss Essie said, "This evening is not the first time I have given this matter thought. For quite a time I have wondered when you would try to do something about it. In my opinion there is but one balm that will cure the social malady with which we are suffering and that is to start a project of common concern to all the people and secure their participation in its accomplishment. Such a project is the construction of a building to house the Institute. You, Chaplain, have advocated this for some time and you promised at a school meeting a long time ago to organize a committee to promote this project. But you have never done anything about it. I suggest that you now fulfill your promise." After thinking a while the Chaplain said, "Of course, with you all problems are solved by promoting education but I am of the opinion your plan is the most meritorious that has been suggested. I would like to hear what the rest of you think about it."

Mr. Davidson said, "I realize the project will have to be a large one in which all of us will be vitally interested, but I wonder if this community is able to build a large enough building to accommodate our present enrollment of students as well as the extra student body that would result from increasing the curriculum." Dr. Alston said, "Everybody knows we are compelled to provide a larger building for what we are doing now. It will not be asking for more than we are compelled to do. An increased curriculum would furnish an opportunity for some to secure the education they need but never would receive unless it were available locally. If the Chaplain and Mr. Matthews will undertake the promotion of the project, I believe we can do it."

Miss Essie said, "I'm sure it can be accomplished if these two preachers take the lead." The Chaplain said, "The community is so desperately in need of something to restore normal conditions I am willing to give the project all my time if those present here decide to adopt the plan and pledge their support." Mr. Matthews said, "I will place myself at the disposal of the Chaplain." Mr. Davidson responded, "All right, I will go along. I move we adopt the plan." It was adopted and the Chaplain was requested to proceed to organize the campaign. He asked those present to remain as a committee with whom he could consult about ways and means.

In a week the committee met and finalized the plans for the first move to promote the building of the Institute. The Chaplain reported that it would be necessary to follow the practice of holding a meeting of the citizens to determine whether or not a proposal for the community welfare should be adopted. He said the success of the undertaking would depend on the attendance of this meeting. In an effort to assure a successful meeting he would give an outdoor dinner at which he would serve barbecued meat, camp stew, bread, cake, ice cream and coffee. He had a sufficient supply of meat given him by some of the members of one of the churches he served. Mr. Blossburg and Mr. Davidson were purchasing the other ingredients and he had requested Miss Essie and Mrs. Davidson to arrange for bread, coffee, cake and ice cream.

Mr. Matthews was asked to undertake the responsibility of inviting every man and his wife to attend. In order to quiet the fears of some that they might be required to sit at a table with a person to whom they had rather not converse, Mr Matthews had prepared a chart showing how the tables would be arranged and who would sit at each table. Mr. Matthews' father had an interest in a printing business and he had printed a large number of these charts as a contribution. When a person was invited he would be given a chart and shown where he and his wife would sit and who would be at the table with them. The Chaplain also reported that there was a group that had quite a reputation as performers with fiddles and banjos, and that they agreed to contribute the music for the occasion. The committee agreed that everything had been done to get the meeting well attended.

The Methodist preacher went personally to every house inviting and urging each family to attend. It is said he wore out a new pair of shoes. An amusing incident happened in this connection. Lon Williamson noticed that Mr. Matthews was wearing a pair of new shoes and accused him of buying them from a Jew instead of purchasing them from the Chairman of his Board of Stewards. He was not entirely pacified when the preacher told him that his father had sent him the shoes.

When the evening for the dinner arrived, the committee had all preparations fully completed and anxiously awaited the guests, uneasy as to what might happen. However, they did not have to wait long. It was soon evident that there would be a full attendance. Many arrived early. The groups were kept separated by the Chaplain, Mr. Matthews, Dr. Alston and Mr. Davidson. When all had gathered they were invited to serve themselves. In order that they might be seated as arranged, they were escorted to their tables. Before and during the meal the musicians played and talked in a humorous manner.

When the meal was finished, the Chaplain stood and asked for attention. He said, "I wish to thank the musicians for contributing so much to the pleasure of the meeting." Everybody cheered for they had enjoyed it. Continuing to address the musicians he said, "If you gentlemen will go to the table, the ladies will see that you are well served." The Chaplain waited until the musicians were ensconced at a table, then he said, "Of course, all of you know that I have invited you to come to this meeting to consider a matter of extreme importance to us all. So that the meeting may be conducted in an orderly manner, I think we should name a chairman." Dr. Alston said, "I nominate Ben Davidson as chairman." There were several seconds to the nomination. Without waiting the Chaplain said, "All who favor Mr. Ben Davidson as chairman say "Aye."" There was a chorus of "Ayes" and the Chaplain said, "With that many 'Ayes' there could not be any 'Nos' so I declare Ben Davidson duly elected chairman." Mr. Davidson stood and said, "Thank you. We will need to keep a record of our proceedings. I am asking Miss Essie to act as secretary." There was some applause for this appointment. Then he said, "The Rev. Peter Matthews will state the purpose of the meeting." Rising, Mr. Matthews said, "This meeting has been called to give the citizens of Landsee an opportunity to take some action to remedy the inadequate housing of our school children. I think we should first hear from Miss Essie. I am asking her to describe to you the situation at the school."

Miss Essie in her direct and matter-of-fact manner said, "As you know, I am teaching my last year. I have taught in that room in the Masonic Building for twenty-five years. For the last three years we have been so cramped for space because of the number of students attending, that it has been impossible to teach properly. Some of the students have had to sit in chairs along the wall without any desk. It would take four times the space now available to properly house the present student body. Even this would not care for the normal annual increase of students. There are no blackboards. The black paint put on the walls to serve as blackboards has worn or peeled off. Many of the seats are broken and uncomfortable. I have called Mr. Williamson's attention to needed repairs repeatedly but there has been no response. Since he said he was Chairman of the Board of Trustees, I thought he was the proper person to whom to report. You are cheating your children by not providing better housing and equipment."

When Miss Essie concluded her remarks Mr. Matthews said, "A few weeks ago several of us were discussing the need for a school house and decided that we could not afford to wait any longer to start definite action to provide for this public need. Miss Essie urged us to submit to you plans that would provide housing and equipment which would not only care for present needs, but also for the future increase in the student body. She also stressed that we should provide for higher grades than are now being taught in order that our children may secure locally their preparation to enter college. It is realized that this will be a herculean task for a community of this size. This will mean adopting the plan advocated for some time by the Chaplain, which is to make Landsee the educational center for an area encompassing many miles around our village. This will require providing housing and equipment for an Institute of much higher learning than we now have. As I said, this will require the cooperation of each one of us and a sacrifice by many, but those of us who were discussing it know it can be done if you wish to do it, and we also thought you would want to do it. Consequently, we decided to call this meeting and submit the matter to you. However, before we discuss the question I think we should hear from the Chaplain. He has a plan by which he is confident this project can be accomplished."

The Chaplain said, "No one will deny that we are forced to provide better facilities for what we are now doing. I propose that we give our children better and higher educational advantages than we have offered them in the past. This is a large undertaking for the money that would be available from us. We are not a wealthy people financially, but there are other contributions than money that will be just as valuable in completing such a project. For instance, I cannot donate as large an amount of cash as Lon Williamson, but I am willing to donate my labor as a carpenter from the beginning to the completion of the building. In fact, I believe we can secure the donation of sufficient labor and most of the material to do all the work. This is the proposition we are asking you to consider."

Mr. Davidson said, "We would like to hear from each of you. It must be everyone's project." One citizen got up and said, "The best way to ascertain if the proposal is practical is to see how many here will contribute to the accomplishment of it. I have been told I own the most desirable tract of land for such a building. I will donate the site and some cash." The man who operated the sawmill said, "I am sure those who work at my mill will donate their labor to manufacture the lumber and I think I know who will donate the logs." The man who operated the stone quarry said he would give the stone and he would also give some cash. Everyone there except Lon Williamson volunteered to furnish either labor, material or cash, and sometimes all three. The Chaplain addressed Mr. Williamson, "Lon, you are the one wealthy man in Landsee. You have often expressed yourself as being interested in education. Certainly you wish to make a generous donation."

Lon Williamson took advantage of this opportunity to stand and address those present. He said, "For many years I have been Chairman of the Board of Trustees charged with operating our schools. I have had more experience in connection with school operation than any man here. I have also had as much experience, if not more, in financing buildings. Is it not strange that I was not consulted about this fantastic scheme before it was submitted to you this evening? I am sure the reason is that they knew I would not approve it because it would legally bind the persons mutually agreeing to these donations, to pay the whole debt incurred. Do not think there will be no debt. If this extravagant dream is undertaken, a debt could be incurred that would bankrupt every individual taking part in it. Fortunately, there has been no action by this group endorsing the proposition. I move that we postpone the action in order to give everyone an opportunity to think about it and study the legal liability they will assume. As Chairman of the Board of Trustees of the Board of Education, I will call a meeting within two weeks to settle the matter." You could tell from the smirk on his face as he took his seat that he was confident he had dealt the proposal a death blow. Because financial considerations always completely controlled his life, he was sure that the fear of personal bankruptcy, which he was certain he had planted in the thinking of all present, would control their vote.

Mr. Reuben Stone, the Justice of the Peace for Landsee precinct, was employed as a clerk by Mr. Williamson. He was regarded as inherently a good and honest man. Mr. Williamson sought to control his life by constantly reminding him that he could discharge him and that he could foreclose the mortgage he held on his home. Because Mr. Stone felt that he was entirely dependent upon Mr. Williamson for employment, he was not only slavishly subservient to Mr. Williamson's many unreasonable demands, but he endeavored to use every opportunity to please him. Mr. Stone said, "As the plan is entirely new to all of us and could involve each of us in financial difficulties, I think we should follow Mr. Williamson's suggestion. I second his motion."

Mr. Davidson was showing increasing irritation during this assault on their efforts. He stood and started to speak but then seemed to think better and simply said, "Does anyone else wish to discuss this motion?" Mr. Matthews said, "Perhaps I should let Mr. Williamson know that he is mistaken in the details of the proposal. Under the condition which Mr. Williamson thinks exists his fears might be well founded, but those conditions are not present in the plan proposed by the Chaplain. Last year I was assigned as an assistant to a pastor who was undertaking the construction of a large sanctuary. He assigned me the task of raising subscriptions to the needed funds. One of the most able men to donate money raised the same question which Mr. Williamson has raised. The pastor submitted the matter to an excellent attorney for advice. The attorney said that to avoid any question of liability beyond one's subscription, he would prepare a subscription blank to be used which specifically limited the subscriber's liability to the amount he designated. The provisions in the subscription blank also void the subscription in the event of the death of the donor."

Before he continued Mr. Williamson interrupted and said, "That shows how little practical business judgment has gone into concocting this scheme. You could not borrow any money on a subscription list of that character." Mr. Matthews continued as if he had not been interrupted. "We discussed this matter of liability and decided to recommend the using of a similar subscription blank as was used in raising money for that church. I have a copy which we can follow. Mr. Williamson is correct when he says this is not the type of subscription on which to borrow money. Your committee is recommending that we do not borrow any money or go in debt and that we build as we have money, material and labor available." Mr. Davidson waited a few seconds and said, "If no one else wishes to discuss the matter, we will take a vote. All in favor of Mr. Williamson's motion please raise your hands." Mr. Williamson and Mr. Stone raised their hands. Mr. Davidson said, "I see two votes for the motion. All opposed to the motion please raise your hands." All the other hands shot up at once and were held high. Mr. Davidson said, "The motion is so overwhelmingly defeated it is useless to count the uplifted hands."

Then someone said, "In order that Miss Essie's record might show a formal adoption of the plan, I move its adoption." There were several seconds of the motion and it was unanimously carried as Mr. Williamson and Mr. Stone did not vote. To compel Mr. Williamson to disclose his attitude to those present, Mr. Davidson said, "Lon, as the plan has been duly adopted, do you wish to indicate the amount of your generous donation?" He replied, "A large amount of materials will have to be purchased through my store and I will give a ten per cent discount on all the bills. This will amount to a substantial amount." He looked around for approval but, since the coming of Mr. Blossburg, the citizens had become keenly aware that Mr. Williamson marked up his merchandise from fifty to one hundred per cent and that his offer still left him with a handsome profit.

At this point, the Chaplain said, "I was asked by Mr. Blossburg to explain his absence from this meeting. He had an engagement away from Landsee. He said he would make a cash donation of five hundred dollars at the beginning and if we needed to order any material through his store, he would let us have it at what it cost him." There was some applause. Mr. Davidson said, "Lon, do you not wish to match this offer by Mr. Blossburg?" He replied, "I deal in first class not second class material. I do not have the wholesaler to mark up his bill so as to allow a good profit and make the purchaser think I am making nothing."

Mr. Davidson said, "I think the next step is to set up the machinery to accomplish the adopted proposal." Mr. Williamson seemingly unabashed by the rebuffs he had received, and in a renewal of his effort to take control said, "As Chairman of the Board of Trustees, I will appoint the committee to work out the details of how we should proceed to solicit funds and begin construction. I will call a meeting in about ten days to advise you what the committe has decided."

Mr. Drake, who seldom spoke in public meetings, said, "No, Lon, this project is independent of the Trustees of which you say you are chairman. The citizens have never given that board any authority. It is self-constituted and you assumed the chairmanship just as you propose to do here. Furthermore, you have shown you are opposed to the plan and I am sure you would do all you could to kill it. I wonder if those who called this meeting have any suggestions as to how to implement the plan." Mr. Davidson said, "Yes, we have given it serious consideration. I will ask the Chaplain to tell you what we think would be the best way to handle it."

The Chaplain said, "We decided that a committee of three or four should be elected by this group. This committee would incorporate Landsee Institute as an educational organization. In the beginning this committee would act as the officers and directors of the corporation for the first year and would proceed to secure donations and, when feasible, begin building. All people donating to the Institute would have a vote at its meetings which would be as often as considered necessary. The corporation would be the owner of the land and all other donations." Lon Williamson said, "You are suggesting that three or four people have arbitrary power. This leaves all the rest of these people without any voice as to what happens. I oppose it." The Chaplain said, "I hope you listen to your preacher's sermons better than you have listened to what I said. I clearly stated that every person who made any donation would have a vote in running the corporation." Someone said, "I move the plan be adopted." The motion was seconded without delay and it was carried.

As soon as the motion was carried Mr. May said, "I move that the committee be constituted of four people and that the Chaplain be named chairman of the committee and president of the corporation. It is what he has advocated for years and he will be giving most of his time to it. The second person should be Ben Davidson who has no private interest to be served, who is a good business man and who should have charge of all purchases. Next, Mr. Matthews, who should be in charge of soliciting donations and act as treasurer. His past experience qualifies him well for these duties. The fourth should be Miss Essie. It would not be right to have any educational effort without her. She should be secretary and should be allowed some compensation for her services. The others should work without compensation."

Mr. Williamson said, "It is not good practice to vote on several persons at one time. A person might wish to vote for one of the parties included in the group and against another in the group." Mr. May said, "If anyone does not like the manner of election proposed in the motion, they should vote against the motion. If the motion is not carried, then we will vote on each individual separately." He waited a few seconds and said, "As Ben is included in my motion I will put the motion. All in favor say 'Aye.'" It sounded as if everyone had voted for the motion. He then said, "If anyone opposes the motion say 'No.'" No opposition was heard and the motion was declared unanimously carried. At that point Mr. Davidson said, "Unless there are other matters to be considered the meeting is adjourned. We thank all of you for attending."

Dr. Alston, Mr. Davidson, Mr. Matthews, Miss Essie and the Chaplain lingered for a conference after all the others had gone. The Chaplain said, "Miss Essie, you win." She replied, "What do you mean by saying 'I win?' The idea has been yours for several years." "Yes, I have had the idea," he said, "but ideas are worthless unless implemented and you made us implement it." It was the consensus of the committee that the meeting was a success. They had noticed that motions made by one faction would be seconded by a member of the other faction and that in leaving the meeting a number of the men of opposite factions were talking to each other. It was their hope that the community, which for months had been immersed in that which stifled friendships and cordial relations, had seized this opportunity for their better selves to assert themselves and restore normal conditions. They thought a good beginning had been made.

The committee decided not to give the enthusiasm time to lag so they moved at once to incorporate, solicit donations and start to build. Their efforts were rewarded by a response of liberal donations. Quite a number of young people offered to give their services. The Educational Aid Club volunteered for service and the Chaplain found ways to use them. He invited them to the meetings at which were discussed the progress, needs and proposed future action.

In that time when there were no public bond issues to erect schools, and no large industries on which to levy taxes, it is marvelous how much was accomplished with such a small amount of available cash, and largely by individual effort and personal sacrifice. It appears that the men of that day not only took advantage of every opportunity to advance the community's good, but they also created opportunities to do so. The building of the Landsee Institute is an example of how a people of limited means and no public funds can by cooperation, personal sacrifice, and the use of what is at hand, accomplish great things.

The construction of the building progressed rapidly with the Chaplain planning and directing the work. Under the supervision of the Chaplain a number of men did the carpentry and all the heavy work. The Rev. Peter Matthews was proving an effective solicitor as well as a good keeper of the records of donations of money, labor and materials, and of all expenditures. Mr. Davidson was as effective in doing all the buying and seeing that materials and labor were on hand when needed.

The Rumor

At a meeting of the officers of the corporation, which Dr. Alston had been requested to attend, they discussed a report Mr. Matthews made. He said someone was circulating a rumor that some person must be profiting from purchasing materials from firms located outside of Landsee when the same materials were available in Landsee. The rumor went further and implied that an investigation should be made to protect the public. He said that he did not know how general the rumor was but two people had mentioned it to him and expressed the opinion that it should be stopped. Miss Essie said she had heard that such was being circulated. Dr. Alston said he had not heard the rumor, perhaps because he only talked to people about their ills. Mr. Davidson said, "I think it is a safe guess to say that Lon Williamson is its source. He has a philosophy that no project must be permitted to succeed unless he controls it or unless it contributes to his personal financial gain. He is sometimes a little careless in the means he used to accomplish his ends. Few, if any, will credit the rumor but I think it should be killed and Lon be given to understand he had better not repeat it any more. I suggest we call a public meeting to make a progress report and answer any question anyone wishes to ask."

The interest in the erection of the building for Landsee Institute was still so great that the public meeting was well attended. The committee had made detailed preparation to show how every cent was spent. They had also agreed on the tactics they thought would be most effective to silence Lon

Williamson's rumors. Interest was also increased by the fact that Mr. Williamson openly bragged that the committee would have some embarrassing questions to answer at the public meeting. He felt sure of the embarrassment for he could not think of anyone doing anything except for personal gain or aggrandizement.

Mr. Davidson called the meeting to order and said, "We appreciate your attending this meeting. And the committee you appointed to secure donations and erect the building for Landsee Institute appreciates the response to calls for funds, material and labor. We are here to answer any questions. First, I think you would like to hear a general report from the Chaplain." The Chaplain said, "I wish to join Ben in expressing my appreciation for your confidence and cooperation. As you have seen, we are ahead of schedule in our building. All the framing of that large two-story building is in place. Many of you here tonight have worked on it. We do not owe any money. We still have some cash on hand. We have sufficient material to keep us busy for two weeks and promise of enough material to keep us busy for two weeks more. With your continued support, the building will be completed."

The Chaplain had purposely failed to say anything about collections and expenditures, hoping to entice Mr. Williamson to make his attack. One of Williamson's stooges said, "You have not told us how much money you received and how you spent it. I hear that some want an investigation to see if someone received a rake-off for buying materials from firms outside of Landsee when they could have been bought from a firm in Landsee." Mr. Williamson had used someone else to ask his question. Mr. Davidson hesitated and then turned aside to Mr. Matthews and spoke to him in such a low tone that only Mr. Matthews could hear him. When Mr. Matthews looked at his record and answered him, Mr. Davidson returned to the place where he stood when presiding, and said, "Only those who have made some contribution to the Landsee Institute have any right to participate in this meeting. Mr. Matthews says he has no record of your donating any money, material or labor. We will have to ask you not to interfere with the meeting."

Mr. Davidson was attempting to force Lon Williamson into the open with his attack. Mr. Williamson said, "This is a public meeting and any citizen has a right to ask questions. I contend you have no right to hold he can't take part in this meeting." Mr. Davidson replied, "This is a meeting of the shareholders of a corporation. The shareholders are those who donated something of value to Landsee Institute and we do not propose to let someone who has not given one cent of value come here and attempt to run our business. Furthermore, we know he is not speaking for himself." There was applause. Mr. Williamson said, "It seems you object to giving an account as this party requested." Mr. Davidson repled, "That statement intimates facts which are not true. All we have objected to is an interloper meddling in our affairs." Mr. Williamson said, "I am sure the good citizens here want to hear that question answered." Mr. Davidson replied, "I have not heard a qualified shareholder ask the question." Mr. Williamson said, "I guess as a shareholder I am authorized to ask the question."

Before he could go further with a statement, Mr. Davidson asked Mr. Matthews, loud enough for everyone to hear, if Lon Williamson had made a donation to Landsee Institute. In equally as loud a voice Mr. Matthews replied that the record showed he had donated five pounds of nails. Mr. Davidson knew what he had donated but he wanted everyone there to know. Mr. Davidson said, "The size of the donation does not matter. Any donation makes him a stockholder." Mr. Williamson, in an effort to retort to the obvious criticism of his small gift, said, "You should not expect a business man to put his money into a project where there is a rumor questioning the method of purchasing the materials used. I will ask the question. See if you can answer it satisfactorily." Mr. Davidson wanted to make him unequivocally commit himself to the statement that the rumor charged that one of the committee had secured a secret payment for giving the business to firms located outside of Landsee. He said, "I understand that you adopt the question asked by the non-stockholder." Mr. Williamson said, "Yes." Mr. Davidson continued, "In order that we may fully understand your question, both you and the non-stockholder said the question was based on a rumor you heard that someone was securing secret payments to purchase materials from firms located outside Landsee when the same materials could have been purchased here." Mr. Williamson replied, "You have been told 'yes' to that question several times. Are you taking up time trying to think of some way to avoid answering it?" Mr. Davidson said, "One more question, Lon. Who told you about this rumor?" Mr. Williamson answered, "It does not matter who told me. The question is, are you going to explain your transactions?"

Mr. Davidson, in what all recognized as an extremely deliberate and dangerously cool manner, said, "No, for the considerations of this meeting it does not matter who started and promoted this erroneous rumor, but as I am the only one who purchased any materials it matters to me, for it is a dirty lie. I am asking you to remain after the meeting to talk to me about this lie. For your information I have had a private investigation made and, so far, every party interviewed states he heard the rumor from you. If you are unable to give your source, I must conclude you are responsible. My lawyer advises that this rumor constitutes malicious slander and a suit will lie to collect many thousands of dollars of damages. I expect to file such suit. We are prepared to answer your question. Mr. Matthews has kept the records. He, Miss Essie and the Chaplain have been advised of, and have approved every purchase. Mr. Matthews, will you please report."

Mr. Matthews came to the table with an arm full of papers. He said, "When we heard that some person was circulating a slanderous rumor relative to purchases of materials, we decided to make a detailed report so that every stockholder would be informed of every transaction. My father has an interest in a printing business and, as I was involved, he offered to print a large number of copies of this report so that each one of you could have a copy. Will someone give one of these copies to each person here who is a stockholder?"

After copies of the report were distributed he continued, "This is a long report for it covers every donation and every expenditure. The question is about purchases so we will discuss them. In detail you will find the facts about purchases. We took bids on each purchase. Mr. Williamson was asked to bid in writing. This report shows his bid and the amount we paid for the material. You will note that we saved twenty-five per cent by purchasing from the lowest bidder. Mr. Williamson, even after deducting the discount he said he would allow, was much higher than the bid we accepted. There is printed in this report a letter from each wholesaler from whom a purchase was made stating that they never paid anyone to give them the business. In this connection, I might say they have had investigators here to ascertain who is responsible for this slanderous rumor. They are contemplating court action. Our cash went over twenty-five per cent further than it would have gone if we had purchased from Mr. Williamson. Any questions?" As there were no questions Mr. Matthews took his seat.

Mr. Davidson rose and said, "As there are no questions I assume all are satisfied with the report and that we are ready to adjourn. While this closes the corporation's dealing with this matter I assure you, ladies and gentlemen, that it does not close my personal dealing with it. I have been slandered and I do not permit the impugning of my character without holding the person guilty responsible. We are adjourned." Many of the wives had attended this meeting. Mrs. Matthews was near Mr. Williamson and near her was Mr. and Mrs. May. Mr. Williamson said to Mrs. Matthews, who he contended was too pert to be a minister's wife, "It seems that your husband has been influenced to write his report to reflect on me. He had better remember who butters his bread." Mrs. Matthews, acting as if alarmed, said, "Oh, Brother Williamson, don't tell me you are thinking of not letting us have any butter?" Mrs. May, who had heard the exchange, said, "Don't grieve too much. I will share some butter with you."

About that time Ben Davidson called and said, "Wait for me, Lon. I wish to see you." The Chaplain was talking to Mr. Davidson and this delayed him from reaching Mr. Williamson immediately. Mr. Williamson, trying to act as if he had not heard Mr. Davidson, rushed away. Mrs. Matthews and Mrs. May were not alone in being amused at his hasty departure for several men were waiting to see what would happen when he had to face the ire of Ben Davidson. But the Chaplain held Mr. Davidson until Lon Williamson could get away.

The Brush Arbor Meeting

As a young man Paul Gordon, tall, handsome and intelligent, trained himself to be a carpenter. He became a good carpenter and was always in demand. According to his own story, one day while reading his Bible, he felt an urge to become a preacher of the gospel. This urge grew until it became so great he was convinced that he was called to the ministry. He discussed this matter with the pastor of the church of which he was a member, and with the deacons of his church. A committee composed of two ordained preachers and three deacons was appointed to examine Paul Gordon as to his faith and beliefs. After the examination the committee recommended that he be ordained as a minister of the gospel. The church approved the report of this committee and Paul Gordon became an ordained minister of the Baptist denomination.

His call was to a larger field of service than he was equipped to render, and he was keenly aware of this fact. So he gathered his personal belongings and took what cash he had accumulated and went to a place where he could work and make a living and also secure an education. He was in his junior year at a Baptist college and the pastor of a one-Sunday Baptist church when there came an urgent call for chaplains for the Confederate Army. The War between the States was only a few months old when he resigned his church, quit college and began serving as a chaplain. He had served in this capacity almost two years when he became a prisoner of war. He was held as a prisoner until the close of the war. His service was during some of the severest battles fought in the war. He tried to give aid and comfort to the wounded and the dying. Sometimes it was on the battlefield and to a soldier of the Federal Army. It was soon known that as long as his physical strength permitted, he was ministering to those he thought needed him. He knelt beside many a brave man mortally wounded and endeavored to strengthen his faith. His was a ministry of consolation and assurance. In prison he was nurse to the sick and wounded prisoners and sought to bring to them the gospel message.

In the discharge of his duties, both in which he was active in the army and in prison, he found no time or place for theological creeds that divided Christians into denominations. His experiences burned the dross of sectarianism out of his soul. To him the gospel was for "whosoever." So when Paul Gordon returned from prison and was called as the pastor of the Baptist Church at Landsee he was still a loyal Baptist but that did not limit his service to members of that church nor to members of the Baptist denomination. His field was to every human being to whom he could be of any help or comfort, regardless of his financial standing, his church affiliation or race. While he did carpenter work he always had it understood that his work as a minister came first. He was soon recognized as the Chaplain of the countryside.

It was this catholic spirit of working with and for everybody that prompted him to request the pastor of the Methodist Church and the pastors of all the churches within a ten mile radius of Landsee to come to his home for a conference on a very important matter. Because some of the rural pastors would have to drive too far to attend the conference and drive back the same day, he let them know they would be entertained the day of the conference and that night. There was never any trouble in securing some family to care for a preacher for a short period.

After the midday meal, which the Chaplain served, he disclosed to them his proposal that they unite in erecting a brush arbor for holding a revival each summer. He said he had discussed the proposal with the Methodist preacher. They had agreed that a joint revival would accomplish more good than separate revivals in each church and that perhaps the other churches near Landsee might wish to join in this effort. This would not be a camp meeting which was not practical, but if all churches joined in the proposal they could bring a strong evangelist to Landsee every summer and gain great good from the united effort. After a brief discussion the proposal was adopted. They then planned another meeting at which the preachers would have one of the leading members of each church he served to attend. At this meeting each church was allotted its part in constructing the brush arbor, and thus it came into existence.

The erection of the brush arbor claimed the active interest of a wide area. The response for every need to construct it was so generous that it was finished sooner than anticipated. The brush arbor was erected in a grove of shade trees along the brook flowing from what the Indians called the Spring of Living Waters. The frame of the structure stood from year to year, being repaired from time to time as necessary. Each year fresh brush was place on its top to serve as shelter from summer showers and such hot rays of the summer sun as might stray through the boughs of the shade trees.

The brush arbor was oblong and seated over three hundred. At one end was a platform on which was a foot-pumped organ, the pulpit and room for those leading the singing. Seats were arranged by placing planks on risers. Three rows of seats left two aisles running from the rear to the platform. The ground was covered with sawdust, an extra amount being placed in the aisles. Along one side, but not under the main structure, were seats and the ground covered with sawdust for use by Negroes. Because the village was unable to accommodate overnight all those who attended from a distance, the services were arranged to be held during the day. The first service was held from 10 o'clock a.m. to 11:30 a.m. There was an intermission from 11:30 a.m. to 1:00 p.m. during which the midday meal was served. The afternoon service was from 1:00 p.m. to 2:30 p.m. This was the schedule every day except for the last day when the final service was on Sunday evening. In the grove near the brush arbor were erected long tables on which was spread the food brought for lunch. The people stood at these tables. The meals served at the intermission were delicious and lavish. Each family seemed to vie with every other family as to who could bring the most delicious food. Everyone was free to select food from any one of the tables whether he knew the party furnishing it or not.

These meetings were well attended. By common consent during the services all businesses were closed and all work suspended. This was their expression of the supreme importance of a spiritual revival. They took time to attend religious services and to consider and redeem the promises they found in their Bible with a faith that a God of love who watched over and cared for their daily lives would answer their prayers.

Is it fanciful musing of the days of my youth that causes me to be impressed with the opinion that there was a larger percentage of devout men in that long ago in Landsee than there is in the busy world of today? Is it true that more of them were regular in their attendance on church services? Maybe this attendance, for whatever reason, resulted in compelling them to think seriously on the Lord. My memory pictures them as regarding the church as holy ground, a place set aside and dedicated as sacred for the worship of God and the learning of man's duty to the Creator. There was nothing sanctimonious about their worship. They accepted without question the Bible as the inspired and authoritative Word of God. It was a simple faith, but it was a faith held by strong, courageous men who showed mercy, acted justly and walked humbly before God. So the brush arbor meeting was perhaps the most important event of the year.

Each year a different evangelist was secured to conduct the services. At the final meeting on Sunday evening, it was arranged for a large number to bring lanterns which were hung in the arbor and from the limbs of the trees. Thus the place of worship and the surrounding grounds were well lighted, for each person that brought a lantern trimmed the wick, filled it with kerosene and polished its globe. A person would be ashamed to bring a dirty lantern for use at the brush arbor meeting.

It was one of these Sunday evening services that cannot be forgotten. From the very beginning of the service it was fraught with a moving spiritual power. There was something about each prayer that caused one to listen almost in awe, and each song seemed to be an humble petition for God's mercy. A large number of Negroes in the area joined in the singing with their melodious voices. They were careful not to permit their voices to overshadow the singing of the white people. Their singing was like the muted notes of a great pipe organ accompanying the singing by the whites. It added a benign beauty to the music. This was the last service of the meeting. The preacher used for his text the 28th and 29th verses of the 26th Chapter of Book of Acts:

> Then Agrippa said unto Paul, Almost thou persuadest me to be a Christian. And Paul said, I would that not only thou, but also all that hear me this day, were both almost and altogether such as I am, except these bonds.

It was a simple but soul searching sermon, delivered with earnestness and unadorned eloquence. When Paul spoke of his bonds, the preacher said, he was referring to the restraints placed upon him as a prisoner. To the onlookers Paul had no freedom while, to them, Agrippa was a free and powerful man. These saw only the external which was not eternal. In truth Paul was eternally free, for his freedom was spiritual and that freedom exists for us today if we can accept it. Agrippa, like some of us, was a spiritual prisoner. Paul gave him an opportunity to be released from his bonds but he failed to accept the gracious offer. He was almost persuaded but lost. The preacher stressed the fact that to almost succeed was but to fail, and he quoted that familiar verse:

> There is a time, we know not when, a place, we know not where, that seals the destiny of men, either to glory or to despair.

He gave the invitation, saying that maybe the time and place were here this evening for some person hearing a still small voice telling him to now make Agrippa's "almost" Paul's "altogether." There was no other proposition. The invitation song was the old familiar hymn, "Almost Persuaded." It was not sung loudly but softly and beseechingly.

During the singing of the second verse, a man who had been seated on the last seat in the rear moved out to the aisle and came to the preacher. He was laboring under uncontrollable emotions. It was Mr. Stanley, who had killed Mr. Steele. Mr.

Stanley was one of the few men in the community who did not take any interest in religious affairs. After his trial for the murder of Mr. Steele he seldom went to church. When he walked down the aisle in response to the invitation of the preacher, it was the first time that most of the congregation was aware that he had attended any of the services.

When Mr. Stanley reached the evangelist he said, "I have come to beg God's forgiveness for my sins, and the forgiveness of any one who thinks I have wronged him."

One of the most active church supporters in Landsee was Mr. Ennis Thomas. He was highly esteemed. Mr. Thomas was a cousin of Mr. Steele and was also a close friend of Mr. Stanley and had endeavored to reconcile the differences between Mr. Steele and Mr. Stanley without any success. Mr. Thomas became convinced that Mr. Stanley, perhaps because he feared Mr. Steele, had waylaid and killed him and, because of this opinion, had not spoken to Mr. Stanley since his trial.

When Mr. Stanley finished his statement, Mr. Thomas, who was near the front, walked forward and offered Mr. Stanley his hand. At first, Mr. Stanley hesitated to take the outstretched hand, but when he looked straight at Mr. Thomas he must have read the old friendship that once existed between them, and suddenly the two men embraced. That evening, tears were shining in the eyes of many adults.

Grown men whose bodies were toughened by hard physical toil, whose faces were tanned by working in the sun, and whose characters were that of just and courageous men, were not ashamed for people to see tears in their eyes when their emotions were profoundly aroused. Their tears on this occasion were tears of happiness and gratitude. Whatever had been their attitude toward Mr. Stanley theretofore, he was now a new man standing forgiven by God and man.

There had not been many to join the church during the revival services but, as they sang as usual as a benediction, "God be with you 'til we meet again," there was a general feeling that it had been one of the most successful meetings ever held.

The Fight

When youthful friends fight, the fight is generally furious, but bide a little while and they will be friends again. It has been observed that youth is quick to take offense and quick to forget and forgive. Fortunately, such was the instance in the fight between John Alston and Donald Hughes. It was one of those peculiar circumstances in which the fight did not result from any personal hatred for each other. When we consider the circumstances leading to this fight, which bruised and bloodied both of them, we find illustrated two truths often present in hostilities great and small which we frequently overlooked.

First, it illustrates that the combatants, although they are voluntary combatants, are not always responsible for creating the influences which result in the violent action, and that the person or persons morally accountable are seldom blamed. It appears that the law is lame in dealing with those who deliberately create an atmosphere that induces and incites injustices and violence. Certainly, such a person is a more contemptible criminal than the person who, driven by such influence, strikes the blow that kills.

John Alston and Donald Hughes had always been good friends. They grew up together; they hunted together; went swimming together and played ball together. Their parents were friends. They had never had any serious differences.

Donald was the bass in the church choir that Ina led. He was deeply devoted to Ina and at every opportunity he was attendant upon her, always endeavoring to anticipate her every wish. He attached great significance to her slightest suggestion. Constantly hearing Ina speak of Sarah as "that Jew girl," and her avowing that if the Jews had their way there would be no Christian churches, that the Jews crucified Jesus, etc., it is not surprising that Donald became incensed against Sarah, although at times he acted as if he liked her. It was this atmosphere that controlled Donald in his fight with John Alston.

Second, it illustrates that many persons affirm an undying commitment to some high ideal and then are guilty of expressing their loyalty to that ideal by actions flagrantly opposed to the principles of the ideal. The life of some is a strange mixture of contradictions between the lips' profession and life's actions. The records of the past disclose that some of the most cruel torture was inflicted upon their fellow man by those who professed a religion that taught that you should do good to those who despitefully use you. As difficult as it is to understand, many such persons do not consider themselves to be hypocrites, pretending to be something they know they are not. According to their conceptions they are sincere crusaders for the right.

The fight between Donald Hughes and John Alston occurred about two weeks after the close of the Brush Arbor Meeting, a meeting heralded as deeply dedicating the entire community to a devotion of the faith that required one to think charitably and act kindly. Just before the beginning of the meeting, Ben Davidson, Jr., was the victim of a severe attack of illness. For two weeks he was in bed with a fever which the doctor feared might be contagious. The doctor advised that he have no visitors, which prevented his close friends from seeing him. Even after he was free from fever the doctor advised him to remain in the house for a week. It was at the end of this period of time of confinement that John, Ellen and Sarah went with him on his first walk after his sickness.

As they were walking along the road they noticed Donald Hughes and two of his friends who had been walking ahead of them, step off of the road and wait for them to pass. Just as Ben and his friends came opposite where Donald was standing, Donald shouted, "Ben, I see you are still in the clutches of the Christ killer." Ben whirled around and stepping toward Donald said, "Donald, apologize for that rude and false statement!"

Sarah grabbed Ben's arm and in a voice choked with emotion said, "Please, Ben, let's go. I don't care what he says. You have been sick. You must not get into a fight." Donald, who had worked himself into a state of anger before he shouted at Ben, became frenzied when Ben accused him of lying. Donald shouted, "Instead of me apologizing, I will make you not only apologize for calling me a liar, but make you sorry you did." Ben started as if to meet him. All the time Sarah was begging Ben to ignore Donald, insisting that she did not want to be the cause of trouble. John caught Ben and said, "Ben, Sarah is right. You are weak from your long illness and you are not physically able to fight Donald and he knows it. I am surprised he would take advantage of your condition to pick a fight with you." In a sneering voice Donald turned to John and said, "All right Mr. Alston, you have not been sick, so how about you resenting what I said and try to make me apologize?"

John lost his conciliatory efforts and replied with considerable heat, "Yes, I do resent your remark for it was an insulting lie that no gentleman would make." Donald's face flared with still fiercer anger and he shouted at John who was standing near Ellen, "You are too big a coward to come out from behind those skirts, because you know if you did I would thrash you until you begged for mercy." It was now Ellen who endeavored to persuade John, Ben and Sarah to leave with her. But the die was cast, the fight was on. John quickly moved away from Ellen and Sarah to the other side of the road where Donald stood. When he was just across the road Donald came charging toward him like a mad bull. Donald was larger and a little taller than John. He looked and was stronger than John and his actions showed that he was confident of his ability to win the fight. He did not doubt his prowess.

Two factors favored John, namely, Donald was so angry he was not at his best, and John was faster. John had not expected Donald to rush him so quickly and was just able to dodge the vicious blow at his head. John saw the coming of the blow in time to side-step so that the blow glanced along his left shoulder. Even then it carried sufficient force to throw John slightly off balance. The failure of his blow to make solid contact with John not only surprised Donald, but it also threw him off balance. John was the first to recover and he moved to a position where Donald would be coming up a slight grade as he approached. Donald never took time to maneuver for position but, confident of his superior strength, advanced speedily and recklessly on him. Both now were firmly on their feet delivering blow for blow, Donald striking ferociously, and John quickly moving so as to parry the terrific force of the blow and then to strike when Donald left an opening. Donald was constantly the agressor, delivering mauling-like efforts to knock John down and each time he failed, he became more angry, more savage and more indiscreet in protecting himself from a damaging blow.

In one of Donald's mad charges he left an opening that gave John an opportunity to strike Donald's head. He had to strike so quickly and move away so fast to prevent Donald from clinching and overpowering him that the blow did not carry much force but it landed just below Donald's left eye and closed the eye. This gave John an advantage and so he constantly and quickly moved to Donald's left or blind side where Donald would have to move almost completely around to see what John was doing. It resulted in John finding another opening to land a blow on Donald's face. This blow had considerable force behind it and it staggered Donald and cut his lip, which bled profusely. When Donald realized that John was effectively avoiding his pile driving punches he rushed and clinched him to throw him to the ground. The momentum of the rush was so fast and furious that John was not able to side-step him nor to brace himself sufficiently to prevent being shoved back and off balance. When Ben saw what was happening, he started to John's aid. Ben had taken only two steps when Jake Wilson, who had arrived on the scene just as Donald shouted at Ben, laid his hand on Ben and said, "Don't interfere. It's their fight." His command, for Ben realized it was a command and that Jake was able to enforce it, surprised Ben. He obeyed him because he knew he was John's friend and also he felt so tired from the two quick steps he had taken he knew he could not be of any help.

While John and Donald were severely punishing each other physically, the ones who were suffering most were Sarah, Ellen and Ben. Ben was ashamed at being helpless. Ellen and Sarah were standing as close to each other as possible. Sarah had one hand over her slightly open mouth as if it was holding back a cry of pain which showed in her eyes, eyes moist from tears she could not prevent shedding. Ellen was tense, watching every move with alarm, fearing serious injury to John.

When Donald clinched John, John was able to keep his right arm and hand free. When John realized he was going to fall backward unless he could turn their bodies, he placed his right hand under Donald's chin and thrust his head back so violently that Donald's grip slackened sufficiently for John, by a supreme effort, to turn their bodies so that each fell on his side, but John was still locked in Donald's arms. When they hit the hard graveled ground Donald's left arm, which he had around John, was crushed against the brick-like surface.

This fall pained Donald so much it caused him to loosen his hold and John twisted himself free of Donald's vice-like clinch. He hurriedly gained his feet. Donald with all his injuries was not thinking of being subdued. He was on his feet as soon as John was. John moved away from Donald again seeking an advantageous position for maneuvering. Donald, still confident of his superior strength, and constantly growing angrier because he had failed to knock John down and so had permitted John to close one of his eyes, moved rapidly toward John. His onslaught was terrific but somewhat blind. He intended to clinch John again, throw him to the ground and hold him helpless until he apologized. But this time John knew what to expect and was in good position to take advantage of any carelessness in Donald's attack. As Donald approached, John took a posture that indicated he would meet Donald headon. Donald knew that he would be able to overcome John in such a tussle, so he increased the speed of his approach. When Donald got near him, John quickly stepped aside, grabbed Donald's arm and violently yanked him in the direction he was going. This added so much to Donald's already rapid momentum that he was unable to control himself and he went sprawling to the ground. The increased impetus was so great and unexpected that he failed to break the force of the fall and he hit the ground so hard that all the breath was knocked out of him.

Before Donald could recover from the shock of the fall, John was on top of him and secured a full Nelson on him, a locked hold that enabled John to prevent Donald from rising.

All at once there was a cry of alarm from Ellen. She saw one of Donald's friends with an open knife in his hands and murder in his face advancing on John. But Jake had also seen him and he stepped between John and the knife wielder and said, "I said this was their fight. Put that knife in your pocket in a hurry." The boy looked at Jake towering over him, closed his knife and put it in his pocket.

But Donald, though almost breathless and physically exhausted, with his left arm injured and paining him, even though he was left handed, was not quitting without a final effort. He put all the strength he could muster into an effort to free himself from John's immobilizing clutch. John realized that he must retain the advantage he had if he was to win, so he tightened his hold as Donald tried to break it, and in the struggle Donald's face was being cut by the gravel.

Jake, seeing the futility of Donald's effort and the physical damage he was doing to himself, reached down and took hold of John's arm and said, "Let go, John. Donald is sorry he unthoughtfully made an ugly remark. Am I right, Donald?" Donald grunted, which was about all he could do, held as he was. The grunt was accepted as consenting to Jake's statement that Donald was sorry for his remark. John loosened his hold and moved off Donald. Donald had fought valiantly and lost. By all physical comparisons he should have won. But anger possessed him during the fight and anger is a defeating ally. Also he was wrong. The combination of the two constitute such a great handicap it is extremely difficult to overcome. The battle over, fatigue overtook them. Perhaps Donald was the more exhausted as he had expended more energy than John in his efforts. They rose slowly and wearily to their feet. A rock had gashed John when Donald threw him to the ground the first time. Both were bloody and their clothes were torn and dirty.

When they got to their feet they stood with Jake between them, looking at each other, lifelong friends who had just been engaged in a fierce fight with each other. As John looked at Donald he was startled at how seriously injured Donald's bleeding lip, closed eye and swollen face appeared. The thought came to John, "How much courage and determination Donald had to have to press the fight so vigorously when so severely handicapped by blindness on one side, a painful bleeding lip, and his strongest arm injured and lessened in its usefulness." He recalled that during their friendship Donald had always exhibited the qualities of a gentleman. He was sure Donald's action was the result of some delusion which temporarily created an irresistible impulse to say what he did.

Donald was standing there chagrined, thinking of their friendship and wondering why he suddenly lost his temper and invited a fight. He also marveled that one lighter in weight, and not as strong as he, could bring him to such a helpless physical condition. It is a blessing that youth does not harbor hatred very long. There is usually a mercurial quality in the character of youth that enables it to forget offense and change attitudes quickly. So when Jake said, "I think you two should shake hands and be the friends you have always been," John held out his hand and said, "I am sorry you are so badly hurt." As Donald took his hand he said, "I guess I had it coming to me."

Donald was making an effort to wipe with the torn sleeve of his shirt the blood that still oozed from his cut lip and he was having little success because of the coarse material out of which the shirt was made. When Sarah noticed this she gave Ellen her handkerchief and told her to give it to Donald. She said, "He might resent my offering it to him." Ellen, after being certain John was not seriously injured, promptly recovered her usual optimistic self and undertook to implement Sarah's request with alacrity. She went to Donald and said, "Wait, Donald, you're merely making your lip worse. Hold your breath while I clean it. I will try not to hurt you." After she had cleaned the wound she handed him the handkerchief and said, "Hold it to the cut until it stops bleeding." Donald said, "I must not keep your handkerchief." Ellen said, "Oh, you keep it for you need it. You know we know you are not as mean as you tried to sound and act even though you did fight like you were going to tear the world apart, including John." Ellen's ministrations to Donald, her smiling face and her good natured and bantering talk relieved the tension that had gripped all of them.

When Donald looked at the handkerchief Ellen had left with him, he saw in one corner of it the letter "S." He knew then that Sarah had given her handkerchief to Ellen to bring to him for his use. He realized Sarah was looking at him and knew he had noticed the initial on the handkerchief. It seemed to him everyone there was looking at him and that it was very quiet. He was glad in his heart it was this way for he wanted all of them to hear what he was going to say. It was then he made what sounded like a great confession and a plea for forgiveness. He said, "Sarah, I am sorry."

The Dedication Of The Institute Building

For some time the center of interest of the Landsee community was the construction of the Institute. The Institute building was being used although the work on it was not complete. Its furnishings were mostly makeshift. The auditorium had been completed and was properly furnished. This had been accomplished so that Landsee would have a good hall in which to hold large public meetings. The balance of the work was being done and furnishings acquired as funds, labor and materials were available.

The building committee decided that, under the circumstances, it would be appropriate to hold a ceremony dedicating the building. This would promote interest in finishing it. The committee did not have authority to arrange for the holding of such a ceremony so they placed the consideration of such action on the calendar of the next regular meeting. They gave notice that at the regular monthly meeting, in addition to the usual financial report and information as to progress of the project, there would be discussed the desirability of holding a ceremony to dedicate the building. As at the previous meeting Mr. Matthews distributed copies of his report showing in detail all transactions. Mr. Davidson asked if there were any questions about Mr. Matthew's report. There were none.

The Chaplain made a brief statement as to the progress of the building and what was needed to complete and furnish it. Mr. Davidson then said, "The building committee thought that, as the building is almost finished, free from debt and being used, it would be appropriate to hold a service dedicating the building. As our committee does not have authority to decide this matter we are submitting the question to you." It was voted to hold the ceremony.

Lon Williamson had anticipated that this action would be taken. He had had several men whom he controlled to donate a day of work so as to be eligible to vote at the meeting. Mr. Stone stood and when recognized said, "Since the beginning of a school at Landsee, Mr. Lon Williamson has been chairman of the school board and has carried the responsibility of that position to the satisfaction of the community. He has presided at its meetings and appointed its committees. It would only be proper for Mr. Williamson to have charge of arranging this program and presiding at the ceremony. Therefore, I nominate him for the performance of these duties." Mr. Stone had read his statement and everyone knew that Lon Williamson had written it and had required him to make the motion. The motion was immediately seconded and then another called for any questions in an effort to secure action on the motion before there could be any other nominations made.

Mr. Davidson said, "We should take matters in proper order. We have not decided whether arrangements are to be made by a committee or by one individual." Mr. Stone said, "My motion decides that it be by an individual and that the individual be Mr. Williamson. You should put my motion."

Someone else then said, "I offer as a substitute to Mr. Stone's motion that all arrangements be made by a committee of three elected by this meeting." This motion was carried. Then another said, "In my opinion the three largest givers should have charge of the program and these three are Isaac Blossburg, Ben Davidson, and the Chaplain." Mr. Williamson said, "If you are going to place the appointments on the basis of value of donations, I again call your attention to the fact that I have donated services of more value than amounts credited to any of the three mentioned. Furthermore, as the present chairman of the school board, I have the authority to arrange the program."

Ignoring Mr. Williamson's statement Mr. Davidson stated that the building committee decided that no member of that committee should serve on the committee of arrangements and that he had a letter from Mr. Blossburg stating that he did not wish to serve on the committee. Mr. Stone then moved that Mr. Williamson be made chairman of the committee. The motion was lost. Instead they elected Mr. John Nelson, the school principal, as chairman, and Mr. May and Mrs. Matthews as members of the committee.

Mr. Williamson was not only incensed at not being placed in charge of the ceremony, but he was especially angered because Mrs. Matthews was a member of the committee. He often said that she flounced around in a manner not in keeping with a minister's wife and that he felt it his duty to so advise the Bishop when he had his conference with him. Mrs. Matthews, who was aware of Mr. Williamson's attitude and remarks, would smile her sweetest smile whenever she met him and would greet him in her most honeyed tones. In her heart she held him in contempt.

Lon Williamson, usually cool and calculating in all his actions, let his anger control him in his efforts to prevent the ceremony to dedicate the building from being a success. He made the accusation that a majority of the committee members were foreigners who knew nothing of Landsee, and such a program as they would arrange would be a farce. He became so reckless in his efforts that he began to alienate those who previously tolerated him. Ina was broadcasting her father's views.

Mr. Nelson was disturbed that there should be active oppositon to the committee. He told his committee of Ina's constantly repeating to the students her father's comments. He asked if they had any suggestions as to how it could be stopped. Knowing the extreme dislike Mrs. Matthews and Mr. Williamson had for each other they were surprised when Mrs. Matthews said, "If you two will approve of what I do, I will attempt to annul this effort of Mr. Williamson." Mr. May said, "You have our approval in advance." Mr. Nelson nodded in agreement.

In those days it was not popular to denounce the government and burn or tread on the flag. The citizens recognized the truth that they enjoyed the greatest liberties of any country in the world, that those liberties had been bought at great sacrifice and that the government was necessary to preserve these liberties. In virtually every public program of civic nature, there was some expression of patriotism. It was planned that a part of the dedication program should be of this character.

The next day Mrs. Matthews purposely ran into Ina. She said, "I would like to talk to you." Ina answered, "I am in a hurry and have little time to talk." This was about the answer Mrs. Matthews had expected for she knew Ina would not want to talk to her. She said, "It will not take long. You know we want an impressive patriotic act at the beginning of the program dedicating the Institute. We hope to make it the most important part of the program. We plan to have 'Miss America' draped in our nation's flag to sing 'The Star Spangled Banner.' We had hoped you would take this part. We were told your father will not permit you to accept this role and that we would have to ask Sarah to accept it. We decided we would not ask Sarah until you said you would not participate in the program."

Poor Ina, all her self-importance yearned to take this important part in the program. She did not know what to say. She suddenly wished her father had never opposed the program. Mrs. Matthews understood her embarrassement and said, "Suppose you let me know tomorrow if you will take the part. Of course, if your father objects we do not want you to do anything against his wishes. Also, we would like to know if we should replace Lon, Jr., as an usher." The next morning Ina told Mrs. Matthews that her father had consented for her to take the part and for Lon, Jr., to act as an usher. Soon everyone was supporting the program of dedication.

There are some things about the program I will never forget. It was well attended. There pervaded the gathering a sense of pride and satisfaction at having accomplished so much with so little. They had made Landsee the educational center of a large part of the state. And I remember Ina bedecked in Old Glory carrying herself in her confident manner as if she were a queen to the manor born, singing in her strong clear voice, "The Star Spangled Banner." Whatever one might think of Ina as a person, she made her part a premier performance, and spontaneous and long applause evidenced the audience's appreciation and brought a glow of exultation and joy to her countenance.

Mr. Nelson, who presided, paid a tribute to the building committee and presented Mr. Davidson, its chairman. His response was an expression of thanks for being permitted to serve the community and praise for the support of the project by about ninety-nine per cent of the citizens. Mr. Matthews spoke next. "I recall," he said, "if it had not been for Miss Essie and the Chaplain the Institute would never have been built." He continued, "I am sure I have been able to render more lasting service to my people as a member of the building committee than I have preaching against the devil from my pulpit."

Mr. Nelson then said, "Both the program committee and the building committee thought that the students should be given some recognition for the valuable contribution they have made in supporting and working for the construction of the Institute. It was decided that this recognition should be made by presenting a certificate of appreciation to the student who had contributed the most personal effort to the undertaking as the representative of the student body. We will ask Ellen Green to come forward at this time and make the presentation."

Ellen came to the stage and said, "A committee consisting of a member of the building committee, two members of the faculty, and three students, selected the student to receive this certificate. They took into consideration Mr. Matthews' records, and they secured the opinions of many who were familiar with the work done on the building and the committee was unanimous in their selection. I am asking Jake Wilson to come to the stage." Jake usually wore homemade jeans, a calico shirt and brogans. But on this occasion he was attired in his Sunday clothes. Jake was the student most often called upon when some chore needed to be done, and he always responded readily. If it was a table to be moved, Jake was asked to move it. If the stove needed wood, Jake brought it in.

When Jake went to the stage he evidently thought he was needed to perform some chore for he asked Ellen what she wished. He never thought of himself as playing an important part. Ellen said, "Stand here by me a minute. Jake, you are the student unanimously selected to receive for the student body this certificate of appreciation for the support the students have given the building of the Institute. So it is my pleasure to present this to you. The certificate is on parchment and beautifully lettered. It is an honor you justly deserve." The applause was strong. It was a popular selection.

Mr. Nelson then said, "The history of education in Land-see is the record of one dedicated and efficient life. No one need introduce Miss Essie Gill to this audience. She has taught here for over twenty-five years. Miss Essie." Miss Essie with her graying hair, her clear blue eyes shining through her steel rimmed spectacles, standing erect, five feet six inches tall, was the picture of a just and intelligent character. Many years of teaching had given her voice a note of authority. Perhaps she had the confidence of more of the young people in Landsee than any other person.

When Miss Essie marched to the lectern she was smiling one of her rare smiles that made everyone feel she was smiling at them. She was given respectful attention because she was talking from the heart to a people she loved and who loved her. She talked about school days of the past. She concluded her remarks by saying that it was the Chaplain who had conceived the idea of the Institute and it was the Chaplain's leadership that had achieved the Institute and she was happy to have had a little part in working with him.

Mr. Nelson said, "I am now going to present the other member of the building committee. The man who dreamed of establishing a great educational institute in Landsee and has worked unceasingly until he has seen that dream become a reality. It was this man's vision, his leadership, his promotion, his planning, his supervision of the construction, his physical labor, and the faith everyone had in his integrity and ability that made possible the building we are dedicating today. I present our beloved Chaplain." The entire audience stood and cheered as the Chaplain walked to the lectern.

Although he walked with steady step, I realized for the first time that the years were taking their toll of this large, energetic and kindly man. The record of his life was one of concern for the welfare of his fellow man. When he reached the lectern he gripped each side of it with his hands. They were large hands, strong hands with callused palms, the hands of a carpenter. Yet, as strange as it might seem, those hands could bring consolation to the grieved by the tenderness of their touch. It was a beautiful lectern. Mr. Green had employed his greatest skill as a master cabinet maker in building it.

The Chaplain spoke in appreciation of the introduction,

the value of the services rendered by Mr. Matthews and Mr. Davidson. He emphasized the contribution Miss Essie had made and how great the citizens had responded. I will never forget the illustration with which he closed. The Chaplain said, "I would not be honest if I took all the credit which Mr. Nelson in his remarks attributed to me. I do not want anyone to think I am so egotistical as to consider that I am entitled to such credit. It is to the community as a whole to whom the credit is due. The part I played was merely as a tool used by the community. Permit me to tell you about a picture I saw one time and the message it brought me. Perhaps the picture might not have been considered an outstanding production by a trained artist, but there was one article in the picture that arrested and held my attention. That article was a chisel. The picture represented a sculptor standing by, and looking with approval at, a marble statue he had just completed. In his right hand he held the mallet he had used in carving the statue, but the chisel he had used with its now pitted and dull blade, its handle crushed by many heavy strokes to drive it into the hard marble, lay on the floor among the chips and other trash. As I looked at this discarded chisel I thought that if that chisel could speak it would say something like this, 'The sculptor has finished a masterpiece which will claim the admiration of thousands of people for many years to come. I know I cannot claim any credit for its grace and beauty, and I know there were thousands of other chisels the sculptor could have used as efficiently as he used me. But,' said the chisel, 'I will always be glad I was the one he used.'" Pausing a moment the Chaplain said, "Thank you for letting me serve you."

The Arrest

When cupidity, that insatiable, avaricious craving to acquire more and more riches, dominates the life of a man he often resorts to means and methods that forfeit the regard of respectable people. Any means, regardless of how offensive to a right sense of justice, or how disgusting to others, are readily employed if he considers their use necessary to the accomplishment of his purposes. Link with this cupidity an intolerant hatred of some individual and he will resort to means and methods to injure and hurt and to satisfy his base cravings that any normal person would disdain.

Lon Williamson had permitted himself to become a victim of this type of madness. He never felt remorse for the misery he wrongfully caused others in his zeal to effect his ends or wreak his vengeance. His hatred of Isaac Blossburg so absorbed his thinking and so prostituted his motives that he became willing to resort to any action which he thought would bring damage or suffering to Mr. Blossburg. Innocently and unwittingly Sarah became the victim of his venality.

One afternoon when Ben was helping Mr. Blossburg in his store the deputy sheriff came in and asked for Sarah. Sarah was in the rear of the store and heard him ask for her. She came to the front where he was standing. The deputy sheriff said, "I am sorry, Sarah, but I have a warrant for your arrest on the criminal charge of having violated the Sunday law. It is my duty to take you into custody and carry you to jail unless you make bond satisfactory to the justice of the peace who issued the warrant." Sarah asked, "Mr. Allen, are you not joking?" Mr. Allen replied, "No, I am not joking. I have no choice in this matter. I act under orders."

Mr. Blossburg said, "May I ask who issued this warrant and who made the complaint on which the warrant of arrest is based?" Mr. Allen hesitated as if deciding what to say and then answered, "Edgar Stone as justice of the peace issued the warrant on a complaint signed by Amy White. I was standing where I could hear and see everything that happened when Amy was forced to sign the complaint. Mr. Williamson called Amy into the store and told her to sign a paper he had prepared. When Amy asked what the paper was Mr. Williamson said it charged Sarah with selling goods on Sunday. Amy said she would not sign it. Mr. Williamson threatened her with having her sick father placed in jail with Sarah if she did not sign the complaint. Under his coercion she finally signed it. He instructed me to require a bond of one thousand dollars and that if not immediately made, I was to handcuff Sarah and carry her to the county jail where whe would remain until her trial. He said that Sarah must be handled so as to carry a warning to all Jews that they could not come into a Christian community and flagrantly ignore the laws protecting the Christian Sunday. When I asked Reuben if those were his orders, before he could answer me Lon said, 'Of course they are,' and then Reuben said, 'Yes.'"

Ben, Jr., who had heard the entire conversation, said, "No one is going to put handcuffs on Sarah and no one is going to lock her up in that county jail." The deputy sheriff said, "Listen, Ben, this is not my doings. I am only obeying orders." Mr. Blossburg said, "Yes, Ben, Mr. Allen as deputy sheriff is only doing his duty as required by law. We must not do anything to obstruct him in the discharge of his duty. We must avoid trouble. Anyway, Mr. Allen is not responsible for the charge being made against Sarah. My property here in Landsee is worth many times the amount required for the bond. I will sign the bond."

Mr. Allen said, "It has been the practice to release a good citizen charged with a misdemeanor on their own recognizance. I told Reuben Stone I would follow the custom when I arrested Sarah and release her. It was then that Lon had Reuben to require me to take a bond for her appearance at the trial and instructed me that a bond with Mr. Blossburg as the sole security would not be approved."

Mr. Blossburg said, "I do not feel that I am in position to ask anyone in Landsee to go on the bond with me. If you are allowed to accept a cash bond I could arrange to get that amount if you could give time to go to my bank. I do not have that much money here." The deputy sheriff said, "Mr. Blossburg, I have to remind you that my orders are to make this arrest without delay. I realize the orders are to prevent you from making a satisfactory bond, so Sarah will have to go to jail. I would like to give you the time but I do not have the authority. You know that Lon Williamson is not going to permit Reuben Stone to vary the requirements he has made."

Sarah had become frightened. She said in a plaintive voice, "What have I done to be required to be locked in that musty old jail behind iron bars with murderers and thieves?" Ben, angry and restless, answered, "Sarah, you have done nothing wrong. This is the dirty work of that unprincipled cur, Mr. Williamson. I am going over to his store and make him withdraw this charge or smash his face." Mr. Blossburg said, "No, Ben, that would make matters worse."

Suddenly, as if a new idea had come to him, Ben turned to Mr. Allen and said, "Before leaving the store with Sarah for jail will you give me time to go home and bring my father here?" Mr. Allen answered, "Yes, I will try to do so but you will have to hurry because Lon Williamson is waiting to see that Reuben compels me to arrest Sarah without delay and take her to the county jail." Ben left walking as fast as he could.

When Ben had gone the deputy sheriff said, "Mr. Blossburg, I will do everything I can to give Mr. Davidson time to get here before I carry Sarah to Reuben to be again ordered to take her to jail. If I cannot delay until he arrives and am forced to leave for the jail, tell him I will stop at Mr. Jamison's home and wait until you and he join us to accompany us to the county seat. Mr. Jamison has a large house and he has a daughter who is a friend of Sarah's." Sarah said, "Yes, Grace is a good friend of mine." The deputy then said, "Sarah, I understand there is a room upstairs where you can rest and change clothes. Go to that room and remain there until I call you. I will tell Lon that you are there packing the clothes you will need in jail."

On his way home to get his father, Ben ran by the Chaplain's home to let him know what was happening but found he was away at one of his churches. He also stopped at Dr. Alston's home but he was away on a sick call. John went with him to get his father. When Ben and John reached the home of Mr. Davidson they were out of breath as they had been running. Mr. Davidson asked, "Why are you two in such a big hurry?" As hastily as he could, Ben told his father everything that had taken place, emphasizing the fact that Sarah was to be handcuffed and confined in the county jail. Mr. Davidson said, "Well, I guess we had better go and see what can be done. It looks as if Lon has let his bitter hatred drive him into committing a crime."

A few minutes after Ben had left the store Mr. Blossburg and Mr. Allen saw Mr. Stone and Mr. Williamson come to the door of Mr. Williamson's store and stand there looking across at Mr. Blossburg's store and talking. It was evident that Mr. Williamson was telling Mr. Stone what to do. Mr. Stone came over to Mr. Blossburg's store and said to Mr. Allen, "Mr. Williamson wants to know why it is taking you so long to make the arrest. I suggest that unless you bring the prisoner over at once, you should come and explain to him your inaction. He is threatening to report your failure to do your duty to the sheriff and have him remove you from the office you hold." Very calmly the deputy replied, "Tell Mr. Williamson I will be over to see him as soon as I check on Sarah."

When Mr. Stone was out of hearing, Mr. Blossburg asked, "Do you have to obey the orders of Mr. Williamson?" Mr. Allen replied, "It is like this. I am subject to the orders of Reuben Stone as justice of the peace and Lon controls Reuben. However, my compliance with his demands is really for the purpose of giving Ben Davidson time to get here before I am compelled to actually take Sarah into custody. I will take all the time I can in going and reporting. Mr. Davidson is free to take action which, as an officer, I am unable to do. I expected Lon to get upset when I did not appear at once with Sarah handcuffed and knew that he would send for an explanation of my delay. That is why I told Sarah to go to her room so I could tell Lon I had to permit her to pack the clothes she would need while in jail.

We are playing for time."

Mr. Allen left Mr. Blossburg and walked slowly to Mr. Williamson's store, stopping several times and looking back. He knew Mr. Williamson was watching him. When he reached the top step of Mr. Williamson's store he again turned and looked back toward Mr. Blossburg's. He then suddenly started walking rapidly back to Mr. Blossburg's. As he passed Mr. Blossburg on his way to the back of his store he said to him, "I am going to close your back door and take the key but I will leave the door unlocked. I will return the key later." He then returned to Mr. Williamson.

As Mr. Allen anticipated, Mr. Williamson was so angry he could not control himself. Reaching the door of the store, Mr. Allen called to Mr. Williamson who had returned to his desk in the back of his store, "Don't you think you should come here to the door to talk?" He was certain he would not agree but Mr. Allen wanted to make Mr. Williamson take the responsibility of having him to come to the rear of the store where he could not see the front of Mr. Blossburg's store. Mr. Williamson shouted back, "Who are you to order me to come to you? You come back here where I am and do it in a hurry." Mr. Allen started as if in a hurry to comply with the demand, stumbled and fell. He slowly pulled himself up, groaning and rubbing his knee, and limped to where Mr. Williamson was sitting. He asked Mr. Williamson what he wanted. Mr. Williamson heatedly replied, "You know what I want. Why were you so long at Blossburg's store without arresting that girl? Why did you stop after reaching my store and turn and return to Blossburg's? And how dare you stand at my door and suggest I come to you instead of coming here to me! If you can't make an arrest without dilly-dallying, I will have you discharged."

Afterwards, Mr. Allen said that it was with difficulty he controlled his desire to tell him to go to hell. However, as the important thing was to give Mr. Davidson time to reach Mr. Blossburg's store, he assumed an humble attitude and, talking slowly and using as many words as possible to describe the situation, he told Mr. Williamson there was no delay in arresting Sarah. He had to wait until she could go to her room upstairs in the store to pack the clothes she would need in jail. He said, "I also had to deal with Mr. Blossburg who insisted his signing the bond was sufficient. He insisted I should give him a day to get a sufficient amount of cash to be used as surety. I told him I could not give him the time. Then Reuben came with your message to report to you. Before leaving I went upstairs in the store to see if there was any way for Sarah to leave the store without coming down stairs. There was not."

Mr. Williamson retorted, "That does not explain your long delay." Mr. Allen replied, "I then started to come to see you when it occurred to me that instead of Sarah having to come out the front door where I could see her, she might slip out the back door. It was when I reached the top step at your store that I remembered the back door. So I returned and locked it and brought the key with me." He showed him the key. Mr. Williamson said, "You still had no reason to summons me to the front door." To this Mr. Allen replied, "I wished to remain at the front door where I could watch Mr. Blossburg's store, but you demanded that I come to the back of your store where I cannot see who leaves there. You have taken the responsibility if she escapes. Perhaps she is still there. I do not know."

Mr. Williamson retorted, "I am not responsible for your actions. You should have handcuffed her and brought her to Reuben to be ordered carried to the county jail. You had better go and take her into custody."

Mr. Davidson was still not in view when Mr. Allen crossed the road to Mr. Blossburg's store. He told Mr. Blossburg he had one more act that would give them a little more time. He went to the stairs leading to the room where Sarah was and called to Sarah to come to the head of the stairs so he could truthfully tell Mr. Williamson he had seen her. When he had seen her he said, "Sarah, I am returning to Mr. Williamson's and telling him you have demanded a copy of the complaint against you. Remain in your room until I call you."

When Mr. Allen reached Mr. Williamson he asked, "Has she escaped?" Mr. Allen said, "No, I inspected to see if she were still upstairs." Mr. Williamson then asked, "Why did you not bring her back with you?" Mr. Allen replied, "They raised a question about the legality of the arrest saying Sarah had a right to have a written copy of the complaint against her. She said that unless she was furnished such a copy she would not submit to arrest and that if I took her into custody over her protest she would sue all of us for false arrest, false imprisonment and several other charges. I have never been asked before for a copy of the charge but I do remember hearing a judge say that an accused had a right to have a copy of the charges against him. As all of us would be financially involved, I thought I had better come and discuss with you what action should be taken." Mr. Williamson replied, "I am not involved. I demand you make the arrest." Mr. Allen said, "Lon, you are very much involved. I saw you make Amy sign that complaint. So did Reuben. You are the complainant. If I make a mistake, the sheriff will suffer. You furnish her with the copy of the complaint or I will not take her into custody until I go and see the sheriff."

Mr. Stone said, "I think the safest way to handle the matter is to furnish her the copy she demands." Mr. Williamson said, "Then make it in a hurry." Mr. Allen said, "I will remain at the front door where I can watch." Just as Mr. Stone finished making the copy Mr. Allen saw Mr. Davidson, Ben, Jr., and John coming. To prevent Mr. Stone from seeing them he said to him, "I will check it with you so both of us can swear she was served with an exact copy." By the time the checking was completed Mr. Davidson was in Mr. Blossburg's store.

When the deputy sheriff returned to Mr. Blossburg's store he told them what he had done in order to give Mr. Davidson time to reach Mr. Blossburg's store before he had to carry Sarah to the justice of the peace. Mr. Davidson said, "Ben, Jr., said you needed me to sign Sarah's bond. Where is the bond? Let us execute it and have Sarah released. This prosecution of Lon's is ridiculous." Mr. Allen said, "Here is the bond. Sarah and Mr. Blossburg have signed it. You can sign under Mr. Blossburg's name. However, I must tell you that Lon had Reuben to instruct me not to accept a bond unless it has two sureties in addition to Mr. Blossburg."

Mr. Davidson said, "The law makes no such requirement. This bond is sufficient. I will take it to Reuben and have him approve it." Mr. Allen said, "To save any argument I am willing to become the surety if a deputy sheriff can go on the bond of a person he arrests." Mr. Davidson said, "Certainly you can act as a surety. Sign the bond and I will go with you to see that Reuben approves it."

When Mr. Davidson and Mr. Allen entered Mr. Williamson's

store, Mr. Williamson asked Mr. Allen in a commanding tone, "Where is your prisoner? Did I not tell you to bring her here handcuffed?" Mr. Allen answered, "She made bond and I released her." Mr. Williamson asked, "Who signed the bond in addition to her father?" Mr. Allen answered, "Mr. Davidson." Mr. Davidson handed the bond to Mr. Stone saying, "Reuben, that is a good bond. Approve it." Mr. Williamson said, "Reuben, do not approve it. There must be two sureties in addition to Mr. Blossburg." Mr. Stone said, "Mr. Allen has also signed the bond." Mr. Williamson said, "He has no authority to sign the bond." Ben Davidson said very deliberately, "Lon, you know he does have a right to sign that bond. Both of you know that bond is good even without his signature. If this bond is not immediately approved and Sarah released from custody, I am going with the deputy and Sarah to the county court house and have the authorities there approve the bond and release Sarah. Then I am going to personally swear to a complaint charging you and Reuben with malicious false imprisonment and any other crime your act constitutes."

Mr. Williamson seeing he had lost began to walk away leaving, as he always did under such circumstances, the responsibility on some other person to act. As he walked away he said, "You Jew supporters will find out the contempt in which the Christian citizens hold you when I show them your actions at Sarah's trial." Mr. Stone seeing he was being abandoned by Mr. Williamson said, "I will approve the bond" and laid it aside. Mr. Davidson said, "Why are you shoving the bond away from you without approving it?" Mr. Stone looked in the direction of Mr. Williamson as if seeking instructions but he was leaving the store. He hesitated a moment and then took the bond and approved it. Mr. Davidson then said, "Now that the bond is approved, instruct the deputy sheriff that Sarah is to be released from custody." Mr. Allen said, "I do not need any instructions. I have seen the bond approved, and I will go and tell Sarah she is free." Mr. Davidson then asked Mr. Stone, "When will the trial be held?" Mr. Stone answered, "Court is held on the fourth Saturday of the month at nine o'clock a.m."

Mr. Davidson said, "That is the day and hour the Masonic Lodge meets. I think the Masons would be interested in attending the trial. The Masons could close their meeting by ten o'clock a.m. Would you consider waiting until that time to begin Sarah's trial?" Mr. Stone, wishing to consult Mr. Williamson before acting on the request answered, "I will consider it and let you know."

Mr. Allen and Mr. Davidson went to Mr. Blossburg's store and Mr. Allen called to Sarah who was still upstairs saying, "Sarah, you are free." Mr. Davidson said to Mr. Blossburg, "You will have to prepare for the trial. It will be held the fourth Saturday of the month. That gives you three weeks. If I can help let me know. I am afraid Lon has contol of Reuben and will compel him to convict Sarah. However, you will have the right to appeal." Mr. Blossburg said, "Thanks for all you have done. I think I will confer with the Chaplain before I decide what course to pursue." Mr. Davidson said, "That is a splendid idea. Let me know what the Chaplain advises."

Pretrial Activities

When the Chaplain returned Tuesday afternoon from one of his churches about ten miles from Landsee he found two men sitting on his porch waiting for him. One was Mr. Blossburg and the other was Mr. White, the father of Amy White, the girl who signed the affidavit charging Sarah with the violation of the Sunday Law.

The Chaplain spoke to them and said, "Gentlemen, as soon as I can put my horse in the stable I will be with you." He returned in a few minutes and as he walked out on the porch he said, "What gives me the good fortune of having you two gentlemen visit me?" Mr. Blossburg answered, "We did not come together but we came about the same matter. As Mr. White has been sick I will withdraw so he can talk to you."

Mr. White replied, "I would like for Mr. Blossburg to be present and hear what I have to say." The Chaplain said, "You two talk as if we are to discuss a very serious matter." Mr. White said, "Chaplain, have you not heard of the arrest of Sarah Blossburg on the charge of violating the Sunday Law?" With surprise the Chaplain said, "The arrest of Sarah Blossburg? I have been away several days and have not seen or talked to anyone since my return. Tell me about it."

Mr. Blossburg said, "Mr. White, I suggest you tell him what you know about the matter and if I know any additional facts I will advise him of them." Mr. White said, "In the beginning I want you and Mr. Blossburg to understand why Amy signed the complaint against Sarah." The Chaplain interrupted saying,

"You mean to say Amy made a complaint charging Sarah with the criminal offense of violating the Sunday Law?"

"Yes," said Mr. White, "but she did not want to do it. That is what I wish to explain. On account of my ill health I have been unable to work for some time and have become delinquent in the payment of a small account I owe Mr. Lon Williamson. Two weeks ago Mr. Williamson came to my house and demanded payment. I told him he knew I had been sick and that I would pay as soon as I was able to work. He said the account was past due and that he could sue me but he would be considerate and give me an easy way to settle it. He said he would accept my hunting dog, Blazer, as part payment and agree to wait on the balance. The dog was worth more than the account but he was going to give me only half of the account as a credit."

The Chaplain interrupted, "Do you mean he was trying to use this small indebtedness to get possession of your dog?" Mr. White replied, "You know Mr. Williamson has always bragged that he had the finest hunting hounds in the state. Recently, in an important hunt Blazer was judged the finest hunting dog in the pack and since then Mr. Williamson has tried to get him. I told him Blazer belonged to Amy. She had raised him from a pup and I was sure she would not want to sell him. Mr. Williamson said that I had better accept his offer or in the future I would wish I had. Of course Amy knew all of this when he made his demands that she sign the complaint against Sarah." Mr. Blossburg said, "I am surprised that anyone would be guilty of such action."

"Last Sunday," continued Mr. White, "I was seized with an extremely painful sickness. I was suffering so much I sent Amy to Mr. Blossburg for some medicine I had used before. I knew the medicine would cost fifty cents but we only had twenty-five cents. I thought Mr. Blossburg would credit me for the balance. Amy said that when she explained the situation to Mr. Blossburg he said he would give her the medicine. He told Sarah to go to the store and give the medicine to her. The medicine was on a shelf near the front door. Sarah opened the front door only partly, went to the shelf and got the medicine and gave it to Amy. When Amy offered Sarah the quarter Sarah said her father told her to make her a present of it. Amy said,

'No,' and placed the quarter on the counter and told Sarah we would pay the balance as soon as we sold some eggs. Then Amy hurried home with the medicine for me. She said she saw Mr. Stone watching her when she came out of Mr. Blossburg's store.

"The next day, Monday afternoon, when she was passing Mr. Williamson's store he called to her to come into his store. When she entered Mr. Stone was also there. Mr. Williamson told her that Mr. Stone had said he saw her make a purchase at Mr. Blossburg's store the day before and that Sarah had made the sale to her. Pointing out that it is a criminal offense to sell goods on Sunday, he accused Amy of being a party to the effort of those Jews to ignore the laws protecting our Christian Sunday. He declared that not only were she and Sarah guilty, but that Mr. Blossburg and I were also guilty. He insisted that he could have all four of us arrested and sent to jail, but that he had decided that if Amy would cooperate with him he would only prosecute Sarah and make an example of her so as to prevent them from constantly breaking the Sunday Law.

"Amy said they already had written out the paper she was told to sign. She told them Sarah just let her have some medicine her father needed and she did not want to make a complaint against Sarah. Lon Williamson demanded that she sign this complaint and cooperate with them or he would call the deputy sheriff and turn her over to him and have him also arrest me. She said she was afraid to refuse to sign the paper and did so. She was afraid if I were jailed in my weak physical condition it might prove fatal. I want Mr. Blossburg to know we regret we have caused him this trouble.

"Chaplain, I have come to you for advice. I thought you might persuade Mr. Williamson to drop the prosecution of Sarah if we would give him Blazer. I wonder if you would make him the offer for me. I thought of sending Amy to my brother so she would not be here to testify. But I guess we would be fined if we did that. I don't know what to do."

After a short silence the Chaplain said, "Perhaps I had better hear what Mr. Blossburg has to say." Mr. Blossburg responded, "First, I wish to assure Mr. White we do not hold any ill will against him and Amy." Then he stated what had happened at his store and what Mr. Davidson had told him with reference to having to force the approval of the bond.

For a short time all were quiet as if thinking. Then the Chaplain said, "I guess I should be surprised at Lon Williamson being guilty of such despicable conduct but I am not. He has always posed as the leader in the community. Permitting him to have his way has not required any sacrifice of anyone's rights or any principle and he has grown to believe he has the power to dictate whatever action he wishes. It is strange how little minds can so easily convince themselves that they are great. It is stranger still that often they labor under the delusion that they are justified in using evil means to accomplish selfish ends. Probably he thinks he now sees an opportunity to strike at both of you and at the same time popularize himself as a defender of our religious heritage. I am of the opinion that on the handling of this case will depend much of the future of our community."

The Chaplain looked at Mr. White and said, "Go home and go to bed and get well. Keep your dog, Blazer. Tell Amy not to discuss this matter with anyone but me. Tell her also that Mr. Blossburg and Sarah know she does not want to hurt them. I will talk to her before the trial. I will look after your interest and report to you." Mr. White expressed his gratitude and left.

The Chaplain then said to Mr. Blossburg, "Of course we know that Reuben Stone is completely subservient to Lon Williamson, otherwise he could not hold his job as clerk in his store. It is rather certain he will convict Sarah regardless of the defense we make." Mr. Blossburg said, "You know I have a brother in Chicago with whom I am going in business in a few years. Is it advisable to send Sarah to him? I can pay the bond. I can't let Sarah go to jail."

The Chaplain replied, "I do not think such action would be advisable. No jury is going to convict Sarah. I doubt if the prosecuting attorney would let the case come to trial. The crushing of this effort of Lon Williamson in the courts is necessary for the future of our community. As soon as Reuben Stone finds Sarah guilty we will make an appeal bond. While it still is not generally known that you are a Mason, the members of the lodge do know it. The lodge meets the Saturday on which the trial is set. I will get word to the Worshipful Master to ask Lon Williamson to postpone beginning the trial until after the lodge meets in order that the Masons can attend. Lon will not know we had anything to do with the request and he will grant it so as to increase the spectators. At the lodge meeting I will work out the details. I will also get the sheriff and prosecuting attorney to attend the trial as we might need them. Both of them belong to this Masonic Lodge."

Mr. Blossburg said, "One more question. Ina and some of her followers are talking in Sarah's hearing about that Jew trying to break down the Sunday Law. Could you arrange for her to be permitted to remain away from school until this is over?"

The Chaplain said, "Sarah will have to remain in school. She will have to ignore the remarks. It will be only two more weeks and Sarah has character enough to bear the outrage without letting the tormentors know they are hurting her. I guess this is all we can do this evening. I promise you to do everything I can to help."

Student Reaction

John, Ben, Ellen and Sarah met at Sarah's home to discuss what they could do to help Sarah. Sarah told them her father had been to see the Chaplain and that he was going to help them. She said she dreaded attending school where some were branding her as a criminal, but that it was not as bad as she had expected. She said, "Yesterday I had a surprise. I was standing looking out one of the windows at the school when I heard someone in a rather low tone call my name. When I turned Lon, Jr., said, 'Sarah, I want you to know I am sorry you are being prosecuted.' He looked embarrassed. I told him I knew he opposed having me arrested because Amy had told me what he had said when she was being made to sign the complaint. About that time Ina came into the room and, seeing Lon, Jr., talking to me said, 'Well, has Sarah also bewitched my brother?'

"All the embarrassment seemed to leave Lon, Jr., and he answered, 'Sarah and I were having a very agreeable conversation. Would you like to join us?' Ina did not have an opportunity to reply for the mathematics teacher entered the room just then and said, 'Sarah, I will be at your trial Saturday to testify to your good character.' So you see, I am not faring too badly. What we need to do is get Miss Essie's advice."

John said, "I heard her say she was leaving Monday to visit some relatives but she did not say where they lived. She said she would be away for a week or ten days which means she will not be here for the trial."

Ellen said, "We must get her here for the trial. Aunt

Mymee will know where she is and how to get her to return. Suppose we go to see Aunt Mymee and ask her if she will help us." They all agreed to seek Aunt Mymee's aid and went in a group to see her.

When they reached her home and were seated Ben said, "Aunt Mymee, Sarah is in trouble." "I know," said Aunt Mymee. Ben continued, "She is being prosecuted by old Lon Williamson and it is an outrage." Aunt Mymee said, "Let Ellen tell me why you came to see me because I expect she suggested that you come."

Ellen said, "Yes, Aunt Mymee, I am the one who suggested you would help if you could and I knew you could. We were trying to think of some way to help Sarah and we thought that if we could see Miss Essie she could advise us. She is away on a visit and we do not know how to reach her. We hope you know where she is and can get her to return before the trial."

Aunt Mymee sat still for a while and then, as if she had reached a decision, said, "Thank you, Ellen, for coming to see me. I am glad of an opportunity to do whatever I can to defeat Lon Williamson. I am also glad if it will aid your friend. We need Miss Essie. I know where she is visiting. I will get a message to her that will bring her back in time for the trial." Then she said, "While I have heard of Sarah's arrest and that she is to be tried Saturday week, I would like to know the facts."

They told her all they knew and had heard about the case. When they had finished Aunt Mymee said, "From what you have said I understand the Chaplain is going to help you. I had better talk to him so as to prevent any action of mine from conflicting with his plans. Ben, will you ask the Chaplain to come to see me as soon as it is convenient for him?" Ben answered, "I will go as soon as I see Sarah home." Aunt Mymee seldom went to see anyone. They all came to see her.

That evening the Chaplain visited Aunt Mymee. The next morning he was at Mr. Davidson's. When he left he and Mr. Davidson rode away together. It was learned afterwards that they went to see the sheriff and the prosecuting attorney to persuade them to attend the Masonic meeting and be present at Sarah's trial. The trial had been postponed to begin at 11 o'clock a.m.

Miss Essie returned Friday afternoon and immediately

went to see Aunt Mymee who told her the whole story. The plan was not to let Sarah testify but appeal from the conviction as soon as Reuben Stone found her guilty. Miss Essie said she was pleased that they had decided to keep Sarah off of the witness stand. She said, "That will deprive Lon Williamson of being able to ask her insulting questions about her religion. I know he is anticipating doing this with much satisfaction."

Sarah's Trial

The Justice of the Peace Court of Landsee precinct was held on the front porch of Lon Williamson's store. Reuben Stone, the Justice of the Peace, had worked for Mr. Williamson for about eight years. Mr. Stone, who was an expert bookkeeper, was persuaded to accept the offer of employment because of the promise that each year as he learned the business, his salary would be increased. He also had been persuaded by Mr. Williamson to purchase a house he owned, Mr. Stone paying his life savings of one thousand dollars in cash and executing a mortgage to Mr. Williamson for the balance.

At the end of the first year Mr. Stone reminded Mr. Williamson of his promise to raise his salary. Mr. Williamson replied he was surprised that he should ask for a raise as he was thinking of discharging him. If he retained him Mr. Stone would have to agree to a raise in the interest rate on the loan on his home. Year by year Mr. Williamson used his economic pressure to make Mr. Stone more servile. Mr. Stone lived in constant dread of losing his job and of Mr. Williamson foreclosing the mortgage on his home. Mr. Stone, being a good but nonassertive man, and not knowing where to turn for employment elsewhere, became more and more submissive to his employer's demands, demands which were sometimes outrageous. Mr. Williamson did not doubt that he would control the conduct of the trial of Sarah Blossburg and direct the verdict.

Lon Williamson's store was a large one-story building about thirty feet wide with a porch across the entire front. This porch was ten feet wide and thirty inches high from the ground, giving those standing on the ground an open view of whatever happened on the porch. A large front door was in the center of the building. As Mr. Williamson anticipated playing an important and popular part in the trial of Sarah, he prepared with considerable care the arrangement of the porch for the trial.

Near one end of the porch was placed a table, and behind this was placed a chair for the Justice of the Peace. On the table was the Code of Laws of the State, the trial docket, the complaint against Sarah and a gavel. A few feet from the table, and between the table and the wall of the store, was a chair for the witness. A short distance in front of the table and to its right was a chair for the defendant. This chair had its back to the wall of the store and faced across the porch toward the road where the spectators would be standing.

A little farther from the table than the chair for the defendant and at about the middle of the porch, he placed a chair for himself. This chair faced the Justice of the Peace and enabled him to look at the defendant and, by a slight turn of his body, look at the assembled crowd. It was a prominent place where all present would see him. At the opposite end of the porch from the Justice of the Peace were two rows of chairs facing the Justice of the Peace. These seats were for witnesses and those considered closely connected with the trial. It was in the front row of these seats that Mr. and Mrs. Blossburg and Sarah were seated. In these seats were also the Chaplain, Mr. Ben Davidson and Dr. Alfred Alston.

Just before the time for the trial to begin someone in the crowd of spectators was heard to call out, "Make room for Miss Essie to pass to the porch." Immediately an aisle opened through the throng and Miss Essie, her clothes starched and ironed as usual, marched through the crowd and up onto the porch. When she was on the porch she looked over the arrangement and then addressing Horace Allen, the deputy sheriff, said, "Horace, place me a chair beside the one provided for the defendant." Mr. Allen did not question her authority. He did as she asked and Miss Essie took the seat.

It is almost unbelievable how fast news could travel in those days when there were no telephones. Before the hour for the trial it looked as if every inhabitant of the countryside was in front of the store. Some were standing and waiting, others were "howdying" with friends they had not seen in a number of weeks. Out in this crowd stood Ben Davidson, Jr. His hair looked redder than ever. Those who knew him could see he was tense with anger. On one side of him was John Alston and on the other side was Ellen Green, standing as if to prevent him from erupting into violent physical action against Mr. Williamson. Sarah said afterwards that she glanced at them once but she dared not look at them again lest she lose control of herself. The homemade poke bonnets worn by so many of the women who lived on the farm were of varied colors and created an attractive scene.

The Masons had finished their meeting and by understanding had moved separately and gradually among the waiting throng. They had agreed on who should go on Sarah's appeal bond when she was convicted. The sheriff and the prosecuting attorney had agreed that the securities selected were sufficient and that they would see that the bond was approved without delay so as to prevent Sarah from being required to remain in custody and being imprisoned.

Promptly at 11 o'clock a.m. Reuben Stone and Lon Williamson, Sr., appeared side by side in the front door of the store. They stood there until they had everyone's attention. Both were dressed for the occasion, wearing their Sunday suits, freshly laundered white shirts, silk ties and highly polished shoes. It was with satisfaction Mr. Williamson noted the large number of people who would see him act the hero's role he had so carefully planned. Mr. Williamson, with a smile and slight bow to the spectators, went to his seat. Mr. Stone proceeded to the edge of the porch, paused as if waiting for his picture to be taken, and then held out his hand for quiet. When he had secured attention he cleared his throat and read from a paper he had as follows:

"Ladies and gentlemen, your presence in such large numbers evidences your appreciation of the great importance of this trial, a trial which is unique in the history of our God-fearing community. On account of the seriousness of the offense charged against the defendant, I wish to be free from any duty except to listen to the evidence so that I might reach a just and proper verdict. Therefore, I have requested Mr. Lon Williamson, Sr., who has always been active in religious affairs and in enforcing the laws protecting our Christian Sunday from violation, to examine the witnesses and conduct the trial. I am confident you will approve of this arrangement and will appreciate the service Mr. Williamson renders." He then went to his chair.

Before Mr. Stone reached his table Miss Essie, in a voice all could hear, said, "The voice that read that statement was the voice of Reuben Stone, but the words were the words of Lon Williamson who wrote it and required Reuben to read it." An unidentified man said, "Amen," and there was general laughter. Mr. Williamson, who could not countenance criticism, in an angry tone said, "Reuben, that statement of Miss Essie's is in contempt of court and you should place a fine on her." Then looking at Miss Essie he said, "You have no right to have a chair next to the defendant. I have reserved this part of the porch for those participating in the trial. Move to the place for spectators." Miss Essie replied, "Lon, your statement disclosed your ignorance of the law. The court is not in session so there can be no contempt. Furthermore, one is not in contempt for stating the truth. Now as to your order that I move, I remind you this porch is now a courtroom over which you have no control. I shall sit here and take an active part in this trial and I think it wise for you not to attempt to stop or to remove me."

Mr. Williamson jumped up and faced Mr. Stone, evidently to compel him to order Miss Essie away from the defendant, but before he could utter a word he heard Ben Davidson say, "Miss Essie has the right to sit where she is and participate actively in the trial. There are several of us who will see that she is permitted to exercise that right freely." Mr. Stone realized some action had to be taken to terminate this impasse so he struck the table severely with the gavel and said, "Mr. Deputy Sheriff, open court." The deputy cried, "Oyez Oyez, the honorable Justice of the Peace Court of Landsee precinct is now in session. Take notice and govern yourself accordingly."

Mr. Stone opened his docket and said, "I now call for trial the case of State vs Sarah Blossburg. The defendant will please come forward." Sarah, who was sitting between her father and mother, stood. She was attired in a simple white dress, with white stockings and shoes. Her long, soft, black hair fell across her shoulders. Her large eyes, almost as dark as her hair and shaded by long eyelashes, usually radiated warmth and merriment but were now full of anxiety. When Mr. Stone ordered the defendant to come forward everyone looked toward Sarah. So intense had become the stillness and quietness that when Sarah appeared to lose her balance as she stood, you could hear a number of the spectators audibly catch their breath as if afraid she would fall. Sarah quickly steadied herself.

Sarah was a perfect picture of loveliness and innocence, innocence being compelled to walk alone across that long porch, as many curious and perhaps some hostile eyes glared at her every movement, to be subjected to a cruelty which it seemed one so delicate would be unable to bear. She walked slowly, as if in a trance, until she stood in front of Mr. Stone. As she moved across that porch there could not have been a greater lack of sound and motion in that large crowd. It was as if a phantom had mysteriously appeared and glided deliberately across their vision.

It was Miss Essie who broke the spell that appeared to envelop them when she said, "Come sit by me, Sarah." Sarah looked at the Justice of the Peace for orders and he nodded and said, "Yes, take that seat." Sarah then sat next to Miss Essie. Mr. Stone instructed the deputy sheriff to call the witnesses that they might be sworn. Mr. Williamson said, "Call for the State, Amy White." Turning so that the audience could see his smirk he added, "And as I have heard that Miss Essie did not attend church services the Sunday the defendant violated our Christian statute, she probably saw her with the merchandise that was purchased, so I will ask that Miss Essie be sworn as a State witness." Miss Essie said, "Yes, I saw a great deal that morning and I am willing to testify to all I saw." Then Miss Essie turned to the deputy sheriff and said, "Horace, call for the defendant Henry May, Ben Davidson, Sr., Lon Williamson, Sr., Lon Williamson, Jr., and yourself." Mr. Williamson said, "My son and I are not witnesses."

Before Miss Essie could reply, the Methodist preacher's wife, who had been sitting near the Blossburgs, rose and quickly took a stand among the witness and said, "You did not call me. I am a witness for the defendant." She saw many friends among the spectators. She resented the prosecution of Sarah and Mr. Williamson's assuming to control her husband, so she decided to cast whatever influence she might have in behalf of Sarah.

When Mrs. Matthews asked to be sworn as a witness for Sarah, Mr. Williamson said, "You do not know anything about this case. You are out of your place as a witness." She replied so everyone could hear her, "Oh, yes, I can testify. I know Sarah well and I know she is a fine character and would not violate any law. So far as I know she might be a descendant of Joseph and Mary." Mr. Williamson, thinking that she would cringe at the prospect of a person of his influence voicing disapproval of her conduct to the Bishop, said, "I know the Bishop will be shocked when I advise him that you volunteered to aid one guilty of violating our Sunday Laws."

Mrs. Matthews, with a saucy flounce of her head, said, "Brother Williamson, I will be glad for you to tell the Bishop about what I do in this trial. You know, the Bishop is my favorite uncle and he says I am his favorite niece. He says I don't understand much about reasoning but that, somehow, I always land on the right side. I suggest that we go to see the Bishop together and discuss each other's actions in this case." Some farmer in the audience, not intending for everyone to hear him speaking, said to a friend, "Now, John, that offer to go together to see the Bishop be a fair offer. I like a fair offer." Friend John replied, "Yes." The information that the Bishop was Mrs. Matthews' uncle came as such an unpleasant surprise to Mr. Williamson that he looked at her as if something shocking and incredible had happened.

Again Mr. Stone realized that Mr. Williamson had maneuvered himself into an unfavorable position and that he must come to his rescue. Mr. Stone asked, "Is the State ready for trial?" Mr. Williamson announced, "The State is ready." Then Mr. Stone asked, "Is the defendant ready?" Miss Essie answered, "The defendant is ready." Mr. Williamson said, "Miss Essie, you are not a licensed lawyer and have no right to represent the defendant. I request the court to order you not to interfere with the trial of this case." Miss Essie replied, "I am as much a lawyer as you are and I have as much right to participate in this trial as you have. You have forced Reuben Stone to allow you to prosecute this innocent young lady and now you seek to control the procedure of the trial and direct its verdict. I call Reuben Stone's attention to the fact that he is not now acting as your clerk but as judge sworn to administer justice." Mr. Williamson jumped up and shouted at Mr. Stone, "I demand," but before he could utter another word he stopped for he felt a strong hand laid on his shoulder and he turned to see Ben Davidson standing by him. He also saw Mr. May standing by Mr. Davidson and noticed that both the Chaplain and Dr. Alston were standing at their seats as if ready to move forward. Mr. Davidson said, "If the Court please, I thought we had it understood a few minutes ago that Lon Williamson was not to interfere with Miss Essie. If you are willing for Lon to make this a kangaroo court and a stage from which to spew his malicious statements without interference, there are some of us who will not permit it. We want it now understood that Lon is not again to question Miss Essie's right to participate or to interfere with her efforts."

Any discerning person could see that Lon Williamson was wilting under Mr. Davidson's statement. Mr. Williamson made a valiant effort to dull the effect of Mr. Davidson's remarks and regain the initiative by saying in a forced, jocular manner, "Oh, if they want Miss Essie to prattle along, I will not attempt to prevent her doing so. I was only trying to save time by securing an orderly procedure."

The Justice of the Peace again endeavored to take charge. He told the deputy to have all witnesses to come forward and stand in front of him so that he could administer the oath to them. When the witnesses lined up to take the oath, Mr. Williamson noticed Lon, Jr., standing among them. He said to him, "I said that you and I were not witnesses. Take a seat." Lon, Jr., replied, "The prosecuting solicitor told me as I was called as a witness I had to take the oath." Mr. Williamson looked around and for the first time saw the prosecuting attorney. Miss Essie stood and said, "I was called as a witness and am ready to take the oath. I insist that Lon take the oath as I expect to examine him as a witness." To the surprise of some Mr. Stone said, "All persons called as witnesses stand and hold up your right hand." Mr. Williamson said, "Let us all please Miss Essie," and stood and held up his right hand. When he noticed that Sarah was not standing he said, "I notice the defendant is not standing to take the oath. I assume she cannot take the oath we Christians do." Miss Essie said, "Sarah is not taking the oath because it will not be necessary for her to testify." Mr. Stone said, "All of you hold up your right hand. Do each of you swear that you will tell the truth, the whole truth and nothing but the truth, so help you God?"

When he had administered the oath to the witnesses Mr. Stone directed them to take their seats and wait until they were called to testify. Then Mr. Stone said, "The defendant will stand while I read the charge against her." Sarah stood. She did not seem to take a breath while she was being arraigned as a criminal. It was evident that Mr. Stone had often read the affidavit so as to be sure he would read it impressively. Loudly he read, "The State vs Sarah Blossburg, whose name is otherwise unknown." Then he paused and said to the audience, "As we did not know whether Blossburg was the name by which the family was known before they came to Landsee, Mr. Williamson thought it best to state that their name was otherwise unknown." He continued to read the complaint which did not follow the form prescribed by the State Code of Laws but contained statements about the sacredness of the law protecting the Christian Sunday, the heinousness of the conduct of one who would stoop so low as to violate such law, and the duty of the citizens and court to prevent any alien who had no respect for the Christian faith coming to their Christian community seeking to destroy the law. When he finished reading the charge which everyone realized was intended as a tirade against the Blossburgs he said, "Does the defendant plead guilty or not guilty to this crime with which she is charged?" Sarah had been instructed to reply that she had nothing to say when asked how she would plead. Before Sarah had an opportunity to answer, Miss Essie said, "Sarah has nothing to say. I say she is not guilty."

Mr Blossburg was expecting a quick trial, the conviction of Sarah and the making of the appeal bond for her release. The unexpected performance of Miss Essie surprised him and made him wonder if it would upset their plans. He quietly moved to where he could talk to the Chaplain. He asked the Chaplain if he were aware that Miss Essie was going to take part in the trial. The Chaplain told him that Miss Essie was probably the only one who knew she was going to participate in the trial. He told

Mr. Blossburg not to be uneasy about what Miss Essie did because all they could do was convict Sarah and they were prepared for that event. He also said, "Miss Essie generally knows what she is doing and, so far, she has succeeded in exposing Lon Williamson. Just pray she will keep exposing him until the people understand him."

When Miss Essie finished her statement, Mr. Williamson, turning so as to be speaking to the audience, observed, "The fact that she does not deny the charges is a silent admission that the charge is true." Miss Essie said, "You again expose your ignorance, Lon. The county solicitor is standing by the porch. Mr. Solicitor, will you advise the Court that a defendant has a right to remain silent and, in doing so, she does not admit guilt." The solicitor, realizing that everyone was waiting for him to reply, said, "I am sure the Court knows that a defendant does not admit guilt by remaining silent." Mr. Williamson was anxious for Sarah to testify. When the solicitor made his statement Mr. Williamson said, "Of course I know that technically that is the law but all of us know that innocent people deny charges of criminal conduct." Before Miss Essie could reply Mr. Stone said, "We will proceed with the trial. Mr. Williamson, do you wish to state the case before examining the witnesses?"

This was the time for which Mr. Williamson had made his greatest preparation. Assuming what he considered a manner of great dignity he rose and, speaking to the spectators instead of the court, said, "It is usual in important cases such as this one, for a statement to be made before the introduction of evidence, advising the Court what is expected to be proved in support of the criminal charge." Miss Essie interrupted, saying, "If your statement is to advise the Court, why do you not speak to the Justice of the Peace instead of to the audience?" In an effort to ignore Miss Essie's remarks, Mr. Williamson continued, "Because of my long and active efforts to keep inviolate the laws protecting our Christian Sunday, I have been asked to conduct the prosecution of this trial. I gladly accepted the responsibility in this pernicious effort to set these laws at naught. In the beginning, may I remind you that this nation was founded by Christians on Christian principles. In their wisdom they enacted laws to protect our Christian Sunday from being commercialized and desecrated by those by those who care only for money.

"Our community has been free from violations of this sacred law by our native citizens and this defendant is the first to be tried here for this offense. We expect the evidence to show that this defendant, while you and I were at church in holy worship, defiantly and flagrantly violated this law for selfish gain." At this point a tall woman standing near the porch whose face was, when in repose, rather stolid and weathered in appearance, said as if the statement could not be suppressed, "I don't believe it!" When she saw the grateful look of Sarah, that impassive looking face became exceedingly tender when she added in a gentle voice, "Don't pay any attention to him, honey."

Mr. Williamson looked at the woman with a patronizing smile and in a sanctimonious voice said, "My good woman, if you are a Christian, which I assume you are, you will change your opinion before the close of this trial. You are perhaps influenced by the defendant's physical attractiveness. Remember, the devil often uses the most beautiful women to do his dirtiest work. You will join me in demanding the conviction of this defendant." Before he could continue the woman said, "Never!" Mr. Williamson continued, "As a warning to others coming from distant places that they must not defy our Christian laws, this defendant should be convicted, sentenced to hard labor and confined in jail during the serving of her sentence. I thank all of you for your approving attention. I will now examine Amy White for the State."

Miss Essie said, "Wait a minute, the defendant has a right also to make a preliminary statement." Mr. Williamson said, "If the Court please, the defendant has not denied the charges and, therefore, there is not reason for a preliminary statement in her behalf." From his seat, Mr. Ben Davidson said in a commanding manner, "Miss Essie has a right to answer Lon's slander." Mr. Williamson continued as if he had not heard Mr. Davidson, "I make the suggestion in the hopes of securing an orderly hearing. Of course, if Miss Essie wishes to talk, we should permit her to do so." Without waiting for a ruling by the Court Miss Essie stood so she could be heard and said, "If the Court please, Sarah Blossburg is innocent of violating any law. The affidavit on which this prosecution is based is void. It does not follow the form prescribed by the Code, it contains propaganda and libel which its author, Lon Williamson, felt would arouse prejudice against this lovely young lady. Amy White was forced by Lon Williamson into signing it. The statement that 'the name of the defendant was otherwise unknown' is false. I expect the Chaplain to testify that he had letters from the Mayor and other good citizens of Charleston, the city from which they came, certifying to their good character and that he showed these letters to both Lon and Reuben.

"Some issues have been injected into this trial for the purpose of exalting Lon Williamson and making him the popular Christian upholding the Sunday laws. Also, an effort has been made to slur the character of the defendant's family. Justice demands that these false charges be answered and the whole truth be known. We expect the evidence to show that the statement that Lon Williamson has been active in enforcing the Sunday laws is false. On the other hand, he has violated these laws whenever it was to his financial interest to do so."

Mr. Williamson shouted, "Reuben, I am not on trial! I demand you fine Miss Essie for slandering me." Miss Essie calmly replied, "In the statement Lon wrote and had Mr. Stone to read, and in his own statement, Lon asserted that he was active in enforcing the Sunday laws. I am answering that statement." Again Mr. Williamson said, "I demand that she be stopped from slandering me and that she be fined."

Ben Davidson, without moving from his seat, said, "Lon Williamson opened the door to his conduct for his benefit and the detriment of the defendant and Miss Essie has a right to answer the false statements. I wonder if the Court is going to prevent Lon from interfering with Miss Essie's statement or will someone else be compelled to stop him?"

Mr. Stone quickly said, "A great deal has been said that is not relevant evidence. The Court will consider only what is proven." Miss Essie continued, "I will testify that I was near the stores Sunday morning at the time Sarah and Amy went to Mr. Blossburg's store. At that time, a reputed bootlegger from Snake Creek Beat backed his two horse wagon to the side door of Lon Williamson's store and he was delivered from the store one hundred pounds of sugar for which he paid." Mr. Williamson interrupted, "I was at church at that time." Miss Essie said, "I will prove by Mr. Stone that this sale was arranged by Lon Williamson and the delivery was by his orders. He knew this sugar was not to sweeten that bootlegger's coffee."

Miss Essie had been holding a piece of paper in her hand as she talked. She dropped it. Mr. Williamson, with an ostentatious show of courtesy, retrieved the worthless paper and went close to Miss Essie to give it to her. When near to her he said something to her in too low a tone for anyone else to hear. After this happened, Miss Essie stood still and remained quiet for several seconds. Some wondered if she were going to continue. The little satisfactory smile on Mr. Williamson's face indicated he thought he had accomplished his purpose to hush her. When she was sure she had everybody's attention she said, "Perhaps you are interested in what Lon has just said to me?" She paused again and then said, "Lon said that I had better remember that he had a mortgage on my home and household goods which he could foreclose next Monday." Mr. Williamson quickly said, "Miss Essie knows I was joking." Again Miss Essie paused until she knew the crowd was in expectancy and then continued, "It is true he does have such a mortgage on which I have paid for over ten years. It has taken most of my income. He probably will begin foreclosure next Monday. However, I wish to remind him that that mortgage does not cover my soul." In the stillness that followed some old man in the audience said, "Amen."

Miss Essie concluded her statement by saying, "We expect the evidence to show that this is not a bona fide effort to enforce the Sunday laws but that it is a malicious prosecution instigated and conducted by Lon Williamson as a part of his continued attempt to compel Mr. Blossburg to leave Landsee so that he might not have any competition, and also to punish Henry White for refusing to let him have his prize hunting dog, Blazer, for fifty cents." Miss Essie then took her seat. An old man in the audience who was hard of hearing and had a tin horn in his ear, asked in a louder voice than he realized, "Did she say Lon had taken Henry White's hunting dog, Blazer, away from him?"

Mr. Stone said, "The State will call its first witness." Mr. Williamson said, "Amy White will take the witness stand." When she was seated in the witness chair Mr. Williamson asked, "Amy, you have been sworn to tell the truth, have you not?" Amy answered, "Yes sir." Mr. Williamson then said, "I now show you the affidavit on which this case is founded. Is that your signature to that affidavit?" Amy looked at the signature and said, "Yes sir." Then he asked, "Was Mr. Stone, the Justice of the Peace, present when you signed that paper?" Amy answered, "Yes sir." Mr. Williamson said, "This is what she signed before the Justice of the Peace," and then read to the audience the affidavit with all its surplus prejudicial propaganda.

Mr. Williamson asked, "Three weeks ago Sunday did you go to Mr. Blossburg's home and ask him to sell you some merchandise?" Amy answered, "I went there and asked him..." Mr. Williamson abruptly stopped her and said, "Answer the question yes or no." Miss Essie said, "Let Amy answer in her own way. Stop telling the witness how she must testify." Mr. Williamson insisted it was a simple question and should be answered "yes" or "no" and asked the Court to compel her to answer in that manner. Amy, who had never been a witness in a trial before and had never been present during the trial of a case, showed that she was intimidated by a fear she would do something wrong and so said in a hesitant manner, "Yes, if medicine is merchandise."

Mr. Williamson, in a reprimanding tone said, "When you are told to answer 'yes' or 'no,' answer that way without adding any statement or I will ask the Court to fine you for contempt. You answer my next question in that manner. Did Mr. Blossburg send Sarah, this defendant, to the store with you to get the merchandise you wanted, and did Sarah open the store and did both of you go into the store? Answer 'yes' or 'no.' Did Sarah give you the merchandise you wanted and did you place some money on the counter in part payment for it? Answer 'yes' or 'no.'" Amy said, "Yes sir." Mr. Williamson then said, "Was not the front door of Mr. Blossburg's store open and this sale by Sarah to you made while religious services were being held at the Methodist Church where I was engaged in worshipping? Answer 'yes' or 'no.'" Amy said, "I am unable to answer the question 'yes' or 'no.'" Scoldingly Mr. Williamson said, "Do you swear that you did not know religious services were being held at the Methodist Church? I ask the Court to order her to answer 'yes' or 'no.'"

Before the Court could rule, Mr. Ben Davidson had moved

to where Mr. Williamson was sitting, carrying his chair with him. He placed the chair beside Mr. Williamson. When seated he said in what was a calm voice for him when mad, "If the Court please, the browbeating method of examining this girl is outrageous." Mr. Williamson started to say something but, realizing that Mr. Davidson's calm might be the calm that could erupt into a violent storm, stopped. Mr. Davidson continued, "Any fool knows that question cannot be answered 'yes' or 'no.' So far as Amy knows, Lon was hidden in the back of his store seeing that Reuben was carrying out his orders to deliver a hundred pounds of sugar to be used in the illegal manufacture of whiskey, and being sure that Reuben secured the cash and a bottle of bootleg liquor for him." Mr. Williamson shouted, "I say I was at church at that time." Mr. Davidson, still speaking calmly said, "I challenge you to take the witness stand and deny you ordered Reuben, on threat of firing him as clerk, to make this sale." Then he said, "Amy, answer the question your own way." Amy said, "Of course, I knew it was the time religious services were generally held. But as I was not there, I could not swear where Mr. Williamson was. I did not see him that morning." Mr. Stone said, "I think that answers the question. Proceed with the case."

Mr. Williamson said, "That proves the case and, as there is no denial by the defendant, that closes the case. The Court is compelled to convict the defendant. Come down, Amy." Miss Essie said, "Wait, Amy, I want to ask you some questions. What did Mr. Blossburg say when you told him your father was sick and needed medicine to relieve the severe pain he was suffering?" Mr. Williamson said, "There is no reason for repeating the testimony. She has sworn that she asked to buy merchandise and he sent Sarah to let her have it." Miss Essie said, "That was your statement. I want Amy to state the entire conversation." Mr. Davidson said, "The defense has a right to call for the entire conversation and Lon has no right to suppress it." Mr. Williamson said, "If everybody is going to take part in this case and call for all kinds of conversations we will be here a week." Mr. Davidson said, "Just remember, Lon, I have as much right as you have to take part in this trial. I am going to exercise that right. Your tactics to suppress the truth are not going to be tolerated."

Mr. Stone hastily said, "Gentlemen, we must have order in the Court. Mr. Williamson was only endeavoring to conserve time. If the defendant wishes to rehash the testimony she has a right to do so. Amy, you may answer the question." Amy answered, "Mr. Blossburg said he knew my father had been sick and unable to earn any money and that he would give him the medicine. He told Sarah to go to the store and get the medicine and give it to me." Miss Essie then said, "Amy, tell what happened at the store." Amy said, "Sarah opened the store and got the medicine and handed it to me. I knew the price was fifty cents and we did not have but a quarter. I offered Sarah the quarter and told her we would pay her the balance when we sold some eggs. Sarah refused the money and said her father had said to give us the medicine. I did not want to appear to be a beggar, so I put the quarter on the counter and left. I did not know that what I did was wrong for I had secured medicine on Sunday before from Mr. Williamson when he would credit us." Mr. Williamson called out, "That last statement is made to slander me and the witness should be reprimanded for saying it." The Court said, "The statement will not be considered. Proceed with the examination."

Miss Essie then asked, "Amy, did you voluntarily go before the Justice of the Peace and prosecute Sarah for getting that medicine for you?" Amy answered, "No, Miss Essie. I don't want to prosecute Sarah. Mr. Williamson called me into his store and threatened to put my sick father in jail if I did not sign a paper he showed me. I signed it to save my father."

Miss Essie then asked, "Did he read the paper to you?" Amy answered, "The paper was not read to me and he did not offer to let me read it. I did not know what was in the paper until I heard it read today." Miss Essie asked, "Did you swear to it?" Amy answered, "I was not asked to swear to it. Mr. Williamson just demanded I sign it." Who else was present when this happened?" asked Miss Essie. Amy said, "Mr. Stone and Lon, Jr., were present." Miss Essie asked, "Did they also demand that you sign the paper?" Amy answered, "Both Mr. Stone and Lon, Jr., asked Mr. Williamson not to make me sign the paper." Miss Essie said, "You can now come down, Amy."

Mr. Williamson said, "I want to ask you a question, Amy. You knew Mr. Stone was Justice of the Peace?" She answered,

"Yes sir." Then he asked, "He was present and saw you sign the paper?" She said, "Yes sir." Then he said, "That is all."

Mr. Stone asked if the defendant wished to introduce any testimony. Mr. Williamson, wishing to emphasize the fact that Sarah had not pleaded, and hoping to force her on the stand so that he could interrogate her about not believing as he did, said, "Certainly, the defendant will want to testify to clear herself."

Miss Essie knew that when she decided to openly oppose Lon Williamson she was jeopardizing her home and what little security she had. However, having cast her die to stand by Sarah, a girl whom she had learned to love, she was resolved to let all of Landsee know the truth about this prosecution and Lon Williamson's character. She had wondered if she would have to defy the Court to do this, but when Mr. Ben Davidson intervened on her side, she was encouraged to believe she would be able to do it.

Miss Essie replied to Mr. Stone's inquiry by saying, "Call Mr. May as a witness." Mr. Williamson said, "Henry May knows nothing about this case." Miss Essie said, "I propose to show that this case is not a bona fide effort to enforce the Sunday laws but a malicious prosecution and a part of your continued effort to drive Mr. Blossburg away from Landsee so that you will not have any substantial competition in your mercantile business. Mr. May will testify you had a meeting at your house and endeavored to get those attending to join you in preventing Mr. Blossburg from coming to Landsee."

Mr. Williamson knew he could not deny this so decided to turn it to his advantage, if possible. He said, "That meeting has no connection with this case. However, I gladly admit that, when I heard that one who despises our Christian faith was thinking of coming to Landsee and realized the evil influence he might have on our Christian youth, I attempted to prevent his coming. This case shows I was right."

Miss Essie said, "Will you also admit that at this meeting both the Methodist preacher and the Baptist preacher were present and neither of them supported your effort?" He replied, "No one opposed the action. They asked for more time to consider it." "Did not Mr. May object?" Miss Essie asked. He replied, "Yes, Henry objected. He had made a profitable deal with Mr. Blossburg and did not want to lose his profit." "Did not the Methodist preacher leave the meeting in protest and charge you with being prompted by selfish motives?" He replied, "He left with some statement replying to my reprimand of him. You note he was not sent back." Miss Essie said, "He was not sent back because he had served a four year term here and was not eligible to be returned." Miss Essie asked, "Do you also admit you attempted to compel Ezra White to sell you his champion hunting dog for fifty cents?" "That has nothing to do with this case. I made him a fair proposition." Miss Essie said, "Take the witness chair, Henry."

Miss Essie asked, "Henry, do you know the attitude of the Chaplain, Dr. Alston, Mr. Davidson and the others toward Mr. Williamson's proposal to prevent Mr. Blossburg's coming to Landsee?" Mr. Williamson interrupted, "I object to that question." Miss Essie replied, "I propose to show that your statement that they did not oppose your proposition is untrue. Mr. May, without waiting for a Court ruling said, "I have talked to everyone who was there and all of them were against Lon's proposal. We voted to postpone action as a courtesy to him in his own home." Miss Essie asked, "Do you wish to ask him any questions, Lon?" He said, "No." Miss Essie said, "Dr. Alston, the Chaplain, Mr. Davidson and others will testify the same as has Henry May but, since Lon does not deny his statement, I will not examine them."

Miss Essie then said, "Lon Williamson stated he would use me as a witness but he has failed to do so. I will testify now about Lon's Sunday sale of sugar to a bootlegger." Mr. Williamson shouted, "I told you I was at church at that time. I object to that statement. We know Miss Essie will testify to what she stated but that does not relate to this case nor involve me." Miss Essie said, "It shows that all the bragging about your enforcing Sunday laws is false. I will put Lon Williamson on the stand and ask him if he will deny he ordered Reuben Stone to make this sale." Mr. Williamson said, "I object to that and I will not be a witness." Mr. Stone said, "I don't think you can make Mr. Williamson incriminate himself." This concluded the evidence. Mr. Stone asked if there were any arguments.

Mr. Williamson was callous to other people's opinion of him. The perfidious picture of him which the developments of the case disclosed did not disturb his confidence that, because he controlled Reuben, he would accomplish his goal, the conviction of Sarah Blossburg. Consequently, he was eager to argue the case. He reiterated what he had before stated, posing as the defender of Christian laws. He concluded his self lauding speech by saying, "There is no dispute as to the defendant's guilt. She is a beautiful vampire, at her parent's demand, seeking to destroy our Christian Sunday. This, I know you good native citizens resent and justifies my insisting that the Court find her guilty and sentence her to a term in jail as a warning to any other foreigner who might consider invading our fair land and flounting our sacred laws. I am sure that the Court will make a just decision."

Miss Essie was short and to the point. She said, "If the Court please, the evidence shows without dispute there is no valid complaint on which to find the defendant guilty. Amy White was forced by ugly threats to sign this paper without knowing what she was signing. That she was not sworn and that Lon, Jr., and Reuben Stone protested Lon Williamson's unlawful action is not disputed. Lon Williamson is guilty of malicious prosecution. If you, Reuben Stone, were to convict Sarah on this evidence, you would also be guilty of malicious prosecution. In the second place, the evidence shows without contradiction the medicine was a gift, not a sale. In the third place, everyone knows it is not a violation of the law to sell medicine on Sunday. Every drug store in the state remains open on Sunday to supply needed medicine to the sick.

"It is also clear from the testimony that Lon Williamson is guilty of selling sugar on Sunday to a bootlegger when he knew the sugar would be used to illegally manufacture whiskey. The verdict in this case should be, 'The Court finds Lon Williamson, Sr., guilty of violating the Sunday laws and maliciously endeavoring to stifle competition by an unlawful use of the Court.'"

After Miss Essie was seated Mr. Stone said, "I wish to confer with the prosecuting solicitor as to the extent of my jurisdiction in this case and what character of punishment I have the power to impose if I find the defendant guilty. Court will recess for a few minutes." He requested the prosecuting attorney to accompany him into the store. When they went into the store the Chaplain called Mr. Davidson and said, "Ben, get the bond we have executed to appeal the case and have the sheriff ready to approve it immediately after the verdict." Mr. Davidson said, "I will have everything ready."

In a few minutes Mr. Stone returned to his desk and rapped with his gavel for attention and said, "The Court is again in session. Will you please keep order as I wish to render my verdict." There was no need to admonish the crowd to keep order because they were too anxious to hear the verdict. Mr. Williamson said, "The defendant should stand when the guilty verdict is rendered. Stand, Sarah." Sarah quietly stood, her hands clasped in front of her and her eyes downcast.

Mr. Stone said, "After a careful consideration of the evidence, I find the defendant not guilty." Sarah looked up in surprise and Mr. Williamson shouted, "Reuben, you do not know what you said. Correct that statement." Mr. Stone said, "I repeat, the Court finds the defendant not guilty," emphasizing the word "not." Then he continued, "The defendant is released from custody and court is adjourned." For a few moments all was quiet. Then there was a burst of applause.

It is said there lies buried deep in the soul of the humblest person a spark of courage and nobility, even a person who has lived a life of dependency and servility, which in his better moments may explode into actions of greatness, even at the threat of the sacrifice of his personal security.

A Day Of Reckoning

In retrospect it can be seen that the trial of Sarah Blossburg changed the destiny of several people. It also changed much of the life of Landsee community. The credit for this must go to the courage and intelligent aggressiveness of Miss Essie in championing justice even when she knew that her action threatened her own economic security. Perhaps only a person of her pride and of her deserved respect and prestige could understand how dire was the prospect of her becoming an object of charity. Many times it has been observed that more often than not the gentle person is found to be made of stern stuff when a crucial test of courage comes.

It is probably impossible to describe accurately the various emotions experienced by different people when Reuben Stone announced his unexpected verdict of "not guilty." At first it was not fully comprehended by the crowd and for a few seconds all was very quiet, as if they were endeavoring to realize just what had happened. Someone shouted, "Good for you, Reuben." Another started to cheer, clapping his hands and then it appeared that everybody present joined in the cheering. Lon Williamson considered this reaction a personal affront and he glared his hatred at the cheerers. As he turned from staring at the crowd he saw Reuben Stone walking toward him. He mistakenly thought Mr. Stone was coming to him to apologize for his verdict and to try to explain it. Mr. Stone gave him an object on which he felt he could safely and effectively vent his seething hate. When Mr. Stone drew near, Lon Williamson said, "You fool, don't you ever put your foot in my store again. You have not only lost your job but also your home. I will begin foreclosure proceedings on the mortgage next Monday." Mr. Williamson was chagrined when Mr. Stone walked by him as if he had not heard what he said. He determined to make him suffer for publicly ignoring him. He watched Mr. Stone as he walked off the store's porch and through the crowd to where the sheriff and prosecuting attorney of the county stood together. He wondered with some trepidation what Reuben Stone was saying to these officers but he did not dare to find out by joining them. Instead he haughtily strode into his store. He ignored even the effort of Ina to speak to him as he passed her.

Maybe the reason Mr. Stone walked past Mr. Williamson as if he had not heard what he said was because he was so intent on executing a momentous decision he had made. When he reached the sheriff and the prosecuting attorney he asked if he could speak to them. When they indicated they were giving him their attention he said, "Gentlemen, what Miss Essie said about my delivering sugar to the bootlegger on Sunday is true. I know that I am not excused for my action even though I was acting under the orders of my boss in order to hold my job. I have come to ask that you give me a few days before you take me into custody. Mr. Williamson has advised me that I am discharged from the position I have held in his store for several years, and that he would immediately begin foreclosure proceedings on the mortgage he holds on my home. My wife is ill and I desperately need a few days to arrange for her care." The prosecuting attorney said, "Mr. Stone, no complaint has been made against you and until such complaint is made there can be no arrest. I don't think any such charge will be made. I certainly would not ask the grand jury to indict you." The sheriff said, "Go home and forget about being taken into custody. If an order for your arrest is issued you will be released on your own personal recognizance." Mr. Stone said, "Thank you both for your trust and kindness. I assure you I will not give you cause to regret your action."

Back on the store porch where the trial had been held there were other activities relating to those deeply affected by the trial. Sarah, suddenly realizing she had been acquitted and feeling an overwhelming sense of gratitude to Miss Essie, stood on tiptoe and kissed her. Miss Essie, embarrassed by this show of thankful appreciation, responded by tenderly pushing Sarah into the arms of her approaching mother. The high emotional tension under which she had labored, although controlled during the trial, could be no longer contained. For a few seconds she wept freely in her mother's embrace. When she was again herself and had dabbed some of the moisture from her eyes, she turned to find Ellen, John and Ben standing nearby waiting for her. From her place of observation just inside the door of the store Ina noted with bitterness that John and Ben walked away with Ellen and Sarah.

One of the persons the trial intensely affected was the Chaplain. He thought that he was aware of any unjust condition that affected the happiness of anyone in the community. He was shocked to learn that Mr. Williamson was exacting of Miss Essie subservience to his wishes by coercive economic pressure. For the first time it occurred to him that Lon Williamson took pleasure in making people suffer. The Chaplain was near enough to hear Mr. Williamson's outburst against Mr. Stone and knew from what Mr. Williamson said at that time he was using some power over Mr. Stone to crush him. The Chaplain determined that something had to be done without delay to protect Miss Essie and Reuben Stone from Lon Williamson's vindictiveness.

The Chaplain went to Mr. Davidson and said, "Ben, I think it is urgent that you, Dr. Alston, Mr. Blossburg and I have a conference to discuss an important matter. Will you get Dr. Alston while I get Mr. Blossburg? We will meet immediately at Mr. Blossburg's store." Mr. Davidson replied, "If you will consider some action against Lon Williamson for the manner in which he has treated Miss Essie, I will gladly come." The Chaplain answered, "That is the main purpose." Each went to secure the attendance of the parties suggested by the Chaplain.

When the four had met in Mr. Blossburg's private office which was in the rear of his store, the Chaplain said, "I have asked you here to consider whether or not we should take some action to protect Miss Essie from Lon Williamson's threat to foreclose a mortgage he holds on her home. He must have secured this mortgage ten years ago when both of Miss Essie's parents were ill and she incurred considerable expense. I think it is a safe surmise that Lon has charged her exorbitant rates of interest during this ten year period. Now because she had the courage to oppose his insidiousness, he proposes to punish her by leaving her homeless during her declining years. After the trial I heard Lon, in insulting language, rail out against Reuben Stone because of his verdict acquitting Sarah. He discharged Reuben from his employment and told him he was going to foreclose the mortgage he had on his home. Lon has become a menace to mercy and justice and I am convinced we should do something to prevent him from injuring these people. It is my opinion that we owe both of these parties a debt for their courageous actions to prevent the perpetration of great injustices. I would like to know how each of you feels about this situation."

Ben Davidson was the first to speak. He said, "I was so outraged when Miss Essie disclosed Lon's effort to intimidate her by threatening to foreclose the mortgage he held on her home, that I had difficulty in restraining myself from walking across that porch and thrashing him. I am in accord to do whatever is necessary to stop Lon's persecution of people over whom he has acquired some economic power. I consider him in the same class as a blackmailer. I pledge my full support to whatever plan is adopted."

The Chaplain turned to Dr. Alston and asked what he thought. Dr. Alston said, "I was surprised to learn Lon had secured a mortgage on Miss Essie's home. I never charged her for my services to her father and mother. She offered to pay me but I refused to accept it. It was necessary to send both of her parents away to a hospital. The doctor's bills there and the cost of hospital care was undoubtedly more than I had anticipated. I agree we must take some action to prevent Miss Essie and Reuben from further wrong."

Next the Chaplain addressed Mr. Blossburg saying, "Mr. Blossburg, can you suggest some practical way of solving our problem?" Mr. Blossburg replied, "You flatter me in two ways. First, you assume without asking that I agree with what you three have said and I do. Secondly, you also suggest I am able to present a solution to the problem. The fact is, I have been considering what could be done to protect Miss Essie since her disclosure of Mr. Williamson's threat to foreclose his mortgage on her home. I did not know about Mr. Stone's situation until the Chaplain's statement a few minutes ago. Mr. Stone's problem is the easiest to solve. As you know, I am planning to move to Chicago to join my brother in business there. I need a good man to work here with me in my store, one who can learn the business and take charge of it and run the store in the event I have to leave before I dispose of it. Of course, in disposing of the business, I would see that the interests of Mr. Stone were protected if he should accept my offer of employment. If I am correctly informed as to the amount of salary he has been receiving, I will be able to pay him fifty per cent more than Mr. Williamson has paid him." Then Mr. Blossburg spoke directly to Ben Davidson, "Mr. Davidson, I would appreciate it if after this meeting you would go to see Mr. Stone and submit my offer to him. If he is interested in accepting the offer I will go into details of the employment with him. In the event of a conference to settle details I would like to have you present." Mr. Davidson said, "It will give me considerable pleasure to comply with your request. It will deprive Lon of the one who has carried the burden of his store for him."

Mr. Blossburg continued, "This brings us to a consideration of the situation of Miss Essie. It is impossible for anyone to know how grateful we are to her for the part she has played in Sarah's life. I am willing to furnish the money to pay the mortgage on her home and relieve her of Mr. Williamson's dominance. However, if the surmise that he has been charging her exorbitant and usurious rates of interest is true, a readjustment allowing only the legal rate of interest will probably leave very little, if anything, due. Before we can plan any action, it is necessary that we know the amount due on the mortgages." Mr. Davidson said, "Reuben Stone was Lon's bookkeeper He could furnish this information." Mr. Blossburg said, "Mr. Stone can give you a general picture of what took place but we need to know what the written evidence shows. If receipts were given and preserved, we can calculate the amount due from them. There is no easy way I can suggest of handling this phase of the problem. Some person will be compelled to perform what I think will be the unwelcome task of demanding an accounting from Mr. Williamson. I would undertake it personally but I am sure I am the one person who would fail to succeed."

Mr. Davidson said, "I volunteer to make the demand if I can secure the authority to do so." Mr. Blossburg said, "I was going to suggest that you, Mr. Davidson, secure from Mr. Stone authority to represent him in adjusting and settling his mortgage and that the Chaplain secure the same authority from Miss Essie. Armed with these authorizations you two can go together to see Mr. Williamson and demand a detailed statement of every payment made on the mortgage indebtedness. If he refuses to permit you to audit his books, you then can advise him you will secure a court order compelling him to render such an account. I will pay the attorney if court action becomes necessary. When we determine the true status of the accounts we can than make definite plans." When Mr. Blossburg had concluded, the Chaplain said, "I was sure you could suggest a feasible plan to handle our problems. I know Ben will undertake the work you suggested for him and I will gladly go to see Miss Essie."

Mr. Davidson suggested to the Chaplain that they should begin their work immediately before Lon had an opportunity to force some agreement out of Miss Essie and Reuben that would place them more under his control. "Chaplain, suppose you go with me to talk to Reuben and then I will go with you to see Miss Essie." The Chaplain agreed and they left for Reuben Stone's residence.

When Mr. Stone opened his door to their knock and saw the Chaplain and Mr. Davidson standing on his porch he glanced back into the room and, viewing its disarray, hesitated to invite them to enter. But in a moment he opened the door and said, "Come in. Please excuse the confused condition of the room but my wife is ill and I, myself, am in a somewhat confused state."

After they were seated Mr. Davidson said, "Reuben, I will come directly to the reason for our visit. You must not resent our proposing to intervene in your private affairs. Just remember that the Chaplain and I are your friends." Then Mr. Davidson proceeded to tell Mr. Stone about the meeting of the Chaplain, Dr. Alston, Mr. Blossburg and himself to consider what they had learned about Lon Williamson's threat to Miss Essie and to him and what they proposed to do about it. He told him that Mr. Blossburg had authorized him to offer Mr.

Stone a position which amounted to assistant manager of his store. When Mr. Davidson finished advising Mr. Stone of the employment offer they heard a woman in an adjoining room say, "God be thanked." They knew it must have been Mrs. Stone who evidently had been listening to their conversation. The offer of employment had a magic effect on Mr. Stone. The anxiety that had so clearly shown in his face vanished and was replaced by an expression of hope and relief.

Mr. Stone asked, "When can I go to work for Mr. Blossburg?" Mr. Davidson replied that the employment would begin the next Monday but he need not report until a week later. After Mr. Davidson had secured written authority from Mr. Stone to represent him in the settlement of his account with Lon Williamson they discussed how the accounts were handled. Mr. Stone told them the first year the rate of interest was supposed to be ten per cent per annum, payable in advance, but the way Lon Williamson figured it the rate was more. The legal rate was eight per cent. Soon after the first year the rate was raised to fifteen per cent. He assured them that the book would reflect the date and amount of every payment.

They went directly from Mr. Stone's to see Miss Essie. When they were seated in her neat parlor the Chaplain said, "Miss Essie, the last time I was here you said I never came to see you except when I wanted you to do something. This time Ben and I have come to ask you to let us do something for you." He gave her the information they had given Mr. Stone and what they planned to do. Then he said, "Miss Essie, I am asking you to authorize me to handle the adjustment of your account with Lon Williamson. We are sure he has charged you more than the legal rate of interest. We want to compel him to credit you with this excess. Reuben has already given such authorization to Ben. We wish to make our demands together."

Miss Essie replied, "You do not know what a relief your willingness to help me in this matter brings. Several times when Lon would raise the interest rate I started to ask one of you to help me handle the matter with him but each time decided I had no right to burden you with my private affairs. I am glad to give you full authority to act for me. You will not have to audit Lon's books to ascertain what I paid. I secured and have preserved a receipt for every penny I paid because I did not trust him. I will get the receipts for you." Miss Essie went into another room and soon returned with a shoe box securely tied with a stout twine saying, "This box is full of receipts." She turned the box over to the Chaplain.

When they had left Miss Essie's home the Chaplain said, "Ben, you are better at figures than I am. You take the box of receipts and calculate the status of the account." Mr. Davidson said, "I have a better idea. Mr. Blossburg is better at such calculations than either of us. What do you say to our asking him to perform this task?" The Chaplain agreed. When they approached Mr. Blossburg about analyzing Miss Essie's account he readily consented. The Chaplain handed him the box of receipts. Mr. Blossburg carefully untied the string and opened the box. After he had inspected several of the receipts he said, "It appears this will be easy. Miss Essie has had Mr. Williamson to note on each receipt the amount applied to the payment of interest and the amount credited to payment on the principal." Mr. Davidson said, "Reuben told us that Lon always dictated how much of each payment went to pay interest and what should be credited on the principal indebtedness and he entered it both on the note and on the ledger of accounts." Mr. Blossburg promised to have a report ready for them by noon the next Monday.

On the following Monday afternoon the Chaplain and Ben Davidson met at Mr. Blossburg's store and received a detailed statement showing each payment made by Miss Essie, the amount of the payment credited to the payment of interest at the legal rate and the balance of the payment credited to payment on the principal indebtedness. The result was that Mr. Lon Williamson owed Miss Essie two hundred and twenty dollars. Armed with this statement they crossed the road to Mr. Williamson's store to accost him with their demands.

While the Chaplain and Mr. Davidson were walking from the front to the back of the store where Mr. Williamson was sitting with his back to them, they saw Lon, Jr., enter the back door. As he approached his father they heard Mr. Williamson yell at him, "Did you go and tell Reuben to report here at once?" Lon, Jr., replied, "Yes sir." Mr. Williamson in a scolding tone of voice said, "Why did you not bring him with you?" Lon, Jr., replied, "Reuben said you discharged him last Saturday and that he would not be working for you anymore. He said Mr. Blossburg has employed him at a better salary than you were paying him." Lon Williamson shouted, "So Blossburg bought him before the trial so as to get him to acquit Sarah!" Lon, Jr., said, "Reuben told me he has never talked to Mr. Blossburg about employment and that the employment was made after the trial by Mr. Davidson and not until after Mr. Davidson had heard that you had discharged him. There is Mr. Davidson just behind you. He can tell you whether or not what Reuben told me is true."

Mr. Williamson evidently was unaware of the presence of the Chaplain and Mr. Davidson. When he turned toward them Mr. Davidson said, "We could not help hearing your conversation. What Reuben told Lon, Jr., is true. The Chaplain heard you discharge Reuben so we decided to help him. Mr. Blossburg offered to employ him at a better salary than you were paying him. It has worked out well for Reuben." Sneeringly Mr. Williamson said, "You think it has worked out well for Reuben, do you? How and where do you think he will live when I foreclose the mortgage I hold on his house and on all the furnishing in that house?"

Mr. Davidson said, "Lon, we came here to see you about that mortgage." Mr. Williamson interrupted, "It is none of your business. I will handle it with Reuben directly." Mr. Davidson said, "Reuben has authorized me to handle the matter and I am requesting a detailed statement of all payments made by him in order that I may determine the correct amount, if any, due on it." Mr. Williamson with forced bluster in his voice said, "I told you I would handle the matter with Reuben personally. I do not recognize that it is any of your business. I am leaving." As Mr. Williamson started to rise Mr. Davidson laid a hand on his shoulder and tenderly, but firmly, forced him back into his chair saying, "Lon, you are not going to be so lacking in courtesy to leave while we are transacting important business. I want to know if you are saying I lied when I said Reuben had delegated to me full authority to handle this matter. If that is your attitude stand up and I will see if I can beat a retraction out of you."

The Chaplain said, "Wait a minute, Ben. I think Lon should have the full picture. Lon, I represent Miss Essie." In a feeble effort to maintain his swagger Mr. Williamson said, "So you too are sticking your nose into my business!" With a force in his voice he was seldom heard to use the Chaplain said, "Your rudeness only evidences your moral weakness and your awareness of the unjust and contemptible manner in which you have treated Miss Essie. An analysis of her receipts shows you have charged her illegal interest and that you now owe her two hundred and twenty dollars. I am here to demand the mortgage marked paid and the payment of two hundred and twenty dollars." With a rather lower tone of voice than he had been employing Mr. Williamson replied, "That is not correct. I will collect the balance due on Miss Essie's mortgage."

Mr. Davidson said, "I think it about time to let Lon know what we are prepared to do. I spent yesterday at the county seat conferring with lawyers and the prosecuting solicitor. We are advised that both Miss Essie and Reuben have a clear case against you and by asking the court for an accounting, you and all your books will be carried to the county seat and an audit will be made. In that suit you will not be allowed the illegal rate of interest and a judgment will be rendered against you. You will be charged with all court costs. We have arranged to file such suits unless our demands are met. A little while ago we heard you charge Reuben with selling his verdict in acquitting Sarah. We know this charge is false and constitutes malicious slander. I shall advise Reuben to sue you for five thousand dollars damages. It is clear that the arrest and trial of Sarah was malicious prosecution by you. Our lawyer advises us Sarah has an open and shut case against you for damages. I will advise Sarah to sue you for ten thousand dollars. The prosecuting solicitor says if we bring the evidence to the next grand jury he will have them indict you for selling goods on Sunday and dealing in moonshine liquor. When these matters have gone against you, I am going to lay the facts before your church congregation and urge them to fire you as superintendent of the Sunday School. The only language you understand is force. I promise you it will be applied to you with as little mercy as you have shown to others. Finally, today is Monday. I am giving you until noon next Wednesday to meet our demands to properly adjust these accounts. If we do not hear from you by that time I will personally see that actions are started to compel you to do so. Chaplain, I don't think we should adjourn this conference with prayer, so let's go."

When they were outside the store Mr. Davidson said to the Chaplain, "I know you think I was unduly rough and angry in what I said to Lon. I did it purposely. He has been so merciless for so long in using coercion that you are compelled to use his own methods against him if you succeed in accomplishing anything." The Chaplain replied, "You are mistaken in what I think. You did the proper thing under the circumstances. Lon is a character who convinces you that mercy misplaced is a menace."

The next afternoon Lon, Jr., called on the Chaplain. When the Chaplain asked him if he could do anything for him he said, "As you know, I was present when you and Mr. Davidson had your conversation with my father about the accounts of Miss Essie and Reuben. Although my father told me to keep my mouth shut about what happened, I went home and told my mother because I was disturbed. I trust my mother's judgment. It is not necessary for me to relate what was said during the argument in which my mother took the position that you and Mr. Davidson would not demand anything but that which was just. The result was that my father said he had to leave this morning and that he would be away for several days. When he was leaving he said to my mother and me that we would have to run the store in his absence and added in a rather sarcastic way that we could handle the matter concerning Miss Essie and Reuben in our namby-pamby way. My mother quietly replied she would use the authority he had given. When we opened the store this morning we opened the safe and got Miss Essie's papers and the money you said was due her and I am turning them over to you to give Miss Essie and get a receipt from her. My mother had me to go to see Reuben and ask him to come to the store while my father is away. When he knew my father was not there he came. My mother had him make a detailed statement of his account. I am to leave this account with you to ascertain what is justly due on it. We will settle for the amount you say is correct." Finally he said, "My mother said to tell you that she knows we are not in position to ask any favors but that we hope this will settle all the affairs connected with what has so recently and unjustly happened."

The Chaplain said, "Lon, Jr., you and your mother have shown you want to do right. Tell your mother that whatever influence I have will be used to save all of you from any embarrassment because of what has happened."

Snake Creek Beat

A community can secure a bad reputation just as can an individual. The reputation of Snake Creek Beat was justly considered bad. It is true that there were several families living in this area who were trusted and respected. With these few exceptions, it was inhabited by people who had little, if any, respect for the rights of others or their lives.

Snake Creek Beat was a precinct of the county lying along the river for about twelve miles and something over fifteen miles north of Landsee. By virtue of today's roads and means of transportation the distance of fifteen or twenty miles could be traveled in thirty or forty minutes, but it must be remembered that in oxcart days fifteen miles was quite a distance. It took a good team of horses an entire day to travel from Snake Creek Beat to Landsee and back. Those who drove ox teams generally went one day and returned the following day.

What served as the public road through this sparsely settled section of the county was merely a marked trail through a densely wooded area. The swamp lands next to the river were like a primeval forest. It was a secluded country. The residences of the families who lived in this section were so far apart they were not in sight of each other. Their houses were generally about a half mile from the public road. A person had to be familiar with the way to reach a home from the public road for there were no signs to direct a traveler. What was traveled as a road to a house often was so seldom used that it could only be detected by one trained to find such ways. It was not only a secluded country but also its residents were secluded in the country.

Snake Creek Beat got its name because through it crawled a slow running creek that was said to be a prolific breeding place of water moccasins. Because of the thick growth of trees and bushes along the banks it offered a number of places where a still could easily be shut from view until you were within a few feet of it. It was said that in this section a large amount of whiskey was illegally distilled. It was a moonshiner's paradise.

Two-thirds of the land of Snake Creek Beat was public land. It was full of game and for many years the hunters considered it an open field for hunting deer, turkey, squirrels and other wild game. But suddenly, and very much to their surprise, this long enjoyed privilege was challenged. For some time there had been growing open hostility on the part of the lawless element against men hunting in that precinct. The hunters thought it was because the operators of the illegal stills were afraid they were endeavoring to locate and raid their stills. Twice shots were fired close to a hunter but he thought it was accidental. It never occurred to him that he would be done any serious injury. Then several of the hunters received notes warning them it was dangerous for them to hunt in Snake Creek Beat. These notices were signed, "Hell's Riflemen." The hunters discussed these notes and concluded that it was a waggish effort to frighten them away. They determined not to pay any attention to the notes.

Soon afterwards an incident disclosed that "Hell's Riflemen" was probably a close knit gang and not entirely peaceful in its operation. Every man who hunted in Snake Creek Beat found a note one morning addressed to him personally and signed, "Hell's Riflemen." They found that all their notes were identical and that the notes were in better handwriting and were better composed than the notes previously received. The notes stated that promiscuous hunting in Snake Creek Beat endangered the lives of the children of the families living there and endangered the lives of the hunting parties. Many hunters not familiar with the location of homes and of children's playgrounds were apt to accidentally cause great injury to them. Hunters not aware of others also hunting in the same section were dangerous to each other. Therefore, for the protection of all concerned, the citizens of Snake Creek Beat were requesting everyone who wished to hunt in the Beat to employ one of its residents to act as a guide. Application for the use of the guide should be made at least one full day before the hunt was to begin so all the residents might be notified. The fee was stated to be one dollar each day the guide was used. The notes stated that "Hell's Riflemen" would be compelled to enforce the regulations proposed in the note if the hunters did not volunteer to abide by them. The notes were signed, "Hell's Riflemen."

Mr. Ernest Long, one of the hunters, led the fight against complying with the demand. He called the hunters' attention to the fact that the hunting was in the swamps along the river and that there were no residences within two miles of that area and there could not be any danger to any children. He contended the day's notice was to give those operating illicit stills time to conceal their stills and put out the fires that might attract the attention of the hunters. He declared it was an attempt at extortion and that he would call their bluff by hunting without a guide. A majority agreed with him.

A week after this meeting Mr. Long did as he had promised, went hunting alone in the swamps of Snake Creek Beat. When he returned he reported to his fellow hunters that he had been in the woods less than thirty minutes when he heard a rifle shot and the bullet cut the bark of a tree by which he was standing about three feet above his head. He said judging from the scar the bullet made on the tree he was able to determine the direction from which it came. He looked for some time in an effort to locate the person firing the shot but saw no one. He then continued hunting as if nothing had happened. In about fifteen minutes there was another shot and this time the bullet cut the bark of a tree near him even with his head. Again, he could see no one but he was convinced that he was being stalked. He realized he was at the mercy of the person firing the rifle and that it would be foolish to pursue the hunt so he called his dogs and left. The next morning he received a note signed by "Hell's Riflemen." The note said, "Tell your friends they need a guide when hunting in our backyards." Mr. Long told the hunters that he was mistaken in his estimate of the situation and that it appeared that they would be compelled to comply with "Hell's Riflemen's" demand or abandon hunting in that territory.

The hunters also learned that there had been posted in a prominent place at the post office in Landsee a large lettered notice containing the same statements as were in the notes to each hunter but, instead of being signed "Hell's Riflemen," it was signed, "Citizens of Snake Creek Beat." It contained the additional statement that anyone wishing to secure a guide could mail a letter to Citizen, Pine Tree post office. Pine Tree was the name of the little rural post office which was at a small store located on the public road running through the Beat. This notice had created considerable discussion in Landsee. While they were not in sympathy generally with any proposal by the residents of Snake Creek Beat, they felt that if children were being endangered, it was reasonable that some action be taken to protect them. This attitude was the result largely of the efforts of Mr. Lon Williamson. He would call the attention of everyone who came to the store to the notice and then he would remark that he was familiar with conditions in Snake Creek Beat. He declared that the request was reasonable and that he had advised the people of the Beat he would comply with their request. Mr. Williamson was only a fox hunter. Few people in Landsee ever visited in Snake Creek Beat. It was a foreign land to them. So it was easy for Mr. Williamson to stir their sympathy for the endangered children.

The hunters decided that, under the circumstances, it would be a good policy to comply with the request to secure the guide. They thought their agreeing to so comply might give them an opportunity to improve the relationship with the citizens of Snake Creek Beat and maybe avoid future trouble. So they wrote "Citizen" at Pine Tree that they would comply with their request and also posted a note of compliance under the notice posted at the post office in Landsee.

Approximately three years prior to the foregoing events, a man who called himself Syd Simmons had moved into Snake Creek Beat. No one knew from whence he came or why he came. He always avoided answering any question relative to his past. All they knew was that one day he drove up to the little store at Pine Tree with two fine horses hitched to a wagon loaded with household furnishings and two dogs. He and his wife asked whether there was a place they could secure for temporary lodging until they could acquire some land and build a house. He purchased forty acres of land bordering on the swamps. It was in as secluded a place as he could find. He paid cash for the land and paid cash for the material and labor used in constructing his home. He was reputed to always have plenty of cash money. He was often seen by the residents riding with a rifle strapped to his saddle in a manner ready for use. It was said he was soon familiar with every trail in Snake Creek Beat including the trails in the swamps. He was an expert shot and often spoke of his ability to use firearms as if to warn everyone of this fact. He never came to Landsee. There was a great amount of speculation about who he was. One surmise was that he had been a member of the outlaw organization led by Jesse James and was a fugitive from justice.

Syd Simmons was a forceful leader. It was his leadership that organized "Hell's Riflemen" into a dangerous clan. He dictated and controlled its actions. Under his leadership the clan became more aggressive in their defiance of legal rights.

It was hoped by the hunters that their agreement to comply with the demand to employ a guide when hunting would placate them and lessen their growing hostility. However, "Hell's Riflemen" construed the hunters' submission to their demand as showing that the hunters had been intimidated. They were of the opinion they had won a telling victory and consequently they became more audacious than ever before.

In an effort to increase what they now considered their power of intimidation to the extent it would prevent anyone from interfering with them, they let it be known that the members of "Hell's Riflemen" had each signed in his own blood, and under oath, an agreement to defend each other with their lives. Also, as an organization, they were pledged to revenge any wrong done one of their members even to the extent of taking human life if the organization so decreed. Each one of them bound himself to carry out the orders of the clan or forfeit his life for failing to do so.

It was soon evident that "Hell's Riflemen" were extending their activities to criminal actions. There was no law prohibiting cattle, hogs and other domestic animals from running at large. They were turned loose to graze in the open woods. Each farmer marked his animals so they could be distinguished from those belonging to someone else. As the swamps of Snake Creek Beat were prolific in forage, the farmers would carry their stock to the swamps to feed for a season and then afterwards corral them at their homes. This had been a practice for a long time. This was a valuable privilege for it saved the expense of feeding their cattle for several months. In the fall there was an abundant supply of a soft shelled hickory nut that served to fatten their hogs.

While the farmers always believed that some of their livestock ranging in the swamps was stolen, especially a few of the pigs to which the sows had given birth, they considered the loss too small to register a complaint. However, after the hunters had capitulated to the demand to employ guides, it soon became impossible for the farmers to find over half of the livestock left in the swamps. Part of their cattle would be missing and only a few pigs were found. In passing some of the residences, they would see a pen full of pigs and they were certain they had been stolen from them.

The farmers had sufficient facts to convince them that their missing cattle and hogs were stolen by "Hell's Riflemen." They did not have the character of evidence necessary to prosecute them in a court. They agreed that each one of them would make an effort to secure such evidence. One day, one of the farmers who had lost several head of cattle, was at a place of business where hides were purchased and he recognized the hide of one of his missing cows. From the businessman who ran the store he ascertained that the hide had been purchased from a resident of Snake Creek Beat. The farmer reported this find to his friends and they concluded they now had sufficient evidence to convict a thief. They reported the facts to the authorities and the party selling the hide was indicted.

At the trial the merchant who had purchased the hide testified that he purchased two hides from the defendant, and at the same time purchased one hide from each of two persons who were with him. The defendant and these two parties with him swore the hides the defendant sold were from cows owned by the defendant and that they had never seen the hide the merchant said he purchased from the defendant. After several hours of deliberation, the jury reported they were unable to agree. It was learned afterwards that eleven of the jury were for conviction but one man refused to agree. A mistrial was ordered. The next day after the trial the merchant received a note saying, "You are warned not to try again to swear a lie to convict an innocent." The note was signed, "Hell's Riflemen." The farmer received a similar note.

It was because of this background of the hostile and aggressive attitude of "Hell's Riflemen" that Dr. Alston became seriously alarmed at an incident about which Ooden told him. On one of Dr. Alston's visits to see a patient who lived in Snake Creek Beat he was driven by the boy, Ooden. On their return trip home Ooden told Dr. Alston that while Dr. Alston was in the house seeing the person who was ill, he started to walk to the back of the house to see if he could get a drink of water. Just before he reached the back he heard two persons swearing and talking in an angry manner. He stopped where these two men could not see him and listened to what they were saying. They were talking about Mr. Blossburg and Mr. Green. One of them said, "It is about time we let Landsee know we are tired of their harassment and we are going to notify them by running that Jew and that Yankee and his 'uppity nigger' out of this country." Ooden told Dr. Alston that several times they said "Hell's Riflemen" were making plans of action to make Mr. Blossburg and Mr. Green and his Negro helper leave Landsee. He said he was afraid for these men to know he might have heard their conversation so he quietly returned to the buggy and remained there until Dr. Alston came out of the house.

Dr. Alston was so completely convinced that "Hell's Riflemen" intended to do Mr. Blossburg and Mr. Green serious bodily harm that he felt compelled to attempt to take some action to protect them. While he had full confidence in Ooden's report being accurate, after carefully considering the situation, he decided that before he approached the law enforcement authorities, it would be advisable to secure additional information as to the plans of "Hell's Riflemen." The corroboration came before Dr. Alston had taken any action. A few days after his visit to see his patient in Snake Creek Beat, Dr. Alston was called to see Mrs. Green who was having one of her attacks. As he was leaving the Green's residence Ellen said, "Dr. Alston, Aunt Mymee told me to tell you she was sick and asked that you come to see her when you leave here."

Dr. Alston went directly to Aunt Mymee. When he entered her cabin he was surprised to find Aunt Mymee moving around with no appearance of being ill. Dr. Alston said, "You do not look like a sick person to me." Aunt Mymee replied, "I am not sick." Dr. Alston then said, "Why did you tell Ellen you were sick and needed a doctor?" Aunt Mymee answered, "I needed to talk to you about what I think is an important and urgent matter that at present needs to be kept from general public knowledge. If I had gone to your office looking as well as I do, the busy-bodies would never stop until they learned the purpose of the visit. I told Ellen I was sick so she would have an answer for those who asked her why you came to my cottage when you left their home. Now I will tell you the reason I requested your visit. You are familiar with the Indian basket makers who often spend the night at my house while peddling their wares in Landsee. These Indians go from house to house in Snake Creek Beat to sell their baskets. Probably because they appear uninterested and not listening to what is said, they have heard a number of statements by some of the men who talked as if they were members of 'Hell's Riflemen.' They think 'Hell's Riflemen' are making plans to come to Landsee some night and tar and feather Mr. Blossburg and Mr. Green and Mr. Green's Negro helper and threaten to set them on fire the next time they visit them if they do not leave Landsee." Dr. Alston then told Aunt Mymee what Ooden had heard and that he had asked Jake Wilson to visit his aunt who lived in Snake Creek Beat and see if he could secure any information about the plans of "Hell's Riflemen." He said that while Jake's relatives were not in sympathy with "Hell's Riflemen," he thought it possible they would have some knowledge of facts that would be well to know.

In a few days Jake returned. "Hell's Riflemen" were so open in discussing their plans that Jake had not only secured the overall details but also the date that "Hell's Riflemen" expected to stage their raid to attack Mr. Blossburg and Mr. Green and the Negro. With all this information, Dr. Alston called a conference to decide what action should be taken in defense of this planned assault.

Conference On Hell's Riflemen

Dr. Alston called a meeting at his office to which he invited the Chaplain, Ben Davidson, Charles Green and Isaac Blossburg. He sent John to ask the sheriff to come to Landsee and spend the night with him in order that he might be present at an important conference. Dr. Alston had requested each one of them to have supper with him.

When they had finished the meal and assembled for the conference Dr. Alston said, "Some information has come to me from several sources that convinces me we are going to have some serious trouble at Landsee with the organization known as 'Hell's Riflemen.' I have asked those present to meet for the purpose of considering what should be done to defend ourselves against any violence that might take place. I asked the sheriff to be present because whatever steps are taken must be with his approval and under his direction. He is our law enforcement officer. I requested the Chaplain and Ben Davidson because we need their advice and cooperation. I asked Mr. Blossburg and Mr. Green because they are personally involved and I think can give us some additional information. I have not mentioned this meeting or its purpose to anyone else because I thought it should be held confidential lest 'Hell's Riflemen' become acquainted with whatever plans we make."

Dr. Alston told them of the conversation Ooden overheard, what Aunt Mymee had reported to him about the Indian basket makers' statements to her and the information Jake Wilson had secured. Then he asked the sheriff if he did not think it was necessary to organize in anticipation of "Hell's Riflemen" attempting to carry out their plans. The sheriff said, "When I saw John, I knew why he was coming to see me. I was already arranging to come to Landsee to advise you of information I had relative to 'Hell's Riflemen's' plans and arrange a way to defeat them. I have reliable information that verifies the reports Dr. Alston has heard. According to the advice I have received, the raid is to be led by Syd Simmons. It is his idea and he assures his men it will be a great success. As he had never been to Landsee, he had one of the men belonging to 'Hell's Riflemen' come with him one night last week and show him the residences of Mr. Green and Mr. Blossburg and where Jim Jones, Mr. Green's helper, lives and also to familiarize himself with the roads and other buildings. He is evidently an experienced man in planning unlawful acts of this character, and he is efficient in his preparations."

Dr. Alston then said, "As the threats are primarily against Mr. Blossburg and Mr. Green, I thought they should tell us whether they have had any trouble with any of the residents of Snake Creek Beat and whether they have any information about 'Hell's Riflemen's' plans. Mr. Green, suppose we hear from you first."

Mr. Green said, "Unfortunately, I have incurred the enmity of 'Hell's Riflemen.' About eight weeks ago one of them brought a machine to me to be mended. I examined it and told him that I would have to order a rather expensive part for the repair. He said he expected that I would have to order the part and that he had arranged with Mr. Lon Williamson, who advanced him during the year until his cotton was ready for marketing, to pay me. I never questioned the truthfulness of his statement. I secured the part needed and made the repairs. He called for the machine while I was away from the shop and told Jim that I understood Mr. Williamson was to pay me. Jim had heard our previous conversation and thought it would be all right to deliver the machine to him, which he did. When I went to Mr. Williamson and requested payment of the bill he said he had not authorized the man to tell me he would pay the bill. I wrote the party at Pine Tree post office requesting payment and telling him that Mr. Williamson said he had never promised to pay the bill for him. I had no reply. As I had a neat sum of money involved by having to purchase the part I used, I asked a lawyer if there were any way I could collect my account. The lawyer said he could file a lien on the machine and when I got judgment in a law suit for the account I could sell the machine to settle the judgment and cost of the suit. I authorized him to write the party stating that unless the account was paid he would have the lien filed. After the lawyer wrote him I found a note which had been shoved under the door to my shop which said, 'Sometimes liens and law suits not only hurt the person starting the suits but his family also. Beware!' and signed, 'Hell's Riflemen.' For fear they might do some injury to Ellen, I asked the lawyer not to press the matter."

Mr. Green continued, "Another time I did some work for a man who lived in Snake Creek Beat. I instructed Jim not to deliver it unless he was paid the bill for the repair. This party also came while I was absent from the shop. He told Jim he would make it all right with me about the payment of the bill for the repairs and to let him have the article which had been repaired. When Jim refused he began to curse him and say that no nigger could tell him he could not have his property. Fortunately, they were standing outside in front of the shop. Jim quickly entered the shop, closed and locked the front door and then went out the back door which he locked and then left the shop. When I got to the shop I found it locked and no one present. Jim, who was watching, saw me approach and immediately returned and told me what had happened. A day or two afterwards there was another note found shoved under my shop door. It said, 'We do not take sass from an uppity nigger. Get rid of him.' Signed 'Hell's Riflemen.'

"About ten days ago a drummer, who drives two horses hitched to a large phaeton in which he carries samples to show to the country merchants on whom he calls, came to my shop for some work on his vehicle. He asked, 'What have you done to antagonize some of the people in Snake Creek Beat?' I replied, 'I do not know. Why do you ask?' He said 'I asked the merchant at Pine Tree where I could get good repair work done on my phaeton and he recommended you. Then one of the men who was playing checkers remarked, 'Yes, he does good work but that Yankee, his uppity nigger and that foreign Jew are going to be compelled to leave sooner or later.' From this I surmised that

Mr. Blossburg had had some trouble with them also. I went to see Mr. Blossburg and found that he had been threatened by 'Hell's Riflemen.'"

Mr. Green went on, "A few days after my talk with the drummer, I received another note. This note said it had been decreed that I should leave Landsee and that I had better leave within ten days after a cross was burned in front of my house. That cross was burned last night. When Mr. Blossburg tells you his experience we will tell you what we have decided to do."

The sheriff, who was a large man, an ex-Confederate soldier with a peg leg which replaced the leg he lost in the war, began to lightly tap the floor with his wooden leg, a habit he had when his resentment began to rise. They thought he was about to say something but he remained silent. He merely looked around at those present with his gray eyes which were usually kind but which sometimes looked like sharp steel swords fixing to pierce you. When Dr. Alston realized that the sheriff was not going to say anything he said, "I think we should hear from Mr. Blossburg."

Mr. Blossburg said, "You know I sell for cash. It limits the amount of business I do but it also prevents loss. Of course, I make exceptions to the rule. Several times some of these men came to the store and asked for merchandise saying they would bring the money the next day. Ben had warned me that they used this scheme to get the merchandise and then not pay for it. I refused to let them have the merchandise unless they paid at the time of purchase. I received a note. It said, 'If you expect to remain in Landsee, you had better learn to trust people who live in Snake Creek Beat like you trust others,' signed, 'Hell's Riflemen.'

"One day one of them was in the store and while my back was turned he slipped a knife into his pocket which I had on display on the counter. He evidently had not seen the deputy sheriff standing in the rear of the store. The deputy saw him and walking to the man said, 'Put that knife back on the counter.' The man replied, 'What are you talking about?' The deputy reached into his pocket and took the knife out. 'This is what I am talking about,' he said. 'I saw you take it from the counter while Mr. Blossburg's back was turned to you.' The man said, 'I was going to pay for it.' The deputy said, 'Then pay for it right now.' The man responded, 'I do not have the money right now.' The deputy said, 'You are under arrest for stealing and unless you can make bond for one hundred dollars I will have to carry you to jail.' He could not make bond. I told the deputy that 'Hell's Riflemen' had already threatened me about the manner in which I treated them and that rather than have further trouble with them I would appreciate the man being released. The deputy said such action would only encourage them in their lawless conduct. He took the man to jail. He is still in jail. I received a note saying, "Have the man released from jail and stop the prosecution of him if you expect your family to be free from harm,' and signed, 'Hell's Riflemen.'"

Mr. Blossburg continued, "As the sheriff knows, I asked him why he was not released on bond and he said he would not approve a bond signed by the men seeking his release. I offered to make the bond but the sheriff said that unless we ceased yielding to their threats there would never be any end to the demands we would be compelled to meet. He would not let me make the bond. I went to the jail and asked the man to tell his friends what I had done and that I was not prosecuting him and would do whatever I could to protect my family. This did not satisfy them for I had another note saying I had lived in Land-see longer than I should have been permitted. It was high time I left. I would be given a certain time after a cross was burned in front of my home to leave. The note was signed, 'Hell's Riflemen.' Mr. Green did not tell you that last night a cross was also burned in front of my home. After Mr. Green and I had these warnings we agreed on joint action to protect our families."

The sheriff was tapping the floor a little faster and a little harder with his peg leg. His eyes had turned cold steel and his voice carried the tone of a reprimand when he asked Mr. Blossburg, "Why have I not been told by you and Mr. Green of the facts you have disclosed here this evening?" Mr. Blossburg, somewhat abashed at the sheriff's question, hesitated and then replied, "Mr. Green and I discussed going to you for protection but, upon consideration we realized that we did not have evidence against any one person sufficient to justify your making an arrest. We also had to realize that I am a Jew and Mr. Green is a Yankee and that we do not have the same standing as the natives. In my case, I know there is one at least who would like for me to be driven out of Landsee." The sheriff said, "You are both citizens of this county, good citizens, and are entitled to as much protection as any other good citizen," and slamming his leg against the floor as if to knock a hole in it, he continued, "and, so help me God, you shall receive it."

Dr. Alston said, "Mr. Blossburg, you stated that you and Mr. Green had agreed on taking joint action in an effort to protect your families. Would you object to telling us what that action is to be?" Mr. Blossburg said, "I suppose it is in order to advise you what we have agreed to do. I hope you gentlemen will not consider us cowards. If only Mr. Green and I were threatened we would defy 'Hell's Riflemen' and risk the consequences. But when your daughter is jeopardized you dare not take the risk. May I tell you of an incident about which Mr. Green said happened a few days ago? One of the men of Snake Creek Beat came to his shop when there was no one present except Jim Jones. As the man did not want any work done, he was sure the man came only to talk to Jim, knowing Jim would repeat the conversation to him. This man asked Jim if he was not afraid not to do whatever 'Hell's Riflemen' told him to do. Jim said he answered that he did not know. The man said, 'Well, you and these whites in Landsee had better be afraid to refuse to do as they say for they are now organized to compel you to do whatever they tell you to do.'

"Then he told Jim that they never killed except when no other method worked. Their leader told them about one man who defied them so they abducted his sixteen year old daughter who had beautiful hair. They shaved the girl's head, cut her skirt off just below her stride and returned her home with the message that, if necessary to compel him to do what they demanded, she would suffer much worse treatment next time. You realize this was a threat to do something as outrageous to Ellen and Sarah. They are ruthless and we cannot risk our daughters being subjected to such humiliating treatment.

"There is another condition that influenced us to agree to meet their demand that we leave Landsee. You are aware that there has existed for several weeks a rumor that 'Hell's Riflemen' were going to raid Landsee and burn such buildings as Landsee Mansion and the Institute. That has taken on stronger life during the last week among the students at the Institute.

Some of the students are repeatedly saying in the hearing of Ellen or Sarah, that there had never been any threat of trouble between the people of Snake Creek Beat and the citizens of Landsee until that Jew and that Yankee moved here and that if they would leave there would be no trouble. It is their opinion this statement is purposely made in their hearing. You can realize the distress they suffer knowing this charge is being constantly discussed by the young people with whom they associate each day. Under the circumstances, Mr. Green and I have decided to leave Landsee and to advise 'Hell's Riflemen' of our decision." The sheriff hit the floor so hard with his peg leg that he apologized for his action.

Dr. Alston said, "You said you were going to advise 'Hell's Riflemen' that you were leaving Landsee. How were you going to communicate with that organization?" Mr. Blossburg looked at Mr. Green as if asking him to reply. Mr. Green said, "Every Friday, which is tomorrow, all the students at the Institute are assembled for notices, announcements and some type of program. We have prepared a statement which Ellen will read to the students tomorrow. There are two students who will be present at this assembly who live in Snake Creek Beat and who will be going home after school to spend the weekend. One of these students is the son of the storekeeper at Pine Tree. We think they will spread the news. If we do not hear from them, we will write to 'Citizen' at Pine Tree advising them of our decision."

The sheriff said, "I am afraid of your having a statement of that nature read. It will put 'Hell's Riflemen' on notice that we are advised of their plans and give them an advantage they do not now have." Mr. Green said, "The statement we have prepared was without any knowledge that you had information about their plans. It is based solely on the current rumors which we say we do not believe but, because some do think they are true and are causing great anxiety on the part of many, we have decided to move to some other community. We will be glad for the Chaplain to read the statement and if he thinks it even intimates we have knowledge of 'Hell's Riflemen's' plans, we will modify it."

The sheriff said, "Perhaps the statement will not hurt but it must be understood here and now that I do not favor your making any concession to this lawless group and I do not favor your leaving Landsee under these threats. It means no one can live in Landsee without their consent. Frankly, I think Syd Simmons is going to have them make the raid because he has made his plans to do so, and because he thinks it will create so much fear of them that Landsee will be at their mercy. While I regret you fear your daughters might be made to suffer more than they have, we must meet their criminal activities sooner or later by rebuffing their challenges. I welcome this proposed raid as a good opportunity to stop them for all time. So you read your notice but we will prepare for their coming. And I will be prepared to use whatever force is necessary to stop them. Now, let us discuss plans to repulse this raid."

Dr. Alston said, "Ben, all of us have had something to say except you and the Chaplain. What do you think of the situation?" Mr. Davidson replied, "I did not know you had definite information of the plans of 'Hell's Riflemen.' This is fortunate. It will enable us to prepare to protect ourselves. I did know about the persecution of Ellen and Sarah. My son has told me that under the leadership of Ina certain students are accusing Mr. Blossburg and Mr. Green of causing all the threats of 'Hell's Riflemen' and saying they should leave Landsee. You know she is encouraged to do this by Lon, who has never abandoned his effort to compel Mr. Blossburg to leave Landsee and thus eliminate his competition. John says they are making certain that Sarah and Ellen hear their comments. He wanted to know if we could not stop them. It occurs to me that this raid might give us an opportunity to check, not only the rumor that we are at the mercy of 'Hell's Riflemen' but also to clean out that gang of thieves and murderers. I volunteer to stand guard and shoot the first one who enters this community on their raid. The sheriff is right; we must not yield them another inch."

Dr. Alston then asked the Chaplain if he would comment. The Chaplain said, "Some of us have seen for some time that some drastic action was necessary to stop this organization. We have endeavored to conciliate them by agreeing to demands that we knew were extortion and that has failed. Of course, we cannot fail to use every lawful means to protect our citizens and our property. I have written some letters trying to find out who Syd Simmons is. He is the leader and if we could get rid of him I think we could control the situation. So far I have not been able to secure any information that would justify his arrest. I would like for us to make one other effort to stop the raid without bloodshed, for I am sure there will be bloodshed if we have to resort to force. Aunt Mymee told me she had told Dr. Alston that she had a plan that would defeat them. It is strange. Although Aunt Mymee seldom leaves her home, she seems to know everything that is happening. Maybe we had better hear from Dr. Alston about Aunt Mymee's plan."

Aunt Mymee's Plan

Dr. Alston said, "I hesitated to mention what Aunt Mymee proposed because it sounds so fantastic and dramatic. However, you would not expect one as matter-of-fact as Aunt Mymee to suggest an impractical plan. And when you seriously analyze it, you find it is based on sound reasoning. Its success depends largely on its execution. Aunt Mymee is confident she can have it effectively executed.

"In each of our minds there lurks a certain amount of superstition and fear of some unseen force of which we are ignorant, deny it as we will. You know people who declare it is ridiculous to give any credence to the old superstition that it will bring bad luck to walk under a ladder are extremely careful to avoid walking under one. Whether we acknowledge it or realize it, this wondering about supernatural powers is what causes you and me to attend Aunt Mymee's recital of the Legend of Landsee. It is common knowledge that the more ignorant a people are, the more readily they believe in ghosts, sorcery, voodooism, enchantment and the like.

"Aunt Mymee says that nearly all the residents of Snake Creek Beat have attended her recitals of the Legend of Landsee every time she gave it. She has had reports that convinced her that they accepted the story as true in every detail. She says this is not surprising because only a few of them can write. The Indian basket makers have told her of their fear of the ghostly inmates of vacant Landsee Mansion and that they fear they might be present when the ghostly rider rushes away from the

Mansion bringing death in his wake. She proposes to capitalize on this fear.

"Aunt Mymee will send the basket makers through Snake Creek Beat to call at every house ostensibly to sell their wares, but at each house they will mention the fact that Aunt Mymee has said the Phantom Horseman is to ride on a certain night. This will be the night 'Hell's Riflemen' plan to make the raid. She will also get Jake to visit his relatives and talk about the citizens of Landsee arranging to remain at home that night to avoid the Phantom Horseman. She says Miss Essie has a friend who lives in Snake Creek Beat who comes to Landsee every Saturday. She thinks the husband of this woman belongs to 'Hell's Riflemen' although this woman is opposed to their unlawful activities. This woman is quite a talker. When she comes to Landsee next Saturday, Miss Essie is going to have her see Aunt Mymee and get Aunt Mymee to tell her fortune. Aunt Mymee says she knows enough to convince this woman that she can tell the future happenings and she will tell her of the Phantom Horseman riding and that great injury is coming to anyone who sees him in the night as he streaks through the village. She is sure that by these methods the clan will be afraid to come to Landsee and that if they do, it will be because Syd Simmons compels them to do so.

"If this does not stop 'Hell's Riflemen,' it will serve to create the atmosphere necessary to the second phase of her plan which is to stage a ride by a Phantom Horseman. As you know, about three-quarters of a mile from Landsee on the road 'Hell's Riflemen' will travel to come to Landsee is a stretch of road from which Landsee Mansion can be clearly seen. From this place she proposed to have a lookout who will signal a party in the Mansion of the approach of 'Hell's Riflemen.' This signal will also give the number of men in 'Hell's Riflemen' for the information of the sheriff's posse. When this signal is given, the lights in all the windows of Landsee Mansion will blaze as this is supposed to happen when the Phantom Horseman takes his last and deadly ride. Aunt Mymee had always emphasized in giving the legend that when the Phantom Horseman made this last mad ride, there would be a light in every window of Landsee Mansion. Until that time the windows would be dark except for the reflected moonlight from the window panes.

"Jake Wilson will be stationed on the road and, as soon as he sees the signal, he will run to meet the clan, loudly calling who he is and shouting for them to run, for the windows of Landsee Mansion are alight and the Phantom Horseman is going to ride. I am to furnish a liquid which she calls 'high life' which causes intense pain when applied to a hairy surface. Under the cover of night, as he runs through the ranks of 'Hell's Riflemen,' Jake will squirt some of this liquid on their horses and this will cause the horses to become unruly. She insists that she organize and execute the plan without 'Hell's Riflemen' being fore-warned of it. She about convinced me it was worth trying."

The Chaplain said, "Any plan that might prevent blood-shed is worth trying. I favor telling Aunt Mymee to proceed with her plans unless the sheriff objects." The sheriff said, "I do not think it will deter Syd Simmons but it may cause confusion with the others. I do not think it will interfere with our defense, so tell her to go ahead. We will prepare to handle the situation if they do not turn back in fear of meeting the Phantom Horse-man. I will need good men to help handle this raid."

The Chaplain said, "Perhaps I have a suggestion that might have some value with reference to the personnel of your posse. Those of you here know that Mr. Blossburg is a Mason. Our lodge meets day after tomorrow. At that meeting I am going to advise our members of the situation confronting Mr. Blossburg and am asking Mr. Blossburg to attend that meeting. I am going to ask their aid in protecting Landsee from these outlaws. As you are a Mason, Mr. Sheriff, you know the character of the men who constitute that lodge and you know that you can depend on them. I suggest you attend the meeting and organize your posse from them." The sheriff said, "That is a good sug-gestion and I will meet with the lodge Saturday." The sheriff then turned to Dr. Alston and said, "Doctor, it looks as if you will have to lodge me Friday night as well as tonight. It would be foolish for me to ride home tomorrow and then get up early Saturday morning in time to ride back to Landsee for the Masonic meeting. Anyway, I wish to attend the assembly of students when Ellen reads her statement to them. Also, I want to ride around the community and see if I remember all its roads and byways." Dr. Alston said, "You know I will be glad to have you. I will be out tomorrow on calls. You make yourself at home."

Mr. Green said, "Mr. Sheriff, you said you wanted to be present when Ellen reads the statement to the student assembly. You do not expect any trouble there, do you?" The sheriff replied, "Oh no, I am interested in the student reaction and I might make a good citizen's pep talk while there, if the principal will permit."

Mr. Green said, "I know that sounded like a foolish question, but I am so apprehensive that some hurt might come to her and I feel so helpless to prevent it that I perhaps cannot think and act normally."

Ellen's Statement

The Institute was the center for the distribution of news and rumor. At the student assembly an announcement of interest would be made and the students would repeat it at home. And sometimes a student would report some rumor and this rumor would be repeated at home and soon the rumor would grow into something almost foreign to its origin. In Pope's "Temple of Fame" is this true and vivid description of rumor:

"The flying rumours gathered
    as they roll'd;
Scarce any tale was sooner
    heard than told,
And all who told it added
    something new,
And all who heard it, made
    enlargements too;
In every ear it spread, on
    every tongue it grew."

So it was with the rumor about "Hell's Riflemen." First, it was a surmise that they would stop anyone from hunting or grazing cattle in Snake Creek Beat. Then they were going to burn Mr. Blossburg's store. Then they were going to burn Landsee Mansion. Then they were going to sack the entire village. This rumor mill was abetted by Syd Simmons as a part of his war of nerves to keep the people afraid not to meet "Hell's

Riflemen's" demands. It was because this method had not produced the results he anticipated he planned the raid to run Mr. Blossburg and Mr. Green away. He knew he had Lon Williamson's good wishes in freeing him from Mr. Blossburg's competition that was reducing his business every day. By having some of his henchmen suggest to Mr. Williamson that, if Mr. Blossburg and Mr. Green would leave Landsee there would be no trouble, he was certain that Mr. Williamson and Ina would peddle the idea vigorously. And they did, with Mr. Williamson making the argument at the store and Ina at school. It was this bombardment of malicious slander that made many of the unsuspecting who did not take time to learn the facts believe that the Jew and Yankee were to blame for all the trouble "Hell's Riflemen" were causing. Sarah and Ellen were the chief sufferers and their parents thought they were endangered. This was what made them decide to leave Landsee.

At the assembly of the students on Friday, after several announcements relative to school work, the principal of the Institute who was presiding said, "Ellen Green has requested permission to read a statement. Ellen, you may come and read your statement now." Ellen went to the stage and as she turned to face the audience, she saw the sheriff enter and ease himself into a seat in the rear of the auditorium. Because Ellen always had so much poise when speaking to the students, the students were aware that today she was having difficulty in controlling her emotions. Ellen thanked the principal for giving her permission to read the statement and turning to the audience she said, "The statement I am about to read has been prepared by my father and Sarah Blossburg's father and signed by them. It is being read to you students with the request that each of you advise your parents of the offer our fathers are making in an effort to prevent 'Hell's Riflemen' from giving Landsee any trouble." She then read as follows:

"This statement has been prepared and signed by Isaac Blossburg and Charles Green and is for the purpose of giving public notice to the fact that we are willing to leave Landsee if it will avert any trouble with those people living in Snake Creek Beat who are organized under the name of 'Hell's Riflemen.' We are all aware that there has been rumor after rumor that 'Hell's Riflemen' were going to perpetrate some serious damage to

Landsee. To that rumor has been added the statement that our families caused this trouble and if we would leave, that would end the threat. We know that we have not been guilty of any act justifying this charge against us. However, there is no way for us to stop this surreptitious slander and many good people are led to believe it is true. Some have intentionally made this charge against us in the hearing of our daughters to let them know they are not wanted. This cruel conduct has hurt them greatly. Under such circumstances, we are arranging to sell our businesses and move to some distant place. Signed."

Ellen said, "That concludes the statement I was to read. Sarah and I wish to express our appreciation to those of you who have been kind and considerate of us. We will always remember and treasure your friendship. Thank you."

When Ellen started to leave the stage, the sheriff stood and held up his hand to attract the principal's attention. The principal said, "I see we have the sheriff of the county with us. Mr. Sheriff, do you wish to speak to the students?" The sheriff answered, "Yes, I have an important statement to make." The principal responded, "Please come to the stage where all the students can see and hear you." The sheriff stumped his way to the stage. Thanking the principal for granting him the privilege to speak, he turned to the students and said:

"Young men and young ladies, please listen to what I have to say. I speak as the chief law enforcement officer of your county and I speak for the welfare of Landsee. Yesterday I was present at a meeting of several good citizens. Mr. Blossburg and Mr. Green were at that meeting. They told us that they had decided to leave Landsee rather than have a number of the good citizens think they were the cause of the threat of 'Hell's Riflemen.' They said if the threat of danger was to each of them individually, they would remain, but as it involved the community, and because some of you students were making their daughters' lives miserable by repeatedly stating in their hearing, and with the intention of them hearing, that there had never been any trouble with people in Snake Creek Beat until that Jew and Yankee came here, and that there would be no trouble if they would leave, that they decided to make the financial sacrifice and move. It was then I learned that Ellen Green was to read this offer. I came to hear her and to talk to you about it and the conduct of those students charging them with prospective trouble with 'Hell's Riflemen.' First, I told Mr. Blossburg and Mr. Green I was opposed to their making this offer and I opposed their leaving Landsee because of this false charge that they were to blame for the threatened trouble. I called attention to the fact that if they could require them to leave Landsee, they could require others like the Chaplain, the principal of the Institute, and even Miss Essie, to leave. While I understand that Mr. Lon Williamson feels safe from any harm being done him by this lawless gang, the day they decided he would not obey them, his store would be closed. Every good citizen I have talked with this morning, and I have talked to quite a number, agree that we should oppose Mr. Blossburg's and Mr. Green's leaving to meet the wishes of 'Hell's Riflemen.' And I hereby serve notice that all the powers of the Sheriff's Office will be used to protect them.

"Now I want to comment on the charge some of the students are making that there was no trouble with any of the people of Snake Creek Beat until Mr. Blossburg and Mr. Green came to Landsee, and that there would be no trouble if they would move away. That charge is absolutely false. Those who make it are either very ignorant or very malicious. There is a student in this audience whose father was assassinated while in the line of duty as a deputy sheriff in Snake Creek Beat. The murderer has never been apprehended because of the protection given the criminal by the lawless element of that Beat. This was before Mr. Blossburg and Mr. Green came to Landsee. There is another student here whose home was fired upon by a rifleman who left a note warning him not to press a suit against one of this gang. This was before Mr. Blossburg and Mr. Green came to Landsee. For several years prior to Mr. Blossburg's and Mr. Green's coming to this community, Snake Creek Beat was considered unsafe for property and life. We have investigated and have found that neither Mr. Green nor Mr. Blossburg have been guilty of any act that would contribute to the hostility of 'Hell's Riflemen' toward Landsee. These facts are sufficient to remind you that whoever states that there was no trouble with Snake Creek Beat before Mr. Blossburg and Mr. Green came, is making a false statement.

"There is a law making slander a crime punishable by both

fine and imprisonment. Slander is making a false statement damaging to the reputation of another person. Those who have been repeating this rumor defamatory of Mr. Blossburg and Mr. Green are guilty of this crime. I have sufficient evidence to have indicted and convicted some of the students in this audience. The prosecuting attorney has advised me not to report the facts to the grand jury for indictment because of the youth of the defendants. However, if this crime is repeated after this warning, the offenders will be prosecuted. Rest assured I will see that such offenders are prosecuted for I have an antipathy for any person who deliberately hurts an innocent party. So I warn you not to repeat the lie." He left the stage and walked out of the auditorium. The principal waited until he had left the auditorium and then he said, "You will stand and I will dismiss you with a prayer."

After the students were dismissed, they moved rather quickly back to their desks. It was noticeable that Ina's close associates moved away from her as if she were contaminated. But Ina was defiant and to the two or three at her side she said, "The sheriff seems to think he is a great power. Just wait and see what my father does to him." She was convinced that her father was the controlling power.

When the students left the auditorium, Sarah and Ellen remained seated. The principal came toward them and Sarah asked to speak to him. She said that she and Ellen did not have any more lessons during the day and they would appreciate his allowing them to go home. He thought a moment and said, "Yes, tell your classroom teacher I have excused you two for the remainder of the day."

The next day, Saturday, the sheriff attended the meeting of the Masons. The meeting was secret and the outsiders did not know what took place. The only comment heard about the meeting was that it lasted about twice as long as it usually did and that it was well attended. It was evidently decided not to have Mr. Blossburg attend as he was seen at his store during the time the lodge was in session.

The Raid

From all external appearances Thursday was a normal, slow moving, middle-of-the-week day. The sheriff had let only a few know that "Hell's Riflemen" planned to stage their raid that night. The sheriff had known of their plan for over a week which gave him sufficient time to notify all the Masons who had volunteered to act as deputies to aid him in protecting Mr. Blossburg and Mr. Green from "Hell's Riflemen."

Every day for over a week "Hell's Riflemen" had one of their men in Landsee to find out whether anyone suspected their raid and whether any preparation was being made to oppose them. These men would always purchase some article to give the impression that they had come to Landsee for that purpose. Their real purpose was known to the sheriff, and Mr. Ben Davidson and Mr. Henry May kept them under constant surveillance. They found they would leave late in the afternoon as if to go home and then return after dark and quietly ride around the village until almost midnight. They spent much of their time during the day at Lon Williamson's store listening to people talk and talking to the visitors at the store. Mr. May and Mr. Davidson made it convenient to apparently accidentally run into them and work their conversation around to the rumor that "Hell's Riflemen" were going to raid Landsee. They would always assure these scouts that only a few thought there was any probability of such an event and that they gave no credence to the rumor whatever. Invariably, they would ask what the sheriff meant when he told the students at the Institute he would protect Mr. Blossburg and Mr. Green from "Hell's Riflemen." Mr. May and Mr. Davidson would answer that they thought the sheriff did not consider that there was any likelihood of any raid and was endeavoring to reassure the citizens. The sheriff had not been seen in Landsee since that particular trip, which indicated that he was not preparing for any expected trouble.

The sheriff had a report about noon Thursday when he arrived at Landsee that disclosed how well his and Aunt Mymee's preparations had been kept secret. The information scouts of "Hell's Riflemen" had unanimously reported that there was no evidence of any preparation to oppose the raid, according to them. They also said that the sheriff did not think there was any probability of a raid and that his speech to the students at the Institute was to allay the apprehension of the few who feared there would be a raid. They also reported that those who believed there might be a raid were complaining that the sheriff was not doing one thing to protect them.

It was revealed at the meeting of "Hell's Riflemen" that Aunt Mymee's propaganda that the Phantom Horseman would ride that week disconcerted some of the more superstitious members of the organization and these sought to postpone the raid. One member agreed that the sheriff did not generally make statements that he did not support so they should know what he was doing at the county seat. Another said frankly he was afraid of the ride of the Phantom Horseman and favored postponing the raid until the time Aunt Mymee said he would ride had passed. Others agreed that the raid should be postponed.

Syd Simmons told them there would be no delay of their plans. They were ready and the moon would furnish the light they needed. He ridiculed them for believing there was such a thing as the Phantom Horseman and said he would ride at the head of the raiders and personally meet the Phantom Horseman first and destroy him. He said he welcomed meeting the sheriff as it would give him an opportunity to show Landsee that the lawman was not able to protect them against the demands of "Hell's Riflemen."

Although all the residents of Landsee, except those secretly involved in preparations to thwart "Hell's Riflemen," were convinced that nothing was being done to prevent the raid, the fact was that the sheriff and Aunt Mymee, who had coordinated their proposed activities, could not have been more energetic in perfecting their methods designed to prevent this lawlessness. At the meeting of the Masons the sheriff had secured the personnel for his posse and given them instructions. Those of us who worked with Aunt Mymee found her to be an exacting taskmaster. She was so determined that her plan should be perfectly performed that she repeatedly drilled each one of us participating in it until he understood exactly what he was to do, when he was to do it, and how it was to be done. John, Ben, Ooden and I were assigned the task of watching for the signal advising the approach of "Hell's Riflemen" and of seeing that the windows of Landsee Mansion were alight at the proper time. Ooden, who believed that Landsee Mansion was haunted, insisted that someone else be given his part, but Aunt Mymee assured him he would not be harmed and made him retain his part on her program. I have often thought that it was because Aunt Mymee was fond of Ooden and thought he would be safe in Landsee Mansion during the raid. The rest of us sympathized with Ooden. Although we did not express any hesitancy in having to be in that long abandoned and musty smelling old house, we did not enjoy it.

Ben and I were assigned the two front rooms upstairs and John and Ooden were given the two front rooms on the first floor. It was the front rooms of Landsee Mansion that "Hell's Riflemen" would see from the high section of the road on which they were expected to approach the village. In spite of the fact that I constantly reassured myself that the Mansion was not the abode of unseen spirits, I could not help having an uncomfortable feeling every time Aunt Mymee took us to the Mansion to practice our parts. After she was sure we would perform our assignments properly, she said, "You do fine in the daylight but we must be sure you will do as well in the dark. In the dark, familiar objects often appear different from what they do in daylight. So we will come back tonight for another rehearsal. Your lanterns will be lit so that you can immediately flash their lights out the windows when the signal comes. Until the signal comes, they will be covered to prevent anyone from knowing someone is in the rooms of the Mansion. We will go over our parts tonight under the exact conditions you will work tomorrow night."

When Aunt Mymee opened the door that night for us to enter, the open door looked like a big black hole even though considerable light was entering it from the moon. Ooden was more nervous than ever. His eyes looked like the proverbial big white saucers shining in his dark face. I was not free from all nervousness for the night gave the place a more uncanny appearance than it had in the day. When I was entering the front door just behind Ooden, he suddenly turned as if to run out. I involuntarily put up my arms to prevent his leaving. As I threw my arms up, I looked just beyond Ooden into the hall of the house and momentarily I all but left with him before I controlled myself. My imagination must have been running wild. For an instant I thought that in the dim light of the moon's rays I saw a tall man with his hat on, standing a few feet inside ready to bar our entrance. A calmer look disclosed it was a man's hat hanging on an old hat rack. Perhaps it had been there every day we had entered the house, but I had not noticed it before and apparently neither had Ooden.

The jittery feeling of this experience was not easily put out of mind in the gruesome surroundings created by the stillness of the house and the semi-darkness that encompassed us. It was perhaps that feeling when I went to the upstairs floor that made me think that I saw the door to the attic stairs ease cautiously open. This made me wonder if someone was stealthily peering through the slight opening to see who was trespassing on his private preserve. This was our last practice and Aunt Mymee was satisfied and we were glad.

There was nothing during Thursday morning to indicate to the public it was the calm before a perilous storm. Early in the afternoon, unnoticed, the Chaplain escorted Jim Jones and his family to the Chaplain's home. A guard was to be placed at the house where Jim Jones lived, but it was decided it would be safer for them to move to the Chaplain's residence. The Chaplain said he did not think "Hell's Riflemen" would attack his home even if they passed the sheriff. The Chaplain also invited Mr. Blossburg and his family and Mr. Green and his family to come to his home until the raid was over. Mr. Green said he could not move his wife and Ellen would not leave them, although Mr. and Mrs. Green made an effort to persuade her to go to the Chaplain's home. Mr. Blossburg said he did not think it right to increase the danger to the Chaplain as their presence in his home would. Early in the afternoon the sheriff and his chief deputy came riding into Landsee but this was not so unusual as to attract attention.

It was late afternoon before it became generally known that trouble was anticipated that night. During the last school period, the principal called all the students to assemble in the auditorium. The calling of an assembly at that hour excited considerable curiosity. When the students were assembled they saw the sheriff sitting on the stage. The principal said, "The sheriff requested me to assemble you in order that he may make an important announcement. Mr. Sheriff, you may speak."

The sheriff stood and said, "I requested the principal to assemble you so that I might give you some important information and request you to communicate this information to all your homefolks as soon as you can. We have reliable information that 'Hell's Riflemen' will attempt a raid on Landsee tonight. They state that the primary purpose of this raid is to kidnap Mr. Green, Mr. Blossburg and Jim Jones. They intend to demand that they leave Landsee and they will treat them so cruelly that they will be afraid of what might happen to their families if they remain. While their declared purpose is to attack the parties I have mentioned, it stands to reason that anyone they think is in their way will be in danger of serious injury.

"My deputies and I are here to use every force at our command to prevent this outrage. There is a possibility there will be the use of firearms on both sides. Anyone about might be hit by a stray bullet. Also, if you were mistaken for the wrong person, you might be intentionally shot. I am asking all good people to be at home by dark and remain at home until they know it is safe to leave. Please take this message home. Thank you." He took his seat. The principal then said, "It is certainly important that you advise your parents of the sheriff's message as soon as you can and we should all heed his advice. You are dismissed for the day."

An hour before sundown there came riding into Landsee from every direction determined looking men, each with his rifle. Each one rode through the village without speaking to anyone. They rode to the Masonic Lodge where the sheriff had his headquarters. Each one dismounted, tethered his horse, then took his rifle and reported to the sheriff. They appeared as if they were in uniform as the sheriff had advised all of them to wear dark clothes so that they would be less conspicuous in the night.

Lon Williamson, Jr., went straight from the Institute to his father's store and told him what the sheriff had said. Mr. Williamson told his son, "I am surprised the principal let the sheriff make such a fool talk to the students." After receiving his son's information Mr. Williamson began to notice that men were riding by his store with their rifles and he soon realized that an armed posse was being formed. He still thought of himself as the person that should govern any civic activity of Landsee. He went to the Masonic Lodge, rushed to the sheriff and shouted, "What is the meaning of all these armed men?" The sheriff replied, "To protect the citizens of Landsee in the event 'Hell's Riflemen' attempt to raid tonight." "I demand to know," said Mr. Williamson, "why I was not consulted before a fool thing like this was done."

Mr. Williamson had not noticed that Mr. Ben Davidson was one of the armed men. It not only surprised him when Mr. Davidson stepped out of the group of men and faced him, but it also reduced his pomposity very noticeably. Mr. Davidson said, "We all know your attitude toward Mr. Blossburg. We even suspected you would welcome his being compelled to leave Landsee because of the violent unlawful acts of 'Hell's Riflemen.' Our suspicion was confirmed by your own words this afternoon. My son was in your store when Lon, Jr., told you what the sheriff said to the students at the Institute and heard you say that if 'Hell's Riflemen' ran Mr. Blossburg out of Landsee, it would be a good riddance of bad rubbish. Because of your sympathy with the purposes of 'Hell's Riflemen,' we advised the sheriff to keep you in ignorance of his effort to protect us. Now go home and remain where it will be safe."

Mr. Williamson retorted in a rather haughty tone, "Ben, neither you nor the sheriff can tell me what to do. All this posse is foolishness. Just to illustrate how foolish your High Sheriff has been, I call your attention to the fact that there were three students at the Institute who live in Snake Creek Beat who heard the sheriff's statement and these students will tell their parents of the sheriff's speech. 'Hell's Riflemen' will then be advised that the sheriff will attempt to frustrate them and they will be ready to make all this armed show look ridiculous. By the way, if you find that 'Hell's Riflemen' are coming, let me know and I will ride out to meet them and ask them not to hurt any of you." With a wave of the hand and a sweeping bow to the men and a smirking smile as if he had scored a great point, he turned and walked away.

One of the men asked the sheriff about Snake Creek students giving word to "Hell's Riflemen." The sheriff said, "Yes, I knew there were three students at the Institute whose families lived in Snake Creek Beat. The families of all three are fine people and not in sympathy with 'Hell's Riflemen.' Anyway, they would not be able to get back home in time to permit 'Hell's Riflemen' to change their plans."

When Mr. Williamson was out of hearing the sheriff instructed one of the men to keep him under surveilance. He said, "I think he is harmless, but a person who has such an exaggerated estimate of his own importance and superiority will sometimes do very unexpected and idiotic things. It is best to know what he is doing."

At dusk the sheriff began placing his men at their posts. Guards were placed on every road and trail entering Landsee. The sheriff, his trusted chief deputy, and two others selected by the sheriff took the guard position on the road he was sure "Hell's Riflemen" would have to travel from Snake Creek Beat to Landsee. He left several men under the direction of Ben Davidson as a reserve stationed where they could quickly reach any guard who needed them.

Jake Wilson, who was to call "Hell's Riflemen's" attention to the lights in Landsee Mansion and warn them that the Phantom Horseman was going to ride, was to be at a place on the road near where Elvin Jackson was stationed to give the signal that "Hell's Riflemen" were approaching. It was hoped that Jake could stop "Hell's Riflemen" before they reached the sheriff. The position of the sheriff and his men was four or five hundred yards nearer Landsee than was Jake's post. It was learned afterwards that when the sheriff was at his post he told those with him that, while Jake Wilson had assured him that he run no danger in acting the part assigned to him as all of "Hell's

Riflemen," including Syd Simmons, knew him personally, he did not feel right leaving Jake unprotected and for them to remain where they were and he would move nearer Jake. In commenting on this action of the sheriff, the Chaplain said it was just like the sheriff to arrange to be the first and perhaps the only one to be exposed to the danger of the clash with "Hell's Riflemen."

At dusk Aunt Mymee saw that all of her personnel were in their places. Elvin Jackson was at his signal point; Jake Wilson was at his post to warn of the riding of the Phantom Horseman and Aunt Mymee accompanied those of us assigned to Landsee Mansion, sent each of us to his assigned place and then took a seat near Ooden. Then came the waiting.

If you wish to experience the sensation of feeling that you had waited many long tedious hours within a period of a few minutes, then try waiting for the probable happening of a momentous event that might be fraught with the danger of destructive violence, and which, if it happened, would charge you with the responsibility of the immediate discharge of an important duty, and when you did not know that if it did happen, at exactly what time it would occur. Under such conditions time plods along with leaden feet while you pray that it will take the wings of a bird and swiftly fly. Under such conditions mental stress tightens your nerves until they are like the strings of a well-tuned violin. It was under such conditions we waited at our posts in Landsee Mansion, listening for the sound of the hooves of the horses striking the road surface as "Hell's Riflemen" rode toward Landsee, and watching for the signal from Elvin Jackson warning that they were coming. So we listened, and we watched, and we waited.

It was almost dark inside the rooms in which we were. We were not allowed to uncover the lighted lanterns nor to open the window shutters until it was time to shine the light out of the windows. Only a little of the moonlight filtered through the slightly opened louvers of the window shutters. We were under too much of a nervous strain even to whisper to each other. The stillness within was oppressive. In the hush that surrounded us, we could hear ourselves breathe and our hearts were like drum beats. Perhaps it was fortunate we heard no sound within the Mansion for our minds were so steeped with Aunt Mymee's insistence that Landsee Mansion was haunted that our imagination would probably have made us think that the noise of a mouse scurrying across the floor was the trailing of the robes of some unseen spirit. All we could do was to listen, to watch and to wait.

As the plateau on which Landsee Mansion was built was much higher than the surrounding grounds, our upstairs windows served as an excellent lookout from which we had a view of almost the entire village. The full moon in a cloudless sky made it possible to distinguish many objects and the movement of men and animals. Through the partly open louvers of the window shutters we scanned the entire panorama within the scope of our view for some telling activity. Once I thought I saw a glint of light reflected from a steel rifle barrel but if it were, the shadows concealed its bearer. No one moved along the roads. As we watched, slowly one by one the lights went out in the various residences of the village. Only the lights in the home of Mr. Lon Williamson remained undimmed. The sheriff had said that in all probability "Hell's Riflemen" would wait until the time for the people to be in bed and asleep before entering the village. In the country, people retired early because they had arisen before sun up and were fatigued from hard manual labor. To us, the village appeared at rest for the night, except we who listened and watched and waited.

From a copse of willows in a far away valley to our left we could hear faintly a screech owl continuously crying its distressing call. It seemed more tremulous and more agnoizing than ever before. Its call always made cold chills creep up my backbone. That night the chills were colder than ever before. Somewhere there was a deep-throated hound howling as if he were suffering some unbearable pain or mourning some inconsolable sadness. In contrast to these melancholy sounds was the beautiful bright moon which gave the entire landscape a soft and peaceful tint, and enabled us to see the graceful movement of the boughs of the trees as they swayed in the evening breeze. Still we listened, and we watched, and we waited.

Although we had been waiting and looking for hours for Elvin's signal of the approach of "Hell's Riflemen," we were startled when suddenly we saw his light flash out of the attic window of the house where he was stationed. It galvanized us into immediate action. We threw open the window shutters, uncovered our already lighted lanterns and instantly the windows of Landsee Mansion were ablaze. While it was expected that the sheriff and Mr. Davidson would understand that "Hell's Riflemen" were approaching when they saw the lights in the windows of Landsee Mansion, we heard leave the two messengers John was to send to advise them of the number of "Hell's Riflemen." For a moment we saw a shadowy movement. It was Mr. Davidson and his men on a run to reach the sheriff and support him if necessary.

It was understood that Elvin's signal would be given before "Hell's Riflemen" had reached the elevated section of the road from which there was a full view of Landsee Mansion. They were to reach this point in about three minutes after he had given the signal. In about this length of time through the stillness of the night we heard Jake Wilson as he rushed out to meet "Hell's Riflemen," crying in a loud frightened voice, "This is Jake Wilson. This is Jake Wilson. Look! Look! The windows of Landsee Mansion are lighted. The Phantom Horseman will ride! The Phantom Horseman will ride!! Flee for your lives!"

From Jake, Elvin and the chief deputy, we afterwards learned what happened. Jake had passed Syd Simmons when he called, "Shut that boy's mouth. He will wake the entire village." Syd Simmons had not noticed that all his men had stopped and were looking at Landsee Mansion as he continued onward. He was about three hundred feet ahead of his men when the sheriff called to him to halt. It was in that instant that two men who had never before seen each other, saw and recognized each other. And each understood it was a fatal meeting which would probably result in the death of one of them. Syd Simmons knew if he were taken into custody by the sheriff that his identity would soon be discovered and he would be executed for past murders for which he had been convicted. The sheriff surmised this was the situation and expected him to resist arrest.

Simmons recognized the sheriff by his peg leg. The sheriff was confident he recognized Syd Simmons because he knew the people who had lived in Snake Creek Beat for a few years and this man was a stranger to him. He also knew he was to lead the men in the raid and he had had described to him the cavalier manner in which he rode his fine horse. Syd Simmons, who always arrogantly asserted that he always shot first and never missed his mark, was already raising his rifle when the sheriff commanded him to halt. There was the crack of two rifles so closely together that many thought only one rifle had been fired. Just as Syd Simmons leveled his rifle on the sheriff and pressed its trigger, his horse, evidently suffering severe pain from the liquid Jake had sprayed on him, uttered a shrill whinny and lunged forward causing Simmons' shot to miss the sheriff. But the sheriff's shot went home to its target and the lifeless body of Syd Simmons was thrown by his bucking horse to the ground.

Syd Simmons had riding next to him the man who had been the leader of "Hell's Riflemen" before he took charge. This man was thought to be the one who had assassinated the deputy sheriff in Snake Creek Beat. At the time the chief deputy reached the sheriff, this man's rifle went off and the chief deputy thought he was firing at the sheriff and shot him. The next morning found the two leaders of "Hell's Riflemen" dead. Four others who had been thrown from their horses and had received broken limbs were under arrest. The sheriff told Lon Williamson that, as he had professed being on friendly terms with some of those involved, he was deputizing him to carry the injured and dead to their homes at Snake Creek Beat and to advise them he had the names of all of "Hell's Riflemen" and that his posse would come to Snake Creek Beat in two weeks to arrest them for assault with intent to murder. If there were any intimation of resistance, they would be shot.

At first Mr. Williamson objected but Mr. Davidson reminded him that he would be doing the men a favor. Also, because they would be leaving the county, he had better arrange with them to handle their property so he could collect what was owed him. This latter suggestion caused him to consent to act as the sheriff requested. Within the two weeks, "Hell's Riflemen" had left without leaving a forwarding address.

Colonel Alvin Foster

The long arm of destiny often reaches across many miles and many years to shape the lives of men. It chooses its own means and methods to accomplish its purposes. Its choice is seldom the result of premeditated plans. Sometimes a chance acquaintance sets in motion circumstances which influence and alter the course of conduct of individuals not connected with it. So it was in the coming of Colonel Alvin Foster and his wife to Landsee.

Colonel Foster, a man of considerable wealth, had never expected to live in any other state than his beloved Vermont where he was born and raised, much less in a quiet and secluded rural village in the deep South. Although he could have escaped combat duty, he had volunteered for service in the infantry when the War between the States first began. He was wounded in one of the war's first battles and, before his wound was entirely healed, he was placed in command of a camp for prisoners of war. It was while serving in this capacity that he met the Rev. Paul Gordon, the Baptist pastor at Landsee.

While the Rev. Paul Gordon was serving as chaplain in the Confederate Army, he was captured by Federal troops when he lingered behind his retreating command to see if any wounded needed his aid. Because he had a pistol in his possession when he was captured, he was sent as a prisoner to the camp under Colonel Foster's command.

Colonel Foster, who took an active interest in persons sent to his camp, was present when the Rev. Gordon was brought to the officers charged with questioning prisoners and making a record for the prison. When he looked at him he said, "This man wears the insignia of a chaplain. I am surprised he would be taken as a prisoner." The soldier who had brought the Chaplain to the camp said, "Sir, my commanding officer considered it important that you be advised of all the circumstances of his capture and, as I was the soldier who took him into custody, he sent me with him with instructions to relate in detail the facts relating to his being taken and sent here as a prisoner of war."

Colonel Foster said, "Very well, suppose you tell us just what happened." The soldier replied, "The intelligence reports indicated that the Confederate unit which was holding that sector in front of our command was withdrawing. I was a member of a reconnaissance patrol to ascertain the enemy's position. My patrol was in an area which had been the scene of hard fighting a few hours before. I came on this man bending over a wounded soldier as if to hear what the soldier was saying. Then I saw him slip his hand into the pocket of the wounded man's jacket and withdraw from it a letter which he placed in his own pocket. As the wounded soldier was one of our command, I thought the letter should be secured and delivered to our officers. Evidently this chaplain was not aware I was covering him with my rifle. I ordered him to stand up and raise his hands, which he did. Then I asked him if he was armed. He replied there was a pistol in his knapsack but that it was not his. His knapsack was several yards from him, but I ordered him to move farther away from it so that I could recover it with less danger. There was in his knapsack this pistol."

The soldier handed to Colonel Foster an ivory handled revolver which had engraving on it. Then he continued, "I asked for the letter which I saw him take from the wounded soldier. The soldier had died and I was not able to secure any information from him. This chaplain asked if I was taking him as a prisoner and I said I was going to take him to my officers. He said that he held the letter at the request of a dying man with special instructions as to its disposition and that he would like to discuss its disposition with my officers before releasing it to anyone. I agreed to permit him to retain it until we saw my commanding officer. When I brought him to my officer and gave him these facts, he decided to send the chaplain to you for decision as to his status and the disposition of the letter."

Colonel Foster then asked, "Did you have any opportunity to talk to the wounded soldier?" The soldier replied, "He had lost consciousness by the time I was able to reach him. He died in a few minutes after I got to him. The Confederates had carried their wounded from the battlefield but this man was virtually concealed by a clustered mass of undergrowth and had been missed."

Colonel Foster asked the Chaplain if the statement of the soldier were correct. The Chaplain said, "Yes sir. If permissible I would like to make a statement giving additional facts relating to my actions." Colonel Foster gave him permission to make his statement and he gave the following account:

"There had been severe fighting when the Federal troops assaulted the position held by the Confederates. The Confederates were arranging to withdraw to a better defense position when they were attacked. When the attack came, they were ordered to counter attack and after several hours of combat the Federal troops withdrew to their former position. Then the Confederates retreated to what they considered a better defense position. This left a distance between the forces of virtually a mile. All of this no-man's land had been the battlefield.

"As was my custom, when conditions permitted, I went back over the battlefield to see if any wounded had been left that I could aid. On my way back, I met a Confederate soldier being carried on a stretcher who recognized me. I had known his family all my life. He requested the stretcher bearers to stop and permit him to talk to me.

"This soldier said he realized that he was fatally wounded and that he had a pistol given him by his father which was a family heirloom and which he wished sent to his son. He asked me to take it and send it to him. Thinking I would not encounter any enemy so soon after a withdrawal of our forces from the area, I took the pistol, unloaded it, tagged it with the name of the party to whom it was to be sent and placed it in my knapsack." Then he asked the Federal soldier who captured him if he did not find the pistol unloaded and so tagged. The soldier answered, "I did. That pistol was in the condition it is now when I found it in his knapsack."

The Chaplain continued his story, "While I was going over

the field of battle, I heard someone calling in a very feeble voice. I found this Union soldier who had evidently concealed himself in bushes. When he first saw me he said, 'You are a Confederate.' Then he added, 'But you are a chaplain and I want you to do me a favor.' He said he knew he could not live. He asked me to take a letter from his pocket and see that it was mailed to his mother to whom it was addressed. He was afraid that in handling his body with many other dead soldiers the letter might be overlooked. I had just placed the letter in my pocket when to my surprise I heard the command, 'Stand up with your hands above your head.' The soldier in charge of me has accurately stated the subsequent events. I now surrender the letter to you, Colonel, and I am certain you will see that his mother receives it." He handed the letter to Colonel Foster.

It was a large envelope on which was endorsed, "Please mail the enclosed letter in the event of my death." Colonel Foster asked the soldier if this were the letter. The soldier examined it and said it was. He had marked it when he took the Chaplain into custody so that he could be able to identify it. The envelope was sealed. Colonel Foster asked the Chaplain if he knew the contents of the envelope and the Chaplain said, "The envelope was sealed when I received it and it has not been opened." The soldier verified the fact that the envelope was sealed when taken from the wounded soldier.

Colonel Foster stated, "It is necessary to ascertain if the letter contains any military information which should not be disclosed, so I will have to read it." He opened the large envelope and found that it enclosed a letter, stamped and addressed. The envelope containing the letter was not sealed indicating that the writer knew the letter would be censored. He took the letter from the unsealed addressed envelope and read it to himself. When he finished, he hesitated a few seconds and then said, "No trust will be violated in my opinion by reading this letter to all of you and I want you to hear it." He read the letter with evident controlled emotion, which was as follows:

"Dearest of Mothers:

"If you ever receive this letter, it will be the last of things earthly for me. But rest assured that I go to Him who created all, clean and unafraid.

"It was soon after I left home that I read a passage in

the Testament sister Elsie gave me that said, 'Fear not them that kill the body' and the rest of the chapter tells why not to fear.

"If by giving my life I can help bring peace to this wartorn globe of ours, you should be willing to give me with a smile.

"Remember me to my brothers and sisters and express to them my hope that the scourge of war will never darken their lives again.

"You have always been my ideal and the strengthener of my faith.

Your affectionate son,
Ernest"*

For a few moments no one stirred or spoke. The Chaplain was looking down at his still hands that were resting on the desk. The soldier was gazing at Colonel Foster with wide, wondrous eyes, and Colonel Foster was motionless, holding the letter in the position he held it when reading it.

Finally the silence was broken by the Chaplain who said, "It reads like a benediction and message from a heavenly host to strengthen our faith."

Colonel Foster then decided he could trust the Chaplain and gave him some authority over the other prisoners. This arrangement worked so well that the Chaplain and Colonel Foster soom became friends and co-laborers in an effort to better the life of the prisoners. This friendship became so strong that for a good many years after the war ended they wrote to each other several times during the year.

*With a change of names this was an actual letter written by a sergeant killed in World War I and is being used by permission of the addressee.

The Fosters
Come To Landsee

One day the Chaplain received a long letter from Colonel Foster. In this letter Colonel Foster told the Chaplain that during the last few years his wife had constantly lost physical strength and the doctors had advised him to move to a milder climate and that perhaps it would be better to locate in a quiet rural community. The letter asked about Landsee and available property. After some correspondence, Colonel Foster and his wife decided to visit Landsee.

The Chaplain invited them to be guests in his home, but the Fosters said they expected to be in Landsee for several days and insisted on staying at whatever hotel accommodations were available. The Chaplain was requested to make reservations for them. He arranged for them to stay at Mr. May's hotel.

Any event out of the ordinary, however small, excited the interest of all the inhabitants of Landsee. Although there were always a number of people who met the passenger train each day, the village became so interested in the coming of Colonel Foster and his wife from a distant state that there was an unusually large crowd at the depot when they arrived. Miss Essie and Ellen were among those present. Ellen had become especially interested in seeing the Fosters when she learned they were from the same section of Vermont where her father and mother once lived. She asked Miss Essie to go with her. As all the people of Landsee deferred to Miss Essie, she had no trouble in stationing herself and Ellen right near where the Fosters would alight from the train.

When Mrs. Foster stepped down from the train's platform, the heel of one of her shoes caught on the last step and the shoe came off. Ellen quickly knelt, retrieved the shoe, and fitted it again on Mrs. Foster's foot. When she arose, Mrs. Foster with a smile said to Ellen in a low voice, "Thank you, dear." Ellen blushed and seemed embarrassed at what she had done.

The Chaplain had met the Fosters and, on the way with them to Mr. May's hotel, Mrs. Foster asked, "Who was that lovely young girl who helped me with my shoe?" The Chaplain said, "She is Ellen Green. Her father and mother came from your state." Mrs. Foster said, "I am going to ask you, Chaplain, to give her an invitation to have lunch one day with me at the hotel. I think I would enjoy knowing her. She is just about the age my daughter would have been if she had lived." In accordance with this request the Chaplain arranged with Ellen to have lunch with Mrs. Foster at the hotel. From this time their friendship grew with the passing of the days.

Although the Fosters lived at the hotel, the Chaplain was there nearly every day with his surrey to drive them arround the countryside. On each of these trips he would arrange for different persons to ride with them. Once he had Miss Essie, often Ellen at Mrs. Foster's request. Mr. and Mrs. Davidson accompanied them on occasions and once even Dr. Alston. When the Chaplain was away on duty, Mr. May saw that they had an opportunity to see the persons and places they wished.

The Fosters became very much interested in the Mansion of Landsee and its acreage. At their request, arrangements were made for them to inspect the premises and look over the inside of the house. They were captivated with the vastness and beauty of the view in every direction. Also, Mrs. Foster was charmed with the interior arrangement, the great chandeliers, the graceful stairs and the other details of arrangements. She said she could not think of any project that would interest her more than repairing and restoring the premises and the Mansion. As the doctors had advised Colonel Foster that Mrs. Foster needed to become actively interested in some undertaking, her evident enthusiasm in restoring the Mansion of Landsee and its grounds appealed to Colonel Foster as meeting this recommendation.

Colonel Foster asked the Chaplain, "Can this property be

bought at anything near a reasonable price?" The Chaplain replied, "It has been for sale for years. I think it can be purchased for much less than its intrinsic value." Colonel Foster then asked, "Why has it not been sold and why has it been permitted to go without proper care?" The Chaplain said he thought there were perhaps two reasons. One was that there were only a few persons able to own the property. The second and perhaps strongest reason was that the place had the reputation of being under an Indian curse and the Mansion was known as a haunted house.

"Whether or not you give any credence to such rumors, the result is that it has been impossible to secure a caretaker to live on the property and look after it. Its reputation has also prevented the securing of labor to work on the premises. Aunt Mymee, who lives nearby and who was brought up at the Mansion as a slave, insists that the curse exists and that the Mansion is haunted. There is a history of several who lived in the Mansion suffering from unfortunate occurrences which gives some support to the rumors, enough to persuade virtually everyone to keep away from the property."

Colonel Foster said, "I would like to know more about the history that gives this property an unsavory reputation, as I am definitely interested in buying it." The Chaplain then said, "The best way for you to learn the history of the property is to hear Aunt Mymee give the Legend of Landsee at one of her recitals of that legend. She has announced that next Wednesday evening she will give her last recital of this legend and, as has been her custom, everyone is invited to attend. This is a unique occasion and besides securing the information you want, I think you will enjoy it." Colonel and Mrs. Foster decided to hear Aunt Mymee give the legend.

It was all new to the Fosters and they found themselves highly interested in everything that happened. The people, the picnic dinner, and especially the group singing held them spellbound. Aunt Mymee had emphasized that this would be the last time she would give the legend and this excited considerable curiosity and perhaps contributed to the attendance being the largest the occasion had ever drawn.

Aunt Mymee as always had selected a moonlit evening. This evening her setting was perfect. When she came to her chair on the porch dressed in white and rapped with her walking stick for order, the silence that immediately followed was almost frightening. She was perhaps at her best and she was always good. Even the doubter's attention never wavered.

At the conclusion of the legend Aunt Mymee paused and then said, "Perhaps you have wondered why I decided this would be the last time I would give the Legend of Landsee when I have been giving it for over fifty years. Many of you perhaps thought it was because I was getting old, but that is not the reason. It is because that property is no longer under an Indian curse and Landsee Mansion is no longer a haunted house. A little personal history and explanation is appropriate.

"Although as a girl I was a slave to the master of the Mansion, I am not a Negro as people have generally thought, but am a full blooded Creek Indian. In the long ago, Indians owned Negro slaves just as did the white man. My mother died and my father, who owned the Negro woman who reared me, was killed in the war. This left me in the custody of the slave without any relatives to care for me. When she became the slave of our master, she brought me along as her child. This slave, whom I loved as my mother, told me just before she died who I was. I could also remember my father. The old Indian who visited us while I was at Landsee Mansion and who taught me the Legend of Landsee told me who I was and gave me my family history, showing that I was an Indian princess.

"It would have been useless for me to go back to the Creeks, for our tribe had been scattered and my family were all dead. It was because of my relationship to the young Creek Chieftain who was buried somewhere on that crest that I was burdened with keeping alive the legend. But an Indian curse can exist for only a limited time and that time was expired. Also, the curse could be abolished by an Indian princess who was a relative of the Indian Chief who placed the curse on the property. As such, I have nullified the curse with the hope and, I think, the assurance that it will become the happy home of some good people. You are all dismissed. Good night."

After Aunt Mymee's meeting, Colonel Foster asked the Chaplain whether he thought they would be able to secure labor to work at Landsee Mansion when Aunt Mymee's statement became known. The Chaplain said he thought they would believe Aunt Mymee and that they would be able to get the needed labor. Colonel Foster then asked the Chaplain to negotiate the purchase of the property for him at as reasonable price as was possible as he would have to spend thousands of dollars in repair. In less than a week, the Fosters owned Landsee Mansion and its broad acres.

They immediately began to repair and restore the property. At first it was difficult to secure labor to do the necessary work. The Chaplain enlisted the aid of Miss Essie, whom everyone trusted, and he and Miss Essie rode with Colonel Foster to see those whom the Colonel wished to employ. With Miss Essie's assurance that Aunt Mymee had lifted the curse, and the Chaplain's statement that he would be working with Mr. Green on the place, they were able to persuade a sufficient number to work for Colonel Foster. In addition to these assurances, Colonel Foster was offering higher wages than was customary.

The Graduation
Class Party

It was nearing the end of the school term at which Ellen, Ina, Sarah, Amy, John, Ben, Jr., and about fifteen others would finish the studies offered by the institute. Those who wished to continue their formal education would have to go elsewhere to college. There were many in this graduating class for whom Miss Essie had a deep affection and she was anxious that no untoward incident take place that would mar the closing days and exercises of the Institute. Such times left long memories.

For the graduating student, commencement always brought a full consciousness that the ties of friendship built through several years of close association and cooperation were soon to be weakened as each student went his own separate way. It was a realization that the happy life that brought them so close to each other during the last several years was about to end. In keeping with this pervading sentiment the commencement exercises were always closed by singing the hymn, "God Be With You Till We Meet Again." And no one endeavored to conceal the tears that came to their eyes, evidencing their deep regret of the ending of their school days. Long ago, the experiences of such days left many cherished memories, memories of friends whose emotions refusing to be constrained, spoke eloquently of their sadness that in the future they would not see and work with each other so often as they had in the last few years.

Miss Essie, whose unflagging interest in youth kept her informed of every current that affected their lives, was so convinced that one of the activities of this year's graduating class would probably be used to hurt Sarah and perhaps Ellen, that she decided to attempt to do something about it. It had become a custom for the Senior Class during the last week of school to have a farewell get-together. Sometimes it was a get-together at the home of one of the students, to which each student brought what they called a "covered dish" to be a part of the dinner for the occasion. Once it was a picnic. The class by vote decided the character of the meeting.

This year there still lingered some of the divisive feeling resulting from the trial of Sarah. Some of Ina's devoted followers had secured her election without opposition as president of the class. While Ina had lost some of her followers, she had not abandoned her "never surrender" attitude. She had, at the expense of her father, arranged several social affairs for the class but none of these were held in her home. Miss Essie was sure that as president of the class Ina would give a senior class banquet in her home and that even if Sarah and Ellen were invited, they would not feel free to attend. She also believed that with Sarah and Ellen not attending, John and Ben would remain away. She did not propose to permit these four to be excluded from this important class activity.

Miss Essie went to see the Chaplain and told him she wanted to give the Senior Class their banquet and why she wished to do this. Then she said, "Some of the class, especially those who without question follow Ina's suggestions, are expecting her to make an elaborate affair of the banquet. She will probably use it to regain some of her lost prestige as well as make it exclude Sarah and Ellen from any participation. Now, if my banquet is not the best any former class has ever had, not only will the students be disappointed, but that disappointment will be turned to Ina's advantage. While I am in much better financial condition than I was when I was compelled to pay unlawful tribute to Lon, what I wish to do is beyond my financial ability. So I have come to you to see if you approve of my effort and if you and your friends will help finance it."

Without hesitating the Chaplain said, "I know all of us will appreciate being given an opportunity to cooperate with you in any effort to prevent these young ladies from suffering further unjust indignities." They then arranged to meet the following

Friday after supper at Miss Essie's home to agree on plans and finances.

When the Chaplain arrived at the home of Miss Essie he brought with him Dr. Alston, Mr. Davidson, Mr. Blossburg, Mr. May and Colonel Foster. They were surprised to find already at Miss Essie's John, Ben, Jr., and Amy White. When all were seated Miss Essie said, "Perhaps I should explain to you the presence of Amy, Ben, Jr., and John. As I have told the Chaplain, the Senior Class by vote decides on the character of their farewell party. I am going before the class at its next meeting to give the invitation. We will keep this secret from Ina and her allies. I wanted these to be ready to quickly get a vote of acceptance. They felt sure they could trust a sufficient number to cooperate with them without Ina's knowledge." She then told John and Ben, Jr., they could escort Amy home.

When the young people had left, Miss Essie said, "We had better get to work. I do not know to what extent the Chaplain has informed you of the reason and purpose of this meeting." She looked at the Chaplain for a reply. He said, "First, I wish to explain the absence of Mr. Green. Dr. Alston said he was needed at home on account of the condition of his wife. I would also like to explain Colonel Foster's presence. You know his deep interest in Ellen. Heretofore, I had given him some background history of the Williamson's war on the Greens and the Bloss-burgs, especially as it related to Ellen and Sarah. I confidentially told him of this meeting and he asked to participate." Then turning to Miss Essie he said, "I have briefed each of those here as to the reason and purpose of this meeting. We are anxious to aid you in your plans. The only question is, how much money do you need and what do you wish each of us to do?" Miss Essie told them something of her plans and her estimate of the expense. They doubled the amount suggested by Miss Essie and gave her the cash.

Miss Essie went to the meeting of the Senior Class. For some reason Ben, who was vice president, was presiding instead of Ina when John entered and announced that Miss Essie was outside and wished to speak to the class. Ben invited her in to the meeting and told her they would be glad to hear her.

Miss Essie said, "Thank you for giving me this opportunity to speak to you. I will be brief. I am asking for the privilege of giving this graduating class their senior banquet. Thank you." Jake Wilson immediately arose and said, "It is wonderful that Miss Essie offers to do this. I move the invitation be accepted." Two others said they wanted to second the motion. Ben said, "Of course all of us are in favor of accepting Miss Essie's invitation but we will vote on the motion." Without waiting for any discussion Ben called for the vote. There was a loud "yes" vote and no one voted "no" but Ben noticed that Ina and a few of her close friends did not vote.

When Miss Essie had left, Ina said, "Ben, do you not think you should have postponed action on that invitation to find out if some other person wished to offer a better plan?" Ben replied, "Personally I do not think there could have been a better invitation. Anyway, the unanimous vote has settled it." Ina said, "As president of the class I should have been consulted before any such proposal was submitted. I have been so completely ignored in this matter I doubt if I will attend the banquet. I had hoped to plan an outstanding occasion." Ben said, "We will regret your absence. Is there any other matter to be considered?" When no one said anything Ben declared the meeting adjourned.

A few days after the class had accepted Miss Essie's invitation Sarah went to see Miss Essie and told her that she remembered that in Charleston the seniors had class rings. She had talked with her father about securing class rings and he said if it were all right with Miss Essie he would donate the rings and they could be given as a surprise at the banquet. Miss Essie said that would be fine but she wondered how they would get the right sizes. Sarah told her that she had talked to Ben and John and they had a plan to get the finger sizes. Miss Essie was glad to get this extra contribution to her banquet plans. She requested the Methodist minister's wife, Mrs. Matthews, to assist her. She knew she would have good ideas for planning the program for the banquet and would know how to please the students. Miss Essie also advised Mrs. Matthews the reason she had volunteered to give the banquet and by whom it was financed. She found Mrs. Matthews an enthusiastic ally and as anxious as she to make the banquet a great success. Miss Essie asked Mrs. Matthews to arrange the program of entertainment and she would devote her efforts to the food.

In the meantime Ina, smarting with resentment of Miss Essie's exposing her father at Sarah's trial, was making her plans. She told Ben that as president of the class she had the right to plan the program for the banquet and that to give Miss Essie notice that she was going to exercise this right. She was going to have the next class meeting pass a resolution stating that she was to exercise this right. Ben made no reply but went to see John and told him of Ina's plan. They went to see Miss Essie and fortunately found Mrs. Matthews at Miss Essie's home when they arrived. After they had discussed this problem Miss Essie said, "This is what we will do. John and Ben will go to see Ina and tell her you have told me of her plan and that I said that the vote of the class that I should give the banquet meant that I would have charge of the program and that I have already asked Mrs. Matthews to arrange it. Also, tell her that was your understanding and the understanding of the students with whom you have discussed the matter and that you will have to oppose her proposition. Remind her that it would be difficult for her to take charge of a program in my house without my approval. As soon as you have had this conversation with Ina, let Mrs. Matthews know and she will make it a point to talk to Ina. I realize I would be the wrong person to approach Ina." With this understanding, they adjourned.

The next day John reported to Mrs. Matthews that he and Ben had had their conversation with Ina. He told Mrs. Matthews that Ina was indignant at their statement that a majority of the class would concur with their understanding that Miss Essie was given the right to arrange the program and she charged that it was a deliberate plan by Miss Essie to humiliate her. He said after considerable heated talk Ina said, "All right, just count me out and let them have their dinky affair."

After John's report of the conversation with Ina, Mrs. Matthews purposely ran into Ina. She said, "Ina, I am so glad to see you. Miss Essie has asked me to talk to you about the senior banquet." In a rather huffy tone Ina said, "What does Miss Essie want you to talk to me about?" Mrs. Matthews, ignoring Ina's attitude, proceeded as if Ina had spoken in a pleasant manner saying, "You know we are keeping the program secret so as to make it a surprise to the class. But it is necessary for the presiding officer of the class to be advised of what is expected.

Miss Essie had presumed that you as president of the class would preside and she has suggested that you lead the singing. But John tells me you are not going to attend. If you are not, we will be compelled to rearrange the program."

Ina hesitated. It was evident to Mrs. Matthews that she wanted to have the prominence this opportunity offered but realized that it would be difficult to explain a change of attitude to the students. So Mrs. Matthews decided to give her a way out of her dilemma. She said, "In order that the class might understand that its officers will be duly recognized, I wish you would announce at the class meeting that, while the plans for the banquet are being kept secret, Miss Essie had asked me to confer with you because, as president, you would be presiding and all class officers would be expected to function in their official capacities." Mrs. Matthews was correct that Ina could not resist this opportunity to bask in the limelight. Ina said, "Well if that was the arrangement, I will notify the class." Mrs. Matthews then said, "Well, that is fine. Come a little early, Ina, so we can go over the program and familiarize you with just how the program should be handled."

The students were surprised when, at the next meeting of the senior class, Ina announced that she had found that she was mistaken in assuming that she was being purposely slighted because she had not been consulted as president. She had found that all plans were being kept secret so as to surprise all of them. However, she had been consulted and advised that she would preside as president and all other officers would act in their official capacities. There was considerable excitement among the members of the class because of the report that great preparations were being made but kept secret.

Miss Essie lived in a big old house with a large dining room and a spacious parlor. It was well adapted to accommodate the senior class. With the help of some friends it was decorated, which gave it a festive appearance. Mrs. Matthews had secured some of the students to collect a small amount of money from each student to be used in purchasing a gift for the president and the best student. She knew the sum so secured would be small and would have to be supplemented but she wanted to be able to say it was from the students. The students raising the fund were requested to keep Ina and Sarah ignorant that they were involved. It was remarkable that both Ina and Sarah came to the party without any suspicion that they were to be given any special recognition.

As requested Ina arrived early to confer with Mrs. Matthews about the program. When Ina learned that she was to follow a written set of instructions she demurred. Ina said she had prepared her own remarks. The fact was that Ina had prepared to take advantage of her position as presiding officer to vent some of the resentment she still felt. Mrs. Matthews readily agreed with Ina that she should have the opportunity to express herself and called her attention to the last item on the dinner program which called for remarks by the president. Ina finally agreed to follow the script.

Then Mrs. Matthews said, "Ina, Miss Essie said that as president of the class you should stand at the door with me to greet the guests as they arrive." Ina looked at her in astonishment and asked, "Miss Essie said I should greet the guests?" Mrs. Matthews replied, "Yes, she said you had done much for the class and should be given every recognition possible as president." In one of those rare moments when truth suddenly becomes vividly clear, Ina realized that this was the first time someone other than herself had proposed that she be given recognition. She had always arranged her own recognition. In a tone full of appreciation she said, "I will be glad to do so. Please tell Miss Essie I appreciate her thoughtfulness." Ina was aglow as she stood with Mrs. Matthews and greeted the seniors as they arrived.

When Mrs. Matthews told Ina that dinner was served, Ina following the script called for order and said, "Miss Essie says dinner is served. Each of you will find a place card indicating where you are to sit. When you have found your place please remain standing behind your chair until Mrs. Matthews has said grace. After grace each young man will assist the young lady to his left in being seated. At each plate there is a small package with your name on it. I do not know what is in the packages but we will find out by opening them as soon as we are seated. We will now have grace." Mrs. Matthews asked them to bow their heads and then she gave a brief but full thanks for their blessings.

The students were not long in opening their packages and

were greatly surprised at finding that each package contained a beautiful class ring. There were many expressions of admiration. One of the students said, "And they all fit. That was why they were measuring our fingers and we did not guess why it was bging done!" But Ina was silent. She knew that rings were suggested by Sarah and given by her father, for the boxes containing the rings were from the jewelers from whom she knew Mr. Blossburg purchased jewelry. And the president's ring was especially beautiful. Again she thought someone else besides herself was seeing that she be given special recognition. Ina looked at Sarah with wonderment in her eyes, as if she were seeing someone she had never seen before. John, who was one of the students who knew about the gift of rings, knew that a special ring had been made for the president of the class. He asked Ina to hold up her hand with her ring on her finger. When she did, there were many expressions of admiration. Ina said, "Yes, it is beautiful and I shall wear it with appreciation all my life."

It was a sumptuous meal and the youthful appetites greatly enjoyed it. Between courses one of the students arose and when he had attention said, "All of us recognize that during the last three years Ina as president of the class has often rendered services to the class. Miss Essie called our attention to this fact. So we took a small collection to purchase something to be presented to you, Ina, as a token of our appreciation of you and your efforts for the class. Fortunately the amount we raised has been supplemented, which enabled us to purchase a token which we hope will last you a long time. It is my privilege to present this token to which every class member contributed hoping it will many times remind you that we enjoyed the occasions you arranged for us." Again Ina thought, "Someone other than myself is interested in seeing that I secure special recognition."

One of the great miracles of human life is that sometimes a person, because of some generous act by another toward them, or some other influence that causes them to understand some vital and neglected truth, becomes aware of a different and better world than that in which he has lived, and determines to change his lifelong attitude.

Through Ina's mind was racing the fact that, in all the

affairs she had sponsored at her expense, she had never before been given any thanks except some formal statement at the close of the party which always impressed her that she was only being thanked for doing her duty. She thought that it was the kind of thanks you bought with money, but the thanks tonight are so precious they could not be purchased with money. The conviction became deeper when, with amazement, she realized all this recognition was sponsored by persons who had cogent reasons to dislike her.

When the cheering ceased and she knew she should make some acknowledgement, she was at a loss as to what to say. She so hesitated that the class sensed that her usual self assurance seemed to have vanished and they cheered again. Ina rose and said, "I cannot remember when anything has ever happened to me that I appreciate as much as what has happened to me this evening. Whether I deserve your good will or not, what you have done makes me deeply desire to deserve it and I will strive to be worthy of it."

Another student rose and said, "The students of this class also wished to give recognition to the member of the class who maintained the highest scholastic standing during the last four years." He paused and asked Sarah to stand and continued, "Sarah, your fellow students wanted you to have some token from them to remind you of their appreciation of your scholastic achievements and your fine character." Now it was Sarah's turn to have surprise make her hesitate and wonder what to say. Finally she said, "You cannot realize how much this token means to me unless you knew how much I have longed for the good will of each of you. Thank you." When Sarah had taken her seat Ina surprised herself and all the students by saying, "All of us know Sarah not only earned the scholarship award but also our admiration and good wishes" but when she saw Sarah's grateful look she was happy she had said it.

When Mrs. Matthews saw that all had finished their meal and were just sitting around the table talking she said, "We will now go to the parlor. For a few minutes each one of you is at liberty to do as you wish. In ten minutes all of us will assemble in the parlor and we will then have a short program before you go home."

After all were again in the parlor Mrs. Matthews said, "We are going to have a program which we will call 'Do You Remember?'" For this program, we have selected some of the highlights of your school years, hoping they will bring pleasant memories of the past. At one time in the program we will vote on some feature to be given. Ellen, you will come to the piano and play the accompaniment and Ina, you stand here by the piano to lead two of the songs the group sang when they went serenading." Ina said, "What two songs shall we sing?" Readily several suggestions were made. They agreed on "Old Kentucky Home" and "Juanita." They had sung these songs many times together and they sang them beautifully.

When they had finished singing Mrs. Matthews said, "Some good people object to dancing but I have seen you play what you call the game of 'twistification' without anyone objecting. So get your partners. Jake Wilson will be in charge and Ellen at the piano and Evan Agee with his fiddle will furnish the music." This announcement was received with glee and Jake had the "the play" soon going.

After several minutes Mrs. Matthews called for their attention and asked them to decide on the next feature. After discussion they decided that Donald Hughes should recite Ella Wheeler Wilcox's poem, "Laska." He became the old cowboy so well in his rendition of the poem that he was cheered for an encore. He asked to be excused.

After another conversation period Mrs. Matthews said, "I have taken the liberty of placing on this program one who is not a member of the class. However, he has so often helped in your class activities that I do not think a program of 'Do You Remember?' would be complete without recognizing him. I have asked Ooden to sing for you, 'Old Black Joe'." Mrs. Matthews called him. He had been serving during the meal. Ooden came into the room with the big smile that showed his white teeth. To the accompaniment of Ellen and Evan he sang the song and was cheered strongly. After Ooden had sung, the group sang one of their favorite songs, "My Darling Nelly Gray."

So the evening moved from one recollection to another until it was time to go home. Mrs. Matthews said, "There always must be an end to the most pleasant experiences. The time has come to adjourn. I suggest you sing, 'Auld Lang Syne'." The evening had wrought a change in Ina. When Mrs. Matthews suggested they sing "Auld Lang Syne" and adjourn, Ina said, "Wait a minute before we sing. We have not seen Miss Essie during the entire evening. John, will you ask her to come in here so we can thank her for what she has done?"

John went to the kitchen where Miss Essie had worked during the entire party and had to force her to come to the parlor. She had accomplished her purpose of protecting Sarah and Ellen and that was sufficient compensation for her. When Miss Essie entered the room, all cheered. When they were quiet, Ina said, "Miss Essie, the class wishes to thank you especially and also Mrs. Matthews and everyone who contributed to this senior banquet. Every one of us will remember it as the most pleasant event of our school days. And Miss Essie, personally, I thank you for the most enjoyable party I ever attended."

Perhaps the dividing bars between Miss Essie and Ina fell when Miss Essie replied, "I very much wanted you to enjoy it, Ina." Someone suggested that Miss Essie play the accompaniment for them to sing "Auld Lang Syne." She demurred but they urged her so strongly that she took her seat at the piano and soon all were singing, including Miss Essie and Mrs. Matthews. They compelled Miss Essie and Mrs. Matthews to stand together where the students could pass them and thank them personally. As usual Miss Essie was embarrassed at being thanked for anything she had done. Each student was profuse in thanks for a glorious occasion.

When Sarah and Ellen came along together, they never said a word but both of them kissed Miss Essie and Mrs. Matthews. And that kiss told them better than words how grateful they were for what they had done for them. One of the last to thank them was Ina. She said, "Miss Essie, thank you for your kindness." And then almost timidly she said, "I would like to come to see you sometime." Miss Essie replied, "I will be happy to see you anytime. Maybe you can come and sing for me." Then Ina said to Mrs. Matthews, "Mrs. Matthews, I know I am deeply in debt to you also and I am grateful." Mrs. Matthews, in that impulsive and attractive manner of hers, kissed Ina and gently shoved her past her.

The Walk
In The Starlight

It was from Miss Essie's party that Ben was seeing Sarah home. Ben was leaving Landsee the next day and would not return before Mr. Blossburg had moved his family to Chicago. Both Sarah and Ben were acutely aware that probably this was the last time they would be alone together for many a day.

The "Do You Remember?" program had awakened many pleasant memories of their association since the Blossburgs had come to Landsee, and the melody of the old familiar songs the group had been singing still lingered with them. They walked along, with her hand resting lightly on his arm as was the custom. They were no longer a part of a distracting crowd. Each was alone with the one with whom they most wished to be.

It was not a moonlit night but the sky was clear and cloudless, and every star seemed to them to be shining its brightest and best to light their way home. Numerous times before tonight they had walked together this way, furrowed by the pressure of the wheels of a heavy loaded wagon, talking lightly of something that took place during the day or of some person they knew, but this evening they walked in silence. Forgotten was the road's rough and uneven surface, for it was tonight a highway of happiness. In that fascinating realm in which two people in love with each other often dwell, language is at a loss to express the ecstasy of their hearts. It is there that their souls silently communicate their love better than words.

A musical sound reaching their ears was that of a mocking bird in some distant tree caroling its good night lullaby. To them this walk was like walking through a land of bliss. In the silvery light of the stars Ben could see a slight smile trembling on Sarah's sensitive red lips, a smile that always caused his heart to beat stronger and faster.

A southern breeze that sighed through the stately long leafed yellow pines and sounded as if it had come a long way and still had a long way to go would lazily lift a lock of her soft, lustrous, black hair that rested on her forehead and then would let it slowly drop back again to where he deeply desired to place a long kiss. He yearned to hold her in his arms but in that time and in that clime a respectable young lady was untouchable.

They walked together leisurely as if time did not exist and as if they were moving in harmony with some melody heard by them alone. Whence comes that mysterious compelling power that so captures and controls emotions that the presence alone of one person brings complete happiness; that causes one to forget the past, plan no future, and live in the paradise of the present with the unreasonable hope that the present will last always without change?

But such hours, like pleasant dreams, have an awakening. Rapture's journey had to end. They reached the honeysuckle-screened porch of Sarah's home. As if by mutual understanding they went to the swing on the porch and sat together. Ben had hoped for this opportunity to be alone with Sarah before their long separation. He had determined at such time to seek her promise to marry him. When he was thinking of this determination he realized that in all their association he had never told her he loved her. He had assumed Sarah knew he loved her. He tried to prepare the way he would ask her to marry him but, now when the time was at hand, he found he had forgotten how to tell her of his consuming desire and hope.

For a few minutes neither of them said a word. Ben was searching for words to seek Sarah's promise; Sarah perceiving his purpose was also trying to find a way to make one she loved very much understand the answer she would have to give.

Finally Ben falteringly said, "Sarah, tomorrow we will separate and it will be several months before we can see each other again. I have never known how to tell you but you must know how much I love you. My very life depends on your caring for me. I have hoped your kindness to me meant that you also loved me and that hope has kept me happy. Is it too much to ask you that we become engaged and agree to marry as soon as practical? I promise I will devote myself to making you happy."

Here it was, the time when all the future course of their relations with each other must be settled, relations between two conscientious people who had a pure love for each other. Ben's proposal did not come as a surprise. Sarah would have to have been an exceedingly dull person not to have recognized what prompted his loyalty and devotion. She had wise parents whose one great goal in life was to make her happy. They were aware of the growing affection between Sarah and Ben and they had thought about it and discussed it often. They anticipated that when the time came for them to part for a considerable period of time that Ben might be pressing Sarah to promise to marry him. So for some time they had been counseling with Sarah about what she should say in such an event.

Sarah was devoted to her parents and knew that they respected Ben for his good character and also loved him because of his staunch friendship to her when Ina was at the height of her campaign against "That Jew Girl." She knew they were aware of her love for Ben and that they would want both of them to be happy. She finally agreed they were right and that she would follow their advice. Knowing the strong emotions under which she would labor in telling Ben her decision, she had endeavored to prepare what she would say. Although she had repeated to herself many times what she would say, when the time came to say it her almost overpowering desire to permit her heart to speak contrary to what she had determined to say made her hesitate. But in a moment or two she had control of her emotions and, with a prayer in her heart that she could make Ben understand, she replied, "Yes, Ben, I know you love me. I have known you loved me truly almost from the first day we met. And it has brought me happiness because I also love you. I do not know whether I will ever love another as I love you. You have stood strong in my behalf when to do so threatened the alienation of life-long friends. There were times when this 'Jew Girl' had only one friend on whom she was sure she could rely, and that friend was you.

"Because I am taking my parents' advice as to what our

relationship should be, I want you to remember that they are anxious that you also should be happy. I hope, Ben, that what I am going to say does not hurt you as much as it hurts me to say it. My parents have convinced me that as much as we love each other, it would be a mistake for us to marry. They say that love is an extremely delicate plant that must have both a favorable soil and environment in which to live or it will die. And where a great love dies, misery is apt to take its place. Youthful hearts, they say, are not always a good guide to lasting happiness. If forever could only be like today, where you and I are alone together, then we could always have a happy married life. But I have come to believe that my parents are right when they say that during the lapse of time, continuing circumstances will conspire to cause both of us unhappiness.

"Marriage is a life-long relationship. As your wife, I would not be living with you alone but I would also be living with your friends. We could not live isolated from all others, and many of our associates would always think of me as a Jew girl, even if they did not think of me as 'That Jew Girl' with the meaning Ina gave that term. My parents are convinced that our social environment would quietly but surely undermine our love as man and wife without our being conscious of it happening. It is the old story of 'water falling day by day will wash the hardest rock away.'

"True unselfish love seeks not only happiness for today but happiness for all the tomorrows for the one loved. The reason I can talk to you, Ben, like giving a lecture, is because I have thought so much about how I can convince you that marriage will not preserve our love and because I so earnestly crave for you to have no doubt that I love you as much as you love me. Tomorrow we will say farewell to each other for a long time, but please do not let it be a farewell for even a minute to our love for each other. That must last forever. So, Ben, our love must be preserved by continuing the friendship we have enjoyed since the first day we met." Sarah had finished and Ben was silent. Sarah could not stand it any longer. She leaned over and kissed him on the cheek and quickly was gone through the front door of her home but not before Ben saw, by the light streaming through the door from the room, that there were tears in Sarah's eyes.

It was several minutes before Ben moved. He sat in the swing, never feeling so alone in all his life. At that moment there was the total collapse of the hope of reaching the one great goal that dominated him. Here was the irrevocable denial of his heart's greatest desire. It left him with a confused mind, a turbulent trembling heart and a feeling akin to absolute despair. His body as well as his reason doggedly objected to functioning.

For those who have not experienced it, it is difficult for them to realize how suddenly and without warning one's world can completely change. The unanticipated new circumstances perplex and often under such conditions it is extremely difficult to get reason and the heart, when at odds, to agree.

After a while Ben realized he should not remain any longer sitting in the swing on the porch of Sarah's home. He compelled himself to start home. He moved at a slow pace, almost as if he were in a daze. He was traveling in an entirely different world from the one in which he had lived just a few hours before when he was escorting Sarah home from Miss Essie's graduating party.

As Ben gradually moved homeward he finally made an effort to take a determined grip on his emotions and assess his new situation. He was bewildered at the complex and contradictory reactions he was experiencing. One moment he thought there was no balm that could bring surcease to the anguish he suffered from the loss of Sarah as his wife and that nothing would ever banish the gloom that enshrouded him. Then without warning there came a gleam of elation that gladdened his heart. Sometimes his heart was like the proverbial pendulum that swung between sadness and gladness. He readily understood why he suffered from despair but at first he was puzzled why now and then a feeling of elation should keep gently tugging at his heart. He was not to remain in doubt very long of the source of this happier feeling. It was the complete assurance that Sarah loved him greatly. This assurance became certain beyond any doubt as he recalled how earnest Sarah was in explaining her decision, the very timbre of her voice evidencing how anxious she was for him to understand why she was compelled to take the action she did. And it was the tears he saw in Sarah's eyes as she left him, and most of all it was Sarah's kiss after her profession of love for him. Although many times Ben had longed to kiss Sarah, he had never attempted to do so.

In that time long ago, the kiss was considered almost sacred. It was a pure and tender caress that attested the sincere devotion of the heart. It was only bestowed where there was a permanent and intimate relationship and esteem and affection. It had not been profaned by being reduced to an indiscriminate manner of greeting almost any casual acquaintance. He knew that Sarah's kiss was a seal of truth to all that she had said. As he thought on these things, it dawned on him that he had not lost everything but that he possessed much that was precious and to be cherished. By the time he had reached his home, he had resolved to cling to the good that was his and that he would endeavor to prevent the public from ever knowing what had taken place between Sarah and him. Plans for tomorrow would have to wait. He needed time to become acquainted with the new world in which he was now living before he could plan for the future.

The next day, when a number of young people gathered at the depot to see Ben board the passenger train, everything was as usual with everyone except Sarah and Ben. But no one suspected that everything was not usual with Sarah and Ben, for they hid deep in their hearts their sacred secret.

Mrs. Green

In a rural village like Landsee where every person was acquainted with or had some knowledge of every other person who lived in the countryside, there was a strong awareness that every individual, young or old, was an important integral part of the whole and that the loss of any one was of interest to all.

The community was interested but puzzled at a gathering of persons at the residence of Mr. Green. At first they surmised that Mrs. Green was critically ill. This would account for Dr. Alston's presence. It would also account for the Chaplain's presence, and for the presence of Miss Essie and Aunt Mymee, the two close friends of Mrs. Green. But it would not account for the presence of Colonel and Mrs. Foster who had not lived in Landsee long, and especially would it not account for the presence of a Mr. Norman, a total stranger in the community who had been at Mr. May's hotel only two days.

The surmise that Mrs. Green was not expected to live through the day was wrong. Mrs. Green had personally planned this meeting and carefully selected those she considered should be present. When all were seated, Mrs. Green asked Aunt Mymee to prop her up in her bed. She then took a written document from the table beside her bed and said, "I have written what I have to say in order to be brief and accurate. I will read it to you and I request that you listen without interruption until I have finished." Then she read as follows:

"This statement is in my own handwriting. It has been carefully and deliberately prepared. I have been in the course of its preparation for a long period of time. It is not an impulsive act. This can be verified by my husband, Miss Essie and Aunt Mymee.

"First, I wish to state why each person here was requested to be present at the reading of this statement. Miss Essie and Aunt Mymee have been asked to be present because I have entrusted to their possession some articles important to the substantiation of some of the facts recited in the statement. And also because they have been present during the preparation of the statement and can testify that while I prepared it I was of sound mind.

"Dr. Alston has been asked to be here because he can testify that, although my body is weak and cannot last much longer, I know what I am doing and am not laboring under any delusion.

"Mr. Norman, the stranger in our midst, is a trained investigator. Sarah secured his services for me to ascertain facts needed to show that my conclusions are correct. Colonel and Mrs. Foster have been asked to be present because what I shall reveal concerns them greatly and because I need to humbly pray their forgiveness. The Chaplain has been my spiritual adviser since I have been in Landsee and I needed his sustaining presence.

"Each of you is able to anticipate the conclusion I have reached because I have discussed with you individually your interest in this statement, but I considered it advisable to present a formal statement of all the facts in the presence of all of you together.

"The purpose of this meeting and my statement is to endeavor to right, as far as I can, a wrong. A wrong I have unwittingly committed. I have been forced to the conclusion that Ellen, as much as I love her, is not my child but the daughter of Colonel and Mrs. Foster. This conclusion has been stated in the beginning because I think that by so doing you will better understand the worth and relevancy of the facts which I will state to substantiate the truth of the conclusion.

"About nineteen years ago when I was nearing the time to give birth to my first and only child, my doctor decided I might have trouble in its delivery and that I should go to a hospital. I went to a hospital about seventy-five miles from where I lived because my sister was a nurse in charge of infants in that hospital. In this hospital was Mrs. Foster. I have attached a statement of the hospital showing the date I was in the hospital. Both Mrs. Foster and I gave birth to a daughter on the same day. A copy of hospital records is attached.

"When Ellen was about fourteen years of age, I had a letter from my sister who was the nurse in the hospital when Ellen was born, stating that she was dying of cancer and she was compelled to tell me the truth about Ellen. Miss Essie has this letter. In this letter she states that about two days after the birth of my child it died. Because of my physical condition she did not think I could stand the shock of being told of the death of my baby. So she reported the death of the Foster infant and, because she was trusted, the doctor signed the death certificate she prepared. One reason my sister wrote me was to assure me Ellen would not inherit any unfavorable mental condition of mine.

"My sister's letter was the first information I had that Ellen was not my daughter, although we had observed that she did not resemble either my husband or me. I did not know what to do. I did not know the Fosters or where they lived. I feared being prosecuted as kidnappers if these facts were known. Until recently, I kept the letter secret from my husband. When I insisted on leaving Vermont, it was to go where the secret of Ellen's identity would never be discovered. Then the Fosters moved to Landsee. At once I wondered if they could be Ellen's parents. When I saw the striking resemblance of Ellen to Mrs. Foster, I was convinced that Ellen was their daughter. Mrs. Foster has the same eyes, the same smile and the same body movements.

"When I considered that the Fosters were such fine and cultured people, financially able to do for Ellen more than we could ever hope to do and, as their child she would not be burdened with the probable inheritance of my mental aberration, I decided to attempt to secure facts to establish the truth or falsity of the statements in my sister's letter.

"I wrote to Sarah telling her the story and asked her to recommend an investigator that could handle the research necessary. She sent us the name of Mr. Norman who is highly regarded for his ability and integrity. We employed him. He came here for one day and discussed all phases of the matter and then went to Vermont to see what he could find.

"Mrs. Foster and I had the same doctor when we gave birth to our daughters. Mr. Norman found that this doctor was still living and that, although retired, his mind was still good. This doctor not only had kept a record of the births but recalled the facts clearly. He said he had not expected my child to live and was surprised when my sister reported the death of the Foster's daughter, but they had so much confidence in my sister they did not question her report.

"The doctor stated that after the first day he decided that neither of us furnished sufficient milk to nourish our child and wrote a prescription for each of them. The prescriptions were different. I still have the old prescription my sister gave me to use with Ellen. It is the prescription which Mr. Norman found was given for the Foster child. The doctor's records and the hospital's records show that the Foster baby had a small mole under her left shoulder. Ellen has such a mole; my baby did not. Another proof that Ellen is the daughter of Colonel and Mrs. Foster is the fact that my husband and I both have brown eyes and Ellen has the blue eyes of both of the Fosters.

"We have had an understanding that the Fosters will have a proceeding filed in court to legally establish them as the parents of Ellen. We will cooperate with them. This will not change our love for Ellen. Both my husband and I have signed this statement." Mrs. Green handed the statement to Colonel Foster and said, "I am very tired. I will have to request all of you to retire." It was Ellen who aided her in lying down in bed and who lingered by her.

When they stood to leave, Mrs. Foster said, "May we have a prayer before we leave? I will lead the prayer." It was a prayer of thanksgiving that they had found Ellen, a prayer of gratitude to the Greens for their tender care of Ellen and a prayer that the new found relationship would make no difference in Ellen's love for the Greens.

It was only one month after Mrs. Green had read her statement that the church bell tolled signaling that her soul had departed the clay housing in which it had dwelt in this life. Few knew her even by sight, but she was to all a part of Landsee and as the bell tolled, everyone who heard it moved more quietly and spoke more softly.

Sarah's Letter

Dear Ben:

Since I returned from Landsee where I went to attend the wedding of Ellen and John, my mind has constantly been recalling the days I sojourned there and it has somehow created an irresistible urge to write to you. Everyone was disappointed that your army duties prevented your attending and your absence caused my expectations of the great pleasure of seeing and talking to you to be wrecked.

As you know, the marriage was at Landsee Mansion. It is surprising the change that has been wrought in a few years in the appearance of the Mansion under the care of the Fosters. It is not only beautiful but also friendly and inviting in appearance. The interior of the house was charming in every aspect. Every glass prism of those large chandeliers sparkled as if it were a prism of diamond. The entire interior smiled a welcome to you.

They say men are not generally interested in how the ladies were dressed or how the flowers were arranged, so I will not attempt to describe how lovely all these things were. However, I must write about some of the people who were there because they are our mutual, precious friends.

Of course, the Chaplain was there to perform the marriage ceremony. It was good to see again his benign face. My family owe him a debt for his kindness and protection that we will never be able to pay. It is so natural for him to endeavor to prevent an injury from being inflicted and to see that right prevails, I was afraid that if I tried to thank him in words he would be embarrassed, thinking I was trying to flatter him.

And there was Miss Essie, my courageous and successful defender who put prosecutor, Lon Williamson, in his place. Perhaps no one else could have done so. You can understand why I almost worship her. I spent one night with her and secured her promise to visit me in Chicago. I am going to send her a ticket. If I can, I shall make her visit such a pleasant event she will gladly remember it throughout the rest of her life.

Of course, Dr. Alston was there, happy and not looking as tired as he usually did. He was best man. Immediately after the wedding ceremony someone came begging him to come to what they deemed an emergency. He excused himself and went. After he had left, someone remarked that Dr. Alston would probably never receive a cent of compensation for his visit. I doubt whether Dr. Alston ever considered his compensation when he answered a call for his services.

The Fosters were aglow with happiness. They did a gracious thing. They permitted Mr. Green to give Ellen in marriage. When the Chaplain asked, "Who gives this young lady in marriage?" Mr. Green replied, "On behalf of Colonel and Mrs. Foster and myself, I give Ellen in marriage to John." Something about it made my eyes become moist.

It was at the wedding I had the pleasure of talking to your father and mother. I knew how much they loved you, and they knew how much I loved you, so it was a mutual choice that you should be the principal theme of our conversation. We talked with pride of your high grades at West Point and your remarkably quick advancement in rank in the army. Your father will always have my deepest gratitude. At a time in my trial when I felt that I could no longer take Mr. Williamson's vicious and slanderous remarks without crying out, it was your father's intervention in my behalf that strengthened me and gave me the courage to endure to the end of the trial in silence.

Mentioning my trial reminds me that Mr. and Mrs. Reuben Stone were also present at the wedding. He is an entirely different person from what he was when he was in the servile employment of Mr. Williamson. Mr. Stone has purchased my father's store and business. I was told he financed the transaction through the bank of which John is president, with your father, Dr. Alston and Mr. May becoming securities.

Jake Wilson was also there. He was as a youth typical of the old saying, "a diamond in the rough." Even as a student dressed in a calico shirt, jean pants and brogan shoes, there was about him an innate dignity. Today, as Sheriff of the County, he appears as a dignified and attractive man.

It would make this letter too long to mention all of our friends who were at the marriage. But I must mention Ooden who, decked out in a white coat, served with that broad smile of his that showed his beautiful, even white teeth. Just before we adjourned we persuaded Ooden to sing. You will remember what a melodious voice he has.

For me, your presence was needed to make it a perfectly pleasant gathering of tried and true old friends. The "auld lang syne" in Landsee could never be complete without your presence. While I realize it is not entirely apt, yet every time I think of my days in Landsee, I recall these lines of Shelley:

> "Many a green isle needs must be
> In the deep wide sea of misery,
> Or the mariner, worn and wan
> Never thus could voyage on."

Of course, my life in Landsee was not on a sea of misery. But I was of a different religious faith from all others there, and to many I was of an alien and unbeloved race. Hardly a day passed but that I was reminded that I was "that Jew girl," as if that appellation carried a stigma. The circumstances made it easy for Ina to promote her prejudices and cause the social sea of life to violently surge and fling angry waves of hate against me, sometimes so angry that my social life would have been entirely wrecked if it had not been for such green isles of love and friendship as you, Ellen, John, the Chaplain and Miss Essie, principally you. You were my friend when being my friend jeopardized your relations with life-long intimate acquaintances. This I shall remember always.

Jacob, my good, handsome and fine husband, has suggested several times that we urge you to visit us. He feels that he knows you well as I have talked so much about you to him. He knows all about our relationship, and he says he is indebted to you for the important part you played in my life. When I told him I was going to write you this letter, he said he was going to write to you also. I hope you will accept our invitation. What a day it would be if you and Miss Essie would visit us at the same time!

When I started to write this letter, I had the idea I would sign it "That Jew Girl, Sarah." But on second thought, I realized that it would be grossly inept to so sign a letter to you who had never used that description of me. Also forcing me to abandon that idea were two other memories. One was the memory of what happened at our graduating banquet. The events of that occasion did something good to Ina. May God bless Miss Essie. The other reason I decided I could not sign the letter in that manner was the cordial way everyone greeted me on my recent visit to Landsee. So I will sign it in the good spirit I was received and with the love I will always have for you. Jacob joins me in wishing you great happiness.

Your devoted friend,
Sarah